We're Still Here

We're Still Here

Pain and Politics in the Heart of America

JENNIFER M. SILVA

OXFORD
UNIVERSITY PRESS

OXFORD
UNIVERSITY PRESS

Oxford University Press is a department of the University of Oxford. It furthers
the University's objective of excellence in research, scholarship, and education
by publishing worldwide. Oxford is a registered trade mark of Oxford University
Press in the UK and certain other countries.

Published in the United States of America by Oxford University Press
198 Madison Avenue, New York, NY 10016, United States of America.

Library of Congress Cataloging-in-Publication Data
Names: Silva, Jennifer M., author.
Title: We're still here : pain and politics in the heart of America / Jennifer M. Silva.
Description: New York, NY, United States of America : Oxford University Press, [2019] |
Includes bibliographical references.
Identifiers: LCCN 2018048646 (print) | LCCN 2018061768 (ebook) |
ISBN 9780190888053 (Universal PDF) | ISBN 9780190888060 (Electronic Publication) |
ISBN 9780190888077 (Oxford Scholarship Online) |
ISBN 9780190888046 (hardback : alk. paper)
Subjects: LCSH: Working class—United States—Social conditions—21st century. |
Working class—United States—Attitudes | Working class—Political activity—United States. |
Coal mines and mining—Social aspects—United States. | Presidents—United States—Election—2016. |
United States—Social conditions—United States.
Classification: LCC HD8072.5 (ebook) | LCC HD8072.5 .S576 2019 (print) |
DDC 324.092/6230973—dc23
LC record available at https://lccn.loc.gov/2018048646

1 3 5 7 9 8 6 4 2

Printed by Sheridan Books, Inc., United States of America

To all the people who invited me into their homes,
looked out for me, and trusted me with their stories.

TABLE OF CONTENTS

ACKNOWLEDGMENTS

The idea for this book started to take shape when I was a postdoctoral fellow at Harvard University. Early conversations with Bruce Western and Robert Putnam expanded my scholarly horizon and pushed me to think about workers' rights, norms of reciprocity and fairness, and distrust. Bruce continues to remind me how vital it is to document the suffering and isolation of the American working class as both an empirical project and a moral imperative. Bob pushed me to a new level of intellectual engagement—modeling relentless perfectionism, confidence, and hard work—and many years later has never stopped being a mentor, still immediately responding to my questions about how to navigate my career. Rosemary Putnam—cooking guru, intellectual companion, kind roommate—read the entire manuscript, offered detailed, careful feedback, caught missing words and typos, and asked for clarification in the way that the best teachers do. Kathryn Edin showed incredible generosity in helping me to sharpen my argument, make the manuscript more empirically defensible, and define the niche I am trying to fill. As I was thinking about political disengagement, Michele Lamont pointed me to the exemplary work of Nonna Mayer and how little we know about the politics of the poor.

I have long relied on the brilliant work of the family demographer Andrew Cherlin as a way to situate my own qualitative work on family change. We met in person at a family symposium at Bowling Green in 2015, where Andy offered, "Send me everything you write." I actually did send many versions of every chapter of We're Still Here, from the very beginning stages of drafting to the final product, and he promptly returned every draft with careful suggestions and perceptive queries, helping to distill my argument and to defend it. Andy also invited me to present in his family seminar, which provided me with early comments on the framing when I was still collecting data.

My brilliant book-writing partner, Simone Polillo, and I skyped every three to four weeks and provided deadlines and feedback for each other as we moved from rough free writing to polished manuscripts. While we (sort of) jokingly created draconian rules—no compliments, no excuses, no personal chatter— this collaboration was in fact a space of support, honesty, and camaraderie in addition to intellectual stimulation.

I was awarded an American Sociological Association and National Science Foundation Fund for the Advancement of the Discipline seed grant for this research. I presented earlier versions of my arguments at several American Sociological Association panels. Along the way, I also presented my work-in-progress at invited talks in the sociology departments of Johns Hopkins University, the University of Connecticut, Bowling Green, and Ohio State; the Graduate School of Public Health at the University of Pittsburgh; University of Virginia's Institute for Advanced Studies in Culture; Penn State's Department of Rural Sociology; UC Irvine's Department of Film and Media Studies; and the American Enterprise Institute. I am grateful to Jeremy Pais, Doug Hartmann, and Chris Bail for seeing early promise and making unexpected connections in my data.

At Bucknell University, where I began work in 2014, I received generous funding from Action Research at Bucknell, the Bucknell Institute for Public Policy, and the Tom Greaves Fund for Research and Curricular Development. The provost, Barbara Altmann, and her husband, John Stacey, were early supporters of this work. The generous funding from Bucknell allowed me to hire talented and hardworking Bucknell undergraduates at every stage of the research process. I began with Jesse Scheimreif, who joined the project in the early, undeveloped stages. Caroline Hompe, who showed great promise as a qualitative researcher as an undergraduate, accompanied me on interviews and wrote useful histories of the coal region. Taylan Stulting transcribed dili-gently. Lizzie Sheprow, an emerging scholar with exceptional talent and work ethic, coded transcripts and analyzed data in intellectually imaginative ways at the busiest time of the semester. Jackie Nicoletti, who worked with me from her first semester freshman year through graduation, brought her extraordinary writing and editing skills to clarify and polish each chapter. Richard Stover in-dependently conducted investigative fieldwork that proved critical in my anal-ysis. Anthony Scrima and I met almost weekly to talk through ideas of injustice and inequality, and I trusted him with organizing and managing references. Both Devon Calhoun and Phebe Alley made time to have honest, frequent, and some-times heart-wrenching conversations with me about poverty, hopelessness, and social change. Chloe Cottineau and Michelle Melville vitally came in at the end for editing. Finally, Kait Smeraldo has worked on this project since she was a college sophomore. She is one of the hardest working, persistent, and authentic people I have ever met, and she never once faltered in the face of a challenge. Her future in sociology is very bright.

Shaunna Barnhart, who organizes efforts in the coal region, was an endless wellspring of knowledge and efficiency. Carl Milofsky read my manuscript, talked through ideas and observations, and brokered many important connections. Being able to chat with Elizabeth Durden down the hall, exchange recipes, and meet for a glass of wine made her into a friend. Tristan Riley read the entire manuscript carefully, sent me respectful and critical comments, helped me work through the reviewer comments, and took it seriously from the beginning. Deb Baney, so much more than support staff, offered guidance and laughter through particularly challenging times. And JJ quickly became a lifelong friend.

Within the professional world of sociology, I have a circle of friends who are willing to read my work seriously and share connections and ideas. Nicole, dear friend since our days at sherry hour in William James Hall, read the entire manuscript through the lens of a smart, careful policy researcher. Kristin, job market and baby partner, reminded me that quantitative researchers need qualitative insights. Deirdre has been a constant voice of strength and encouragement. Kaisa offered indispensable analytical skills and support through life transitions and challenges, always with a sense of humor. Matt offers his intuition at times of creativity and transition.

I am grateful to my editor, James Cook, who understands my strengths, follows his own instincts, and gives me the freedom and space to develop as a writer. Somehow James manages to be honest and critical yet also calm and reassuring. He took the time to read every word. My anonymous reviewers put extraordinary time and energy into making this book more rigorous, streamlined, and clear.

And finally, I want to thank: my dear friends, who are my lifeline; my in-laws, who provide a space of comfort that I needed; my grandmother Jean, who calls to check on how I am doing and never loses the love and awe in her voice; my brother, for his commitment; and my dad, who frequently visited Pennsylvania in the early stages of this research and drove around the coal region with me and Rufus, our beloved boxer, sticking his head out the window. My mom, Paula, knew exactly when to visit in the frantic times and selflessly took care of whatever I needed with a calming, cheerful presence. My parents' pride in me sustains me, humbles me, and energizes me. And most of all Ahrum, my husband and partner, the person I want to spend every day with, who unconditionally and unquestionably supports my goals and puts the hard work in, every day, to help me achieve them.

We're Still Here

Introduction

The Puzzle of Working-Class Politics

I love women, and I think they can do anything a man can do, but that woman should not be the President of this United States, so help me God, but neither should that jackass. So it's like, who the frick do you pick? I'm like, you're not giving us much of a choice here. Either way we're going to be destroyed. Now if there was somebody else worthy, I'd probably go in that direction, because it's a joke. But at the end of the day, I would rather have President Dickhead than President Sellout.

Bree, white, waitress

When it comes to voting, I don't really believe that a President is going to change anything. . . . The government lies to us every day, and people, they listen to it, because they feel like they should. I feel like politicians and the government are the biggest liars in the world.

Eric, black, warehouse worker

This book explores how working-class Americans connect their everyday struggles, triumphs, hopes, and fears to politics. For decades, stable blue-collar jobs have been automated, eliminated, and shipped overseas. Politicians on both sides of the aisle have further gutted the power of the working class by reducing the social safety net, weakening the right to bargain collectively, and protecting corporate profits over workers' basic survival needs. The chance to give one's children a better life—the promise at the heart of the American Dream—is fading away. And yet, rather than rise up together to fight for their fair share of justice and opportunity, the groups who stand to gain the most from mobilizing politically appear the least motivated to act in their own self-interest.

American nonvoters are disproportionately younger, poorer, less educated, and more racially and ethnically diverse. People with lower levels of income and education are also less likely to contact a public official, join a civic and political organization, or donate to a political campaign.[1] Moreover, instead of fostering solidarity, living through the Great Recession of 2008 actually deepened divisions among those fighting to survive, turning some white workers against racial minorities, immigrants, and the poor.[2]

In this book, I begin with the premise that if we want to understand why people act against their own self-interests, we first need to uncover how they imagine the "self" and how this self relates to the larger social world. In this vein, I spent two years interviewing working-class men and women in the southern counties of the anthracite coal region of Pennsylvania. To protect their identities, I refer to this area as Coal Brook.[3] The anthracite industry peaked during World War I, employing 175,000 men and supporting a population of about 1 million. Employment in anthracite mining fell to 17,000 by 1961 and to just 2,000 by 1974. Today, abandoned mine dumps and strip mines dominate the landscape.[4] Neighborhoods that once had a church on every corner now boast tattoo parlors, liquor stores, vape shops, and dollar stores. Meanwhile, over the last decade, rising housing costs, poverty, and crime have pushed black and Latino people out of urban economies and into the coal region, challenging long-standing boundaries of urban and rural, race and place.[5] Banners declaring "Blue Lives Matter" and "Trump Digs Coal" adorn neat window boxes of red geraniums and white and blue petunias as souped-up pickup trucks sporting gun-racks and Confederate flags roar along winding two-lane highways.[6]

While I did not set out to study the 2016 American presidential election, the years leading up to Donald Trump's victory over Democratic nominee Hillary Clinton provided me with a chance to explore the larger phenomenon of working-class political disengagement in the coal region.[7] I spent hundreds of hours interviewing longtime white residents and black and Latino newcomers. I tagged along as they confronted the challenges of everyday life—whether trying to find a ride to pick up their kids at Head Start, struggling to locate an empty bed in drug and alcohol rehab, selling gun bingo tickets to raise money for a school fieldtrip, or figuring out how to buy their daughter a fish tank for Christmas when their lights had just been shut off. I witnessed how the decline of the American Dream was being lived and felt, and listened as they forged political ideas out of realms of experience that are not usually considered political at all.[8] My conversations with these men and women moved my study of political disengagement far beyond the ballot box and into an intricate maze of family troubles, addiction, joblessness, racism, violence, incarceration, and early death.

Most of the people I met are fiercely critical of growing economic inequality and of the politicians who have failed to protect them from poverty, exploitation, and shame. However, the institutions that historically mediated between personal suffering and collective struggle—steady blue-collar jobs, unions, marriage and extended kin networks, churches, social clubs, and political parties—have not only become weak but have also become sites of betrayal.[9] In this emptiness, working-class people cultivate individualized strategies for making their suffering bearable and comprehensible. Stories of triumphing over pain anchor their identities, draw stark moral boundaries between the deserving and undeserving, and stitch together political views that ostensibly conflict with each other. Convinced that democratic processes are rigged in favor of the wealthy, many working-class people search for meaning in internet conspiracy theories or the self-help industry—both of which are solitary strategies that serve to turn them inward or against each other. The imaginative bridges they build between personal suffering, distrust, and political identity often serve to justify disengagement as a safe, empowering, and shrewd choice.

Unexpected Alliances

In early summer 2016, I met Bree Lopez, a white woman in her midthirties. We sat and talked in what was once called the parlor, in a narrow, dimly lit row home, with the windows shut tight and the shades drawn. Bree's grandfather was a coal miner who died of black lung at age fifty. Her mother, a waitress, died of lung cancer at fifty-three, and her father has never been part of her life. In Coal Brook, the jobs that pay almost enough to support a family are seen as "men's jobs"—truck driving, warehouse jobs, construction; working in the numerous federal, state, and county prisons; or driving three hours away to drill on the natural gas pipeline. Graduating high school with poor grades, Bree already knew that "there was nothing here" for her. After a few brief stints in different cities along the East Coast, she returned to the coal region and has been waitressing, on her feet for ten hours a day, ever since.

Bree has been married and divorced twice. Her son's father pays no child support. Her daughter's father, an under-the-table truck driver addicted to Percocet, has contributed just "sixty-five dollars and two packs of meat since last November." When Bree's electricity was shut off last year, she and the kids slept on her cousin's pullout couch for three weeks while she saved up enough money to have the heat turned back on. Bree was devastated when she could not fulfill her daughter's sole request, for "real fishes," for Christmas. "I'm riding the crazy train right now," she confesses. "I'm tired from work. I'm trying to do the right thing, but also what's in the best interest for my kids and for myself, and where we're at right now, I can't move."

"You don't matter in this town unless you have money," Bree asserts. "You can't be poor, no matter what color you are." Bree teaches dance lessons for children on her day off, waiving the three-dollar fee for the poorest kids in town. When I ask her if the government should do more to help poor people, she exclaims: "Hell, yes! We should tax the shit out of rich people." She says angrily: "There's nothing left for our kids. I mean, they took away French from our kids. They tried to cut back on the music program, the arts program. They used to have a skate bus that ran from the old police station back on Friday nights. There's nothing for these children." Bree denounces extreme economic inequality and the lack of opportunities for upward mobility in American society: "You don't just keep them [poor people] under your boot and leave them down there and throw them scraps. Lift them up. Teach them things. Educate them. Get them to work, something. You're killing me. It's like the rich stay where they're at, and the middle class struggle like crazy, living paycheck to paycheck, and the poor people are just fricking poor living off the system."[10]

Bree also suspects that low-income parents seek out diagnoses like ADD (attention deficit disorder) for their children for the money but to the detriment of the children themselves.[11] "It's horrible. Children are supposed to be hyper. Discipline them. Stop medicating these kids," she implores. She recounts the story of a mother who removed half the Adderall from her child's pill capsules, rolling it up in a dollar bill to sell for cash. When Bree confronted this mother, she "cried a little bit, said, 'I need to make some money.' You can obviously tell that this mother was an addict." What makes Bree angry is not that people are poor, unable to pay their bills, or in need of government aid, but that they seem to have capitulated to their suffering rather than fighting back against it. "It's a depressed area, and they just make it more depressed, by doing shit like they're doing," she says disappointedly.

In Coal Brook's surrounding valley, the county coroner has reported an increase in lives lost to drug overdose over the last few years. The postmortem toxicology screenings reveal a deadly mix of heroin, oxycodone, and Fentanyl. It is an open secret in Coal Brook that a prescription for Percocet costs just fifty dollars in cash—and if the doctor, whom Bree calls "the biggest drug dealer in the county," knows your family, you can simply call in your request over the phone. Bree herself lives in constant pain. She points to various spots on her body, physically mapping out her memories of trauma and violence:

> My first husband did this to my teeth [she points to two gaps in her mouth where there should be canine teeth]. He bent me over the baby's crib with her in it backwards. I literally was in half, so I deal with that. I don't go to the doctor for it. They want to send me to this specialist, that specialist, a psychiatrist to deal with the pain, living with pain. I don't even go. I just don't even go, because, honestly, pain medication doesn't really help me. There's really no point, and I can't be all fucked up walking around work, all high on whatever. I need to be where I'm at always. I can't sit up. I have to take twenty minutes to roll onto my side to put a foot on the floor to stand up. It's real bad. It gets real, real bad, and now that I'm waitressing, I'm on my feet twelve hours, ten hours

a day, all the time. Emotionally, I'm a mess. I'm a mess. My God, my poor kids.

Chronic anxiety and a racking cough from twenty years of smoking menthol cigarettes keep Bree up late into the night: "I always have a bad feeling something awful is coming, plaguing my soul." She staunchly refuses to see a doctor. "I'm just afraid of what he's going to say to me," she admits. "I know it ain't going to be good, so I'm just putting if off. He's [the local doctor] the one who diagnosed my mom with the flu when she had fucking lung cancer. That's why they didn't know she had cancer until she was stage-fucking-3, because he was like, here's a Z-Pak. He had a hand in killing my mother. This man is still peddling shit."

Bree's second husband, Manny, the father of her nine-year old daughter, migrated first from Puerto Rico to the Bronx, and then moved four hours west to Coal Brook. Bree implores: "How can I raise a child with the last name Lopez here? My daughter was called the n-word here, her head was smashed into a bus window, and the kid wasn't even suspended."

Bree's current boyfriend, Eric Kennedy, is a twenty-five-year-old black man originally from Southeast DC. Eric hails "straight out of what you would call 'hood or ghetto, projects. My parents were addicts. They were never home. Me and my sister basically scrounging to eat." With his mother gone and his father "in and out of jail, selling drugs, doing drugs," Eric and his younger sister Stacey were raised by his father's girlfriend in southern Pennsylvania. Eric recounts how this girlfriend locked him in a dark basement, where her adult son abused him sexually and physically. In his anguish, often too hungry to sleep at night, Eric would ask himself: "Why can't our dad just stay out of trouble so he can protect us?"

When Eric was ten years old, he and his younger sister ran away. They were caught by a police officer for stealing food from a convenience store. The police officer, Eric remembers, confronted his stepmother before calling Children and Youth Services: "[T]hese kids look like they haven't eaten in months. What are all these welts on them? He looks at the house, and he's like, this is not fit for two children. There's no food in the refrigerator, and that day he went to CYS, and the next day he had us put in foster care." Eric was placed in a Christian foster family nearby: "For once in my life, I actually felt like someone cared about us. Someone loved us. Someone made sure we were okay." But Eric's fear and anger from a lifetime of abandonment and abuse continued to haunt him— "It was my upbringing. I couldn't help it. I couldn't grasp the fact that someone actually cared about me." He got in numerous fights at school, rebelled against his foster mother's conservative rules, and smoked marijuana in the house, behaviors that eventually resulted in a revolving door of group placements and temporary homes.

Eric credits one of his foster placements with offering him emotion management skills, where he "started expressing things that were underlying feelings in my life from when I was younger." He graduated from high school with a football scholarship and enrolled in a regional university. During his first semester, his aunt died suddenly. Eric completely fell apart: "It hit me big, and I told myself that I was going to take some time off from school and try to get my head straight, because stress from playing sports and school work and my aunt passing away, it kind of just hit at once and I just got caught up in stupid stuff and ended up getting locked up." Found guilty of heroin possession, he spent nearly a year in county prison.

When he was released, with no family to take him in, and no money of his own, Eric moved with his former cellmate into a $300-a-month apartment in the coal region. He found a warehouse job that paid $10 an hour. He now reflects on the transition: "It was kind of different to have people just stare at you, or have people drive past and scream '[n-word]' out the window, or tell me they're going to hang me from a tree," he says mildly.

Soon after Eric moved in with Bree, she reports, her food stamps and housing benefits were discontinued. Bree suspects that one of her own family members called the county assistance office and reported that a man with a criminal record was living in her home. Since then, Eric says that he has been subject to constant harassment from the police, many of whom graduated from high school with Bree: "Just the other day, I parked a car, and he [the police officer] drives past me, he slows down, he goes to the end of the block, there's a one-way, so he goes down to the next block and comes around, comes past me again, slows down, goes to the end of the block and makes a U-turn, and then passes me again." When Eric and Bree first began dating, they quickly learned that any public displays of affection at the restaurant where she waitresses—even if Eric were to briefly rest his hand on her back—would be met with customer complaints, threats of violence, and a "screaming boss." A group of white men in town organized an armed march to "take back their streets," Eric tells me, and they walked menacingly by Bree's home. When Eric was arrested again a few months ago on a dog-fighting charge, Bree spoke out against racial profiling at the hearing: "You know if it was me, you never would have arrested anyone!" But, she explains, "the cops are all friends, so it doesn't really matter if one's doing something wrong, because they know half the police force is going to stand up for them. All the judges go to school together or been to school together, or they all go out together, so this town is very corrupted."

Eric powerfully condemns racism, expressing support for Black Lives Matter, a social movement protesting against police brutality, racial profiling, and discrimination in the criminal justice system. He pushes back against the counterslogan "All Lives Matter": "See, no one is saying all lives don't matter. As black people we just saying black lives matter, because it don't seem like they do. When black innocent men are being shot down in the street like a dog."

Eric also praises Colin Kaepernick, the black football player who provoked heated national controversy when he knelt in protest of police brutality during the playing of the national anthem in 2016. "You should see half the videos that are coming up of cops just beating guys," he says passionately. "You're telling me to stand for this National Anthem for justice for all. There isn't. So for me to stand up to that and represent that when you have people of my color not getting that, why would I do that? Then I'd just be doing it because that's what the world says is right."

Still, Eric also tries to transform the vicious traumas of his life into opportunities, thanking God for his resilience and pledging to "do right by" his suffering. He maintains an attitude of hope and resilience when he talks about his future, in stark contrast to Bree's narrative of unrelenting decay. Despite his political critique of the criminal justice system, Eric accepts no excuses for his own personal failures: "I hate when people say, 'Yo I got felonies, so I can't find a job.' That's a bullshit excuse for being lazy. I'm not proud about it, but I have more felonies than a lot of people. But I still scored a job that pays $10 an hour. It's all about your dedication and motivation in making it happen and wanting to really better yourself."

He reflects:

> I can only thank God that he has blessed me with the opportunity to better myself. I really need to do whatever I need to do to make it happen, and one of those things is getting off of my ass, getting out and working. I kind of don't want to be another number, black man on food stamps. I don't want anyone to feel pity for me. I've been through enough in life already. I've been through more than any person could experience in life. I feel like God made me a very strong person. I feel like the things that I did in life that were wrong, they weren't mistakes. They were learning curves, and I felt like I learned from them. I feel like I took the situations that I've done wrong or were affected by in life, and it took me some time to do it, but I was like, you know what? I'm going to take this, and I'm going to do right by it.

Eric ultimately decides to leverage his suffering as an opportunity for self-improvement. He links dignity to a code of self-reliance forged from a long traumatic history. He vows to take advantage of any "opportunity to better myself." He defines himself against the stereotype of "just another black man on welfare," turning his suffering into an individual, moral quest instead of a collective struggle against the injustices he witnesses around him.

Navigating Contradiction and Distrust

Like Bree, Eric expresses right-leaning rhetoric in his suspicions of people who cannot triumph over their suffering through persistence and hard work. On other issues, both Bree and Eric's politics lean to the Left: they are critical of mass incarceration, question the authority of the police, and endorse higher taxes on the wealthy and a downwardly redistributive welfare state.[12] How do Bree and Eric connect their moral convictions to the political sphere?

Bree is a registered Democrat, like her mother and grandfather before her. She does not wholeheartedly embrace conservative or liberal social values. She supports gay marriage and is even reluctantly pro-choice. Her moral calculations meld the repugnance for the idea of abortion (with which she was raised) with the grim necessity of its practice. For young working-class women like Bree, newfound freedoms to escape domestic violence are tempered by the persistence of gender inequality in wages, conflicted visions of masculinity and femininity, and the extreme fragility of family bonds.

She clarifies:

> After my son was born, a couple of months later I got pregnant, and, of course, I wanted to have my baby. My ex-husband literally said, either you get rid of it or I'm going to. This was abuse when it was real thick in the abuse. Of course, my mother was like, I think it's a good thing. You can't have another baby. He's a piece of shit. He's not working. And then I had him threatening me, and I didn't want to lose my family. He would hurt me, and God knows what would have happened, and he would have left. I wouldn't have had a husband or a father for my son, and I went and had that done. It was the most horrible time of my entire life, but for women who don't have a choice, like I felt I didn't, I understand that. Now these girls that go around sleeping with everybody and this is like their fifth time, that's absolutely ridiculous.

Bree does not question men's "nature"—they are assumed to be controlling, promiscuous, and unfaithful—and she holds women to a higher standard of independence and self-control. She accepts that there must be a trade-off between giving her children a nuclear family structure, on the one hand—"I didn't want them to not have a father in the home with the same last name"—and being strong and free, on the other: "I think I was already in that state of mind, that for my children I'll stick it out. No one ever really taught me how to be a real woman." Bree ultimately prioritizes the strength it takes to leave a man. Recalling President Bill Clinton's widely publicized extramarital affair with his aide, Monica Lewinsky, Bree decides she cannot vote for his wife, Hillary Clinton, in 2016 because a "strong woman doesn't let a man get away with that shit." But "Bill, I'd take Bill again. I would take Bill again in a minute. You were a slut, but you're also a male, so I don't judge you."

"Now right now, if I had to vote, I'd probably vote for Trump. I don't think I'm going to vote in this upcoming election. A woman can't be president," she insists. "She [Hillary Clinton] is so easily bought, it's not even funny. I can't see her making rational decisions. We would be terrorized. But Trump's like, kill them all." Her own fight for hard-won independence, alongside deeply ingrained ideas about men and women's nature, inform her reasoning. "But . . . is Trump racist?" I ask apprehensively. "Hell freakin' yes, he's racist!" she roars back. "But you know what? He's not full of shit. You know what you're getting. And *that* woman is in the pocket of too many people. Now if there was somebody else worthy, I'd probably go in that direction, because it's a joke. But at the end of the day, I would rather have President Dickhead than President Sellout."

Bree reflects soberly: "It's funny, because last night I literally posted on Facebook: "trust no one ever." My mother sat me down at the age of eight, said trust no man, don't trust your family. The only people you can trust is me, that's it. Don't trust your father. Never trust anybody ever, ever, ever, and she was right." In her life, Bree has learned to be suspicious of everyone, to draw dignity from facing her problems head-on, and from speaking up for what she believes in despite the risks. This moral vision translates into a halfhearted endorsement for Donald Trump.[13]

For Eric, on the other hand, the idea of voting is absurd: "When it comes to voting, I don't really believe that a president is going to change anything. Because when you think about it, the president can't do anything without going through other people." He believes that the US government is actively and intentionally harming its most powerless citizens. He says excitedly:

> The government lies to us every day, and people, they listen to it, be-
> cause they feel like they should. I feel like politicians and the govern-
> ment are the biggest liars in the world, and the big thing that I tell
> everybody is—remember when Ebola came out? It's wiping the world
> away, then it just disappears. What happened to it? You're telling me
> something that was killing thousands of people. Where'd it go? What
> was the government trying to hide from us? They have our attention
> here, so what were they doing while we had our heads turned? Even
> the Michigan Flint thing, the water. I honestly think that was a man-
> made situation. You pollute the water in basically a poverty-stricken
> area, and you see what it does. You see that a couple hundred people get
> ill. Some people die. You didn't fix it. You tried to see what it does, be-
> cause a lot of people don't think about it. The world eventually is going

to be overpopulated. It's just going to happen. It's just going to happen, and what do you do when it gets overpopulated? You make population control. We're going to dump this chemical in this water supply, have a couple hundred people die, or let's throw this together, make this kill a couple thousand people, then we're going to act like we fixed it.

According to Eric, the US government is already plotting to eliminate powerless people at the bottom of the income ladder like himself. If he does not stay vigilant, or if he lets himself get distracted by the mainstream media, he might fail to spot the signs of impending annihilation. Eric relies on his smartphone to find alternative sources of information: "I read a lot. *They* run everything. They control everything. Maybe they're not out there about it, but everything you do can be watched by somebody, and that's not freedom. The world's messed up." By this logic, a malevolent "they" fabricates events to distract the public from their dissembling. "We're over in Iraq and Afghanistan fighting for our freedom. How did our freedom get over there? Why don't we start here, figure this out, and then we can go over here and figure this out?" he demands. Eric—watchful, isolated, and suspicious—has ceased to believe in democracy at all.[14]

The Puzzle of Working-Class Politics

At first glance, Bree and Eric's politics may appear somewhat incoherent and irrational. Bree endorsed a Republican billionaire for president right after she expressed support for higher taxes on the wealthy, and upheld ideas about masculine dominance even as her own body collapses from years of domestic abuse. Eric did not plan to go to the polls in November even as he spoke with critical awareness about the dangers that haunt low-income people of color like himself in the criminal justice system.

To make sense of these paradoxes requires doing away with the tendency to think about "interests" as predetermined or self-evident.[15] Instead, we need to dig deep into the particular substance of people's worldviews, the processes through which they arrive at such views, the stories that make politics resonate with their life experiences, and the mechanisms that connect their views of the world up to political action—or lack thereof.[16]

Public opinion polling tends to isolate individuals from their social environment, explaining political worldviews in a quantitative language of prediction.[17] They might ask, for example, how a person's level of education predicts their likelihood of casting a ballot or supporting raising taxes. In her groundbreaking study of dozens of political groups across the state of Wisconsin, Katherine Cramer argues that this quantitative approach allows us to see how different kinds of people think, and where their opinions fall on an attitude scale, but it does not allow us to see how they arrive at these positions.[18] Rather, it is the stories people tell about who they are, what they have been through, and how their lives should have been that do the interpretive work of connecting independent and dependent variables.

Stories of the self are not merely factual but also deeply moral. As people select certain life events as formative and pivotal, and discard others as unimportant, they craft a story of discovering and bearing witness to the "right" way to live. People's analyses are often fraught with contradictions and messiness.[19] By taking their accounts of the world seriously, however, scholars have shed light on why people seem to make choices that contravene their own self-interests. Jennifer Sherman's study of a remote logging town, for instance, captured how the deep sense of self-worth that accompanies hard work leads impoverished people to reject any kind of dependence on the state.[20] Robert Wuthnow's immersion in rural America reveals a distinctive moral code of personal responsibility, frugality, and common sense that is far removed from the world of policymakers in Washington, DC.[21] In Arlie Hochschild's ethnography of a white Tea Party stronghold in Louisiana, voters knowingly sacrifice clean air and water, health, and safety in the name of capitalism, equating risk-taking with honor and human freedom.[22] This loss of honor also permeates Justin Gest's study of white working-class men, who turn to radical right-wing politics because they "feel like a peripheral afterthought in a country they once defined."[23] These insights challenge the conventional view of voters who make choices based on the policies that best serve their economic interests. On the contrary, as the political scientists Christopher Achen and Larry Bartels demonstrate, most voters cast ballots based on how "someone like me" should feel, approaching politics through emotion and identity rather than through particular policy details.[24]

Many of the existing studies linking moral identities to political attitudes focus on a particular slice of the American population: people who are tied to a larger community, who articulate clear policy preferences, and who view political participation as meaningful and effective. Most of the people I spoke with, on the other hand, are largely not turning to free-market solutions, championing existing political parties, or even joining community groups to translate their economic grievances into political change. Going forward, we need to uncover the relationships, loyalties, longings, and moral visions that underlie both the political engagement and disengagement of everyday people. We urgently need to create a space for the working class to explain what has gone wrong, to watch them actively take on, negotiate, or reject available political identities, and to listen to how the stories they tell justify their political demobilization.

The Study

I began this endeavor in spring 2015, attending public church services and
festivals, town meetings, drug addiction support groups, volunteer fire-company
shifts, and local sports events in the coal region. I also frequented bus stops, local
businesses, restaurants, and bars. I introduced myself as an assistant professor
hoping to learn about the political beliefs, life experiences, and family histories
of residents of the coal region. I emphasized that there were no right or wrong
answers to any of the questions I would ask, that I was simply interested in what
they thought were the greatest problems facing their communities, and what
kind of country they wanted America to be. I was jokingly labeled "the interro-
gator" at first, but I slowly and painstakingly established trust with local families.

"Working class" is tricky to define in the United States, especially as stable,
good-paying manual labor jobs for people with high school diplomas are dis-
appearing.[25] Although there are more precise ways of measuring economic position than "social class," such as income level or occupation, I have chosen to
retain the more expansive concept of "working class." If social class becomes
the basis of a shared political identity, it is not simply an automatic response to
sharing the same education level, income bracket, or job. Rather, class is something that "happens" through concrete social relationships that generate values,
traditions, and shared interests in ways that cannot be assumed in advance.[26]
The coal region prides itself on a long history of conflict between miners and
mine-owners, high levels of union membership, and loyalty to the Democratic
Party. But as Thomas Keil and Jacqueline Keil astutely observe in *Anthracite's
Demise and the Post-Coal Economy of Northeastern Pennsylvania*, these values
are no longer "generated on the shop-floors" or in "the structures of daily life,"
weakening the link between labor and the Democratic Party.[27] In the southern
counties of the coal region, politicians who advocate pro-business, antiwelfare
policies have gained widespread support over the last several decades. The coal
region thus beckons as a place to investigate how class is not "happening" as it
used to,[28] where previously taken-for-granted ideas about loyalty, civic duty, and
political party affiliation might have to be reworked and reimagined to fit the
changing times.[29]

Against this backdrop,[30] I began conducting interviews with white working-
class men and women—ranging from older people who remember their fathers
"cracking coal" to young adults struggling with its demise.[31] I recruited sixty-
seven coal-region residents who hold less than a four-year college degree and who
work (or had worked) in unskilled and semiskilled jobs that offered little control over their working conditions and schedules. I roughly split the participants
in the study by gender. The white men I interviewed work as carpenters and
painters, soldiers, truck drivers, factory workers, butchers, plumbers, warehouse

distribution workers, custodians, and EMTs. Two men were out of work due to injury or illness. The white women include waitresses, bar-tenders, cashiers, home health-care aides, beauty technicians, hotel maids, and stay-at-home mothers.

In full disclosure, I began this book as a study of white working-class conservatives, but I had trouble finding people who felt strongly enough about politics to fully identify with a political party or advocate for specific policy platforms. Among the twenty-nine white men I interviewed, thirteen men reported that they planned to vote for the Republican candidate Donald Trump, and thirteen of them reported that they would abstain from voting or write in a candidate. Three men planned to vote for the Democratic candidate Hillary Clinton. Among the thirty-eight white women in my sample, twenty-two women did not plan to vote at all, twelve women preferred candidate Donald Trump, and four women planned to vote for Hillary Clinton.

The sociologist Kristin Luker writes that sometimes an ethnographer does not know what she is looking for until halfway through the data collection.[32] In my interviews with white residents of the coal region, I repeatedly heard about the "newcomers," black and Puerto Rican people who were moving into this rural, racially homogenous area that has been famously referred to as "Alabama without the blacks."[33] Rather than write about these ethnic minorities as silent "others," moral foils, and political scapegoats, I wanted to treat the newcomers as active participants in the shifting racial dynamics in the coal region.[34] With the help of people like Bree Lopez, who crossed the stark racial divide in Coal Brook, I interviewed forty-one black and Latino people, also divided roughly by gender. The "newcomers" provided an unexpected opportunity to examine the multiracial coalitions and fractions that exist within the American working class and to witness how new collisions of race and place solidify or disrupt existing racial hierarchies of power and oppression.[35] I was also curious to watch how they confronted and even contested the stigma that awaits them.[36]

Compared to the white residents, the newcomers live in especially precarious households. I intentionally blur the line between working-class and poor, as these groups increasingly share far more work instability and insecurities in basic needs than they do with their professional middle-class counterparts.[37] The newcomers are seeking safe, settled, and stable working-class lives when they arrive in the coal region. They hope to achieve upward mobility for their children by escaping the traumas of inner-city poverty and crime, attaining better-paying, manual labor jobs, and finding housing they can afford. The black and Latino men I interviewed work as line cooks, roofers, day laborers, factory and construction workers, and in shipping-and-receiving departments at large warehouses. About half of these men are actively looking for work. The black and Latina women I interviewed work as bill collectors, cashiers, receptionists, and health aides. No one in the study, regardless of race and ethnic background, reported receiving cash assistance through the Temporary Assistance for Needy Families (TANF) program at the time of our interview. The overwhelming majority of the newcomers did not plan to vote in 2016.

My approach was inspired by the work of the late political scientist Robert Lane, who conducted in-depth interviews with white working-class men in a northeastern city in the 1960s. Lane sought to "relate life experience to social thought, to show how life events made men bitter, passive, defeated, and how these qualities were then used to shape a congenial political ideology." I took an open and conversational approach to the interviews, usually in participants' own homes or in the local coffee shop, allowing people to draw connections between their own lives and their politics.[38] In the writing of this book, I make an effort to not treat people as if they lack the ability to make sense of their own lives. Rather than focus on what they get wrong, I uncover the painstaking, thoughtful reasoning that underlies what they believe to be true to their experiences. I allow the participants themselves to adjudicate between competing definitions of reality. I do not attack their beliefs, as the accuracy of facts would not change the truth of these worldviews. To point out flaws or misinformation in their words feels like a cruel evisceration of their sense of themselves, and the trust they have in me to share it.[39] Instead, I link the personal and psychological accounts in their narratives with the social and historical spaces in which they live. Once we are able to view reality through their eyes, I believe, their accounts of the world become comprehensible, self-evident, and even necessary for survival.

Putting the Pieces Back Together

Let's return to Bree and Eric, as they come to terms with their pasts, envision their futures, and forge moral visions of how the world should work. Both Bree and Eric defy easy categorization and conventional wisdom. There is no obvious, linear relationship between their socioeconomic status, gender, race, and political positions. They do not sound apathetic, passive, or unaware of what is happening around them. They are not single-issue voters who prioritize social issues such as abortion or gun control over economic interests, nor do they place themselves into clear-cut categories of Republican or Democrat, liberal or conservative. Most of the time, as they attempt to come to terms with their past traumas and future anxieties, they do not think about politics at all.

To grasp the complex political landscape, Bree and Eric draw from their own understandings of who they want to be, the hard choices they have had to make, the people they compare themselves to, and the loyalties and betrayals that have defined their lives. Coming to terms with pain—and convincing themselves that transcending pain promises a moral reward—does a tremendous amount of work in organizing their identities. On their own, they create imaginative bridges between painful experiences and political identity in ways that make their suffering feel productive and honorable.

Pain, as experienced, is undeniably personal, but its causes and consequences are often political. Do we blame others for our suffering, or turn it, unforgivingly, back on ourselves? Do we treat pain as a learning experience, or medicate it away? Do we extend compassion to those who suffer alongside us, or dismiss the suffering of others as fraudulent? The historian Keith Wailoo argues that pain management in twentieth-century America became a "fraught political exercise" waged over the question of precisely whose pain counts as valid and in need of government redress versus whose pain should be discarded as fraudulent and undeserving of public intervention.[40] Suffering has been a recurring site for political battle in the United States, from early struggles over disability laws and soldiers' benefits, to welfare reform in 1996 that imposed work requirements and time limits on government aid, to the battle over the Affordable Care Act in the 2000s.[41]

Poverty, inequality, and exploitation are not new phenomena in the coal region. Working conditions in the mines were harsh. Daily risks included suffocation, falling rock, and mine fires, and few miners lived into old age. The United Mine Workers of America Unions united white workers across contentious ethnic lines: John Mitchell, the president of UMWA in the early 1900s, proclaimed: "The coal you dig isn't Slavish or Polish or Irish coal. It is just coal."[42] Workers' demands for safety regulations and steady hours escalated into strikes and open violence. Miners, in this way, expanded their conception of self-interest to include others' pain, creating new visions of social justice that alleviated and held others accountable for it. Thomas Dublin and Walter Licht document how whole communities during the Depression demanded that employment in the mines be equally shared among workers. When work was scarce, miners joined together to illegally "bootleg" coal to survive. As one miner was quoted, "We're miners, without jobs, and our bellies are empty. We don't know and we don't care who's supposed to own the land. God put that coal out there—not the Philadelphia and Reading Coal Company." Miners depended on strong marriages, friendships, fraternal and ethnic societies, unions, and churches to survive.[43]

In his study of Buffalo Creek, a tight-knit mining community in West Virginia, the sociologist Kai Erikson studied what happened when a mining-company dam broke and laid waste to everything in its path. In Erikson's study, people reported feeling "less intact personally," "contaminated" by their surroundings, "emptied by self-esteem and an ability to relate to others," and terrified that something worse would befall them. Erikson suggests that these ailments manifested when the ties between people are eroded, dissolving the "basic tissues of social life."[44] For the people in this book, the stable ties and roles that undergirded working-class life in previous generations have similarly come undone. Detached from mainstream civic and political institutions, they view their social worlds as hostile and broken, leaving nothing larger than themselves to believe in. The categories that served as a compass for earlier generations—whether masculinity and femininity, trust, gender roles, race, fairness, or economic justice—are fracturing into a kaleidoscope of contradictions and uncertainties. In this moment of fracturing, they must come to terms, on their own, with turbulent social relationships, damning economic prospects, and social unmooring.

Individual pain management has become a necessity in an era where family and community ties are fragile, trust is nonexistent, social safety nets are limited, and opportunities for mobility are scarce.[45] The white working-class men in this book feel a keen loss of social recognition, solidarity with other workers, and purpose. For some men, who hold onto a sense of collective economic justice, preserving their sense of authority over women and superiority over racial minorities temporarily stems the tide of social unmooring. Other men abandon their sense of themselves as part of a larger working class, wanting only to be recognized for the risks and sacrifices they make as individual workers. Still other men experiment with dissolving traditional forms of masculinity and finding new, solitary ways to bring purpose to their lives. For white women, whose fortunes still remain tightly linked to white men, narratives of pain and trauma within the family reverberate into larger visions of a political arena where no one can be trusted. Living amid violence and poverty, many of the women turn to food, cigarettes, and drugs to numb their pain, only to decide that they must embrace suffering as a means for self-growth.

The men of color I met combat racism and recast the coal region as a place where their own shameful, traumatic pasts can become their children's redeemed futures. They magnify the positive consequences of their suffering. However, these men frame themselves as the lonely heroes of their individual quests, outrunning the trouble of the streets on their own, and remaining suspicious and watchful of anyone beyond their immediate families. Like the white women, the newcomer black and Latina women recount painful memories of early childhood abuse and neglect, poverty, extreme neighborhood violence, and drug abuse. They vocally fight back against the racism and hostility of the coal region for the sake of their children, but they also protect themselves by limiting their sphere of action to their own immediate families.

What unites these different groups is their inward turn: a focus on self-protection, endurance, and personal redemption. In place of external, collective strategies geared toward social change, they feel empowered by their knowledge that they have not been foolish enough to believe in something larger than themselves. Invalidating the suffering of others—and drawing strength from not depending on anyone to help them—emerges as a moral and necessary choice. Pain becomes a test of individual willpower, empowering working-class people to forge an identity as one who has survived it on their own.

Listening to the Silent

The people in this book are not simply paranoid or delusional. In their lifetimes, they have witnessed the compounding of economic and political interests, as large corporations and wealthy individuals have increasingly made financial contributions that sway policy outcomes in their favor.[46] There is growing evidence that public officials are more responsive to their middle- and upper-income constituents than to their needier ones. In one study, the political scientist Martin Gilens analyzed public policy preferences, as revealed in thousands of survey questions conducted between 1964 and 2006, alongside public policy outcomes. Gilens found that when the policy preferences of low- and middle-income Americans differed from the preferences of the affluent, there was no relationship between policy outcomes and the desires of less advantaged groups. However, the preferences of affluent Americans were significantly related to policy outcomes, regardless of whether their desires were shared by lower-income groups.[47] In another study, the political scientist Larry Bartels demonstrates that senators do not attempt to seek out or respond to the needs of their constituents in the bottom third of the income distribution.

But working-class disenchantment becomes a self-fulfilling prophecy. During impending elections, politicians do show responsiveness to the opinions of the broader public.[48] When Sidney Verba and Norman Nie compared the agendas of ordinary citizens to the agendas of governing elites, they found significantly higher agreement between activist citizens and leaders than between nonactive citizens and leaders.[49] Similarly, research across states by Kim Hill, Jan Leighley, and Angela Hinton-Anderson demonstrates that the more voting is skewed in favor of the wealthy, the less generous state welfare policies are.[50] Without a countervailing power, as the economist Robert Reich powerfully argues, the financial elite has been able to set the rules by which the economy runs in ways that benefit the wealthy few on the backs of the struggling many.[51] In contrast, people with lower levels of education and income, as Kay Lehman Schlozman, Sidney Verba, and Henry E. Brady emphasize, are much more concerned with fighting for government response to basic human needs like housing, food, and health care.[52] Yet without sustained political activity, these needs go unheard.

The title of this book, *We're Still Here*, is a call to listen carefully to the silent ones, even those who deliberately silence themselves. The men and women of Coal Brook speak out as witnesses to the economic and cultural forces that caused their suffering, and they put forth an alternative vision of a world worth belonging to. *We're Still Here* is also a willful insistence that working-class people endure. Their strategies for managing pain will sometimes tear each other apart and deepen that pain as they intersect in irreconcilable and violent collisions. But as visions of a broken America unite people across gender, race, and age, they also give voice to upended hierarchies, creative reimaginings of economic justice, and yearnings to be part of a collective whole. In this way, working-class people spark the possibility of opening up new ways of patching up the brokenness that free us from older divisions, contradictions, and hierarchies. And in this fracturing, there is hope.

1

Fracturing and Revival

To understand how working-class people in the coal region create imaginative bridges between personal suffering and politics, we begin with their desperate, often harrowing attempts to come to terms with the decline of the American Dream. For many families in this book, this decline is lived out not only in poverty, unemployment, and debt, but also in addiction, incarceration, illness, violence, and early death. In this chapter, I chronicle three families, both longtime residents and newcomers: Antonio and Joyce Lorino, the divorced parents of Tori and Ellen; Roger Adams and his wife, Brenda; and Gabrielle Hunter-Jackson and her son, Aydrian Hunter. Moving back and forth between each family's changing fortunes and the broader economic and social transformations that have disrupted working-class life, I trace how each family attaches meaning to their suffering, assigns blame for it, and imagines a way out of it.

As they connect the past to the future, tally rights and wrongs, and weigh their accomplishments and regrets, each family generates political identities that resonate with their pain. Their explanations for their suffering, and their projected solutions to it, emerge in the shifting constellations of family legacies, histories, and hierarchies that envelop their lives. The Lorino family gives voice to the steep decline of the white working class. As economic dislocation and social unmooring compounds with each generation, they struggle to manage their disappointment with themselves and with each other. Roger Adams, unemployed and living in chronic pain, angrily turns away from the Democratic Party of his childhood, accusing them of caring about the wrong people. The explosion of distrust and isolation in his life leads to raging populist visions of "putting a little bomb" on the government and launching a race war in the streets. The Hunters, an African American family, moved to the coal region for a fresh start, trying to escape the poverty, crime, and violence of New York City. Gabrielle tragically throws into relief the tensions between personal resilience and political engagement, as racism proves inescapable for her son Aydrian.

The Lorino Family

When Donald Trump promised to "make America great again," Antonio Lorino, a seventy-year-old divorced veteran with stooped shoulders and a GED, perked up. Antonio has lived through the rise and fall of the American white working class. During the middle decades of the twentieth century, America's dominance in manufacturing across the globe enabled continuously rising wages for workers.[1] The government also protected workers by imposing trade barriers and tariffs on foreign competition and backing labor unions with supportive legislation.[2] During this time, as the historian Jefferson Cowie observes, the definition of human freedom expanded to signify not only the absence of tethers on individuals but also a secure economic foundation on which to build a life.[3] Some of the risks of modern capitalism, such as losing one's income due to old age, unemployment, sickness, or injury, were reconceived as shared social problems from which it was the duty of the nation to protect its citizens.[4]

These protections for working-class people did not last. The following decades ushered in the computerization of routine work, the off-shoring of production, and the decreasing value of the minimum wage. The rise of neoliberalism from the 1970s onward shifted the burden of risk away from the government and back to individuals and families, jettisoning protections for workers in favor of the free movement of capital and trade.[5] In place of collective economic rights, we have witnessed a renewed celebration of the self-made man, with short-term profits for stakeholders taking precedence over loyalty, sustainability, or broadly shared prosperity for workers.[6] In turn, politicians have imposed time limits, budget caps, and work requirements on government aid for families struggling to make ends meet, further stigmatizing dependence on the state.[7]

Antonio's father had only a third-grade education. Antonio dropped out of high school, earned a GED, and got a job painting radio towers. At age nineteen, he was drafted into the Vietnam War. "Everybody was trying to avoid the service," he recalls. "I was an adventurous person. All I thought was glory, and John Wayne, and taking out the enemy. Talking now, I wouldn't recommend that kind of stuff for nobody because the horrors of war, I never knew existed." A surrealness still lingers over his memories of war. "There were definitely times when I was in the jungle that I said, man, I wish I would have gone to Canada," he says wistfully. "I remember once, being in battle. I was hungry for peaches and I had a can of them. I remember thinking, I don't want to sit in mud. So I sit on the dead bodies and I think, boy, this is a nice time to eat my peaches." He shakes his head incredulously: "I'm sitting on dead bodies eating my peaches!" Antonio was wounded multiple times, earned a lifetime disability pension, and made it home alive. Comparing himself to his fellow soldiers, many of whom suffered from posttraumatic stress disorder, he explains, "I was very lucky because I could make sense of it [the experience of war]. We had a saying: '*It don't mean nothing, it don't mean nothing to me.*' That got me through."

Antonio got married and had four children. He and his wife bought a small house in the coal region on his wages as a painter. A devout Roman Catholic, his major regret in life is that his marriage did not last, leaving his children to be raised in "a broken home." Antonio is loud and vivacious, with a bull-in-a-china-shop energy and a generous soul. He insists on treating me to the Chinese food buffet and offers earnest advice on everything from career-planning to married life. But underneath his bluster lies a paralyzing fear of finding his daughter dead with a needle in her arm. Antonio's daughter Tori is currently facing charges for heroin possession. Antonio laments that she is unmarried and unemployed, dependent on food stamps and government-subsidized health insurance, and expecting a second child in July.

Antonio insists that big business has betrayed the American Dream. He questions how "people are supposed to raise a family on nine dollars an hour" and states unequivocally that "Republicans are for rich people." He clarifies: "I am a big entitlement guy," expressing support for generous social safety nets. "I would never, in this great country, have a kid starve. And everybody should have healthcare." He fears that the country he loves has become purely "driven by money." Antonio ponders:

> I think the country lost its spirit somewhere along the way. We lost our pride. My generation, I had it pretty well made. You could do what you wanted to do. I want to paint, I'll be a painter. There was opportunity. Now where's the opportunity? They hand out the opportunity! Do you know what I mean? What would you rather do, work or go fishing and get the same amount of money? Well, I think I'll take the fishing. After a while you can't get up in the morning. That's where it happened. I could look at it politically and I could scream.

While Antonio identifies as a "big entitlement guy," he makes sense of his daughter's troubles by accusing self-serving politicians of winning votes from their constituents by promising endless "handouts" to young people. He resolves the seeming contradictions in his political beliefs with the assertion that pain is good for the human spirit: "I really feel that if I had the power, everyone in America would have a job. It gives you more than purpose. It puts positives and negatives into your life that you have to overcome. We lost that." To protect people from the "negatives," from the pain of everyday life, is to "take the soul out of the person."

Loyal to his country, Antonio detests the people who run it. He fumes, "These politicians, I hate them. I want to shoot them. They're liars. We need jobs and it breaks my heart when I see young people having to pay so much for college. You'll never pay that debt off. Now what kind of rip-off is that? They created college into this big moneymaking con job. There's no reward in helping people, but there is a reward in ripping off people." Antonio is left with the unsettling thought that the bonds between people have broken down, dissolving a shared sense of fate into a cold and meaningless pursuit of profit. He says regretfully: "So now everybody is on their own, and *it's almost like 'Nam again. Like nothing don't mean nothing anymore. It don't mean nothing.*"

Antonio registered as a Democrat at the age of eighteen. Although he has never changed his party affiliation, he fiercely distrusts Democrats who "refuse to rally round the flag" and "hand out too many freebies" to win votes. Today, he trusts only the military. "It makes me feel like somebody is looking over us," he explains. Antonio is not blind to the controversies surrounding the Vietnam War or, more recently, the war in Iraq. He describes his first time encountering protestors when he stepped off the plane from Vietnam: "That was the first time I saw those protestors. When we came in off the planes already the movement was pretty solid. That year the colleges were making a stand. I was like what the heck are they talking about, baby killers? Me?"

In *Chain Reaction*, Mary D. Edsall and Thomas Edsall describe how the cultural liberalism of the Left from the 1960s on alienated blue-collar Democrats, as the liberals who pushed for progressive social change were sheltered from the costs of their own agendas: they sent their children to private schools, avoided the draft through college deferments, and would not suffer wage loss if new environmental protections made industries less competitive.[8] Antonio refuses to collude with the "muckety mucks" who called him a baby killer. "Was Vietnam a stupid war?" he wonders aloud. "I hope there's a bigger picture somewhere. Hopefully, the military is watching over us and national security because that's their job. If I was a general, and somebody told me to go to Iraq, I would say, why should I? You give me a good reason, then okay, let's sacrifice a few for the many." Antonio no longer expects politicians or even the president to know, let alone inform American citizens, of the true reasons underlying military action. "There are seven security clearances and the president only is at level six so you figure it out," he says evenly. "The president's only on a need-to-know basis." He convinces himself that there is a level of authority above even the president that has the nation's, and thus his own, best interests at heart.

Leading up to the 2016 presidential election, a substantial proportion of eligible voters within the working class turned away from solid identification with either the Democratic Party or the Republican Party during the Obama presidency, perhaps leaving them primed for an outsider candidate.[9] Antonio likes

Trump's stance on the economy—"he will put a tariff on Mexico so they can't ship stuff here!" Above all, he is excited that Trump seems to operate *outside* the corrupt system of political bureaucracy: "I think a guy like Trump, who probably has eight billion bucks, he's very intelligent. That Wharton School of business. The guy has a head on his shoulders. He don't even care if nobody donates to his campaign. Now there's a kind of guy that could possibly bring back jobs." His critique of politicians who put personal profit before moral obligation is resolved with the conviction that only a billionaire can rise above the temptation of corruption to save us all. Only a billionaire might resist "taking the soul out of people" like his daughter. In the end, Trump wins Antonio's vote because Trump has "enough guts to not care about a future."

Making Politics Personal

Antonio Lorino's ex-wife, Joyce, is sixty years old. She "work[s] hard like a man" on the night shift at a paper factory, earning about $28,000 a year. Joyce describes vivid memories of her "daddy coming home after trying to fight the coal company, trying to get compensation for his black lung. I remember him sitting on the front steps just wheezing, 'those bastards, they made me climb three flights of stairs and still denied me.' "[10] She weaves these early memories into an indictment of greedy corporations and corrupt politicians: "The drug companies and the banks are making the laws by paying off all the officials, the congressmen, they're paying everybody off. I mean really, how much money do these people need? That's just my opinion. You're talking about all these people making astronomical amounts of money that, I can't even comprehend." For Joyce, lasting memories of her father wheezing for breath, discarded by the coal company, leave her with a deeply rooted belief in economic justice.

Joyce's present family turmoil seeps into her politics in equally intense yet opposing ways. Joyce and her other daughter, Ellen, are currently entrenched in a grueling, protracted legal battle to gain custody of Tori's five-year old daughter, Lacey. On "14 something an hour," Joyce pays for all of Lacey's clothes, activity fees, and toys, and frequently takes care of Lacey for weeks at a time when Tori goes missing. Joyce feels pangs of guilt when she thinks about her daughter Tori's battle with addiction. When I ask her what caused it, she shrugs, "probably me," wondering if Tori's "home life" and especially her parents' divorce may have caused Tori's addiction. Joyce simmers with rage at her own powerlessness: "It is so absolutely horrible, one day I actually threw a coffee cup at the TV screen, and I threw it, and here's how goofy it was. I was stone sober, and I threw the cup and it went flying and it made this crazy noise and I was like oh, that was really cool. And I went and I did it again and again and again."

Over Sprites and the Friday night crab cake special at a local diner, Joyce soundly rejects my assumption that her children have been robbed of the American Dream:

JS: Do you worry about your own kids and their futures? Like, do you worry they won't be able to achieve the American Dream?

JOYCE: I do worry, but not because of the American Dream.

JS: What do you mean?

JOYCE: The land of opportunity gave them too many opportunities. I remember being young having to go out and get a job and being afraid. But if you're not getting through it and you're not going to go through it, how are you going to grow? How do you expect to learn, how do you expect to become a useful part of society?

JS: Who do you think caused that?

JOYCE: I know there was a period of time when my mom had to have food stamps or something through welfare, but back then you had to pay that back. If I lose my job right now, for whatever reason I lost my job, I cannot get food stamps and I cannot get Medicare or Medicaid or any of that stuff.

JS: Why is that?

JOYCE: Why is that? Because you can't. I'm not a drug addict. I don't have a child.

When Joyce condemns corruption on Wall Street and in Washington, DC, she shrugs: "You can't do nothing about that." But when she talks about her disappointment in her daughter—and her frustration at feeling taken advantage of, time and time again—she becomes incensed, weaving together her experiences as a daughter, worker, mother, and grandmother into a tentative political identity. Like her ex-husband, Joyce believes that going through hardship makes people stronger and resents that her own sacrifices have not been recognized. In this way, Joyce's political views are dramatized *within* her already fragile and divided working-class family.

And like her ex-husband, Joyce has decided to vote for Donald Trump. She justifies her choice by condemning the increasing concentration of political and corporate power. "If you want to do good for this country, you either want to do good or you don't want to do good," she asserts. "I can't remember the guy's name, I'll never forget, I was probably only 20 years old, I think he was a mayor of some place, he was a mayor of some place and he turned down a raise. The politicians make these crazy amounts of money, and they're taking it from us who make nothing. I mean, you have people that are probably aren't even making $10,000 a year. I'm like, it's just crazy. I just, why can't nobody else see it? I mean they just take and take and take more." She demands: "What if you only give them money as long as they're in office? All those fringes go, it all goes.

Now let's see who wants to be president and Congress!" And then she turns her vote into a joke. "Anyway, Trump made it," she laughs. "There's a chance. I'm 60, I have 30 more years." When I ask her for her second choice, she names Bernie Sanders—the pro-labor senator from Vermont who advocated universal health care and free higher education and was defeated by Hillary Clinton in the 2016 Democratic primaries.

Breaking with the Past

Tori Lorino, the source of all this anguish, will give birth to a second child in a few months. Tori is hesitant to marry her boyfriend, who is currently undergoing an eighteen-month drug court program for heroin possession: "If it doesn't work, if I don't get married, it's okay," she shrugs. Her employment prospects are grim. She borrowed $16,000 for a one-year certificate in cosmetology from a nearby for-profit college, but calls her degree "worthless" because the teachers at her school were required to pay out of pocket for up-to-date training. "They didn't want to pay for the upkeep of the classes to learn new things," she clarifies. "So we're learning like rollers and stuff and nobody does now. I know how to do grandmothers' hair, you know what I mean . . . old people's hair, that's what I learned how to do."

Tori does not have much to say about the economy or about politics. During our three-hour-long conversation, she weeps steadily as she chronicles the unraveling of her childhood family, the lack of expressiveness and warmth in her intimate relationships, and the horror of being victimized by, and blamed for, unwanted sexual violence. Her parents, before they divorced, "would fight all the time. It was horrible." Tori reports feeling unloved by her mother, who seemed "very distant. She wasn't really what I would want as a mother or I would want to be as a mother. She was not warm." Tori continues: "We never bonded and even now we don't say I love you, we don't kiss. She'll buy me something at a yard sale and that's her way of saying . . . you don't feel it, it's not verbally there, it's just . . . she doesn't know how to be warm."

When Tori was sexually assaulted by a fellow student in high school, she turned to heroin to cope:

> [W]hen I was sixteen I was raped by my friend so that was a traumatic thing that happened in my life. Even with my mom, I went to my mom with that, and she was just like . . . my curfew was eleven and I used to always come in at twelve and I remember her saying to me well, *that is what you get*. So I turned to alcohol and drugs. That was my problem, I didn't know how to deal with past stuff, past trauma, past everything. They put me on pills for depression and ADHD. And somehow I learned how to

be okay with everything. Something that is so simple, that I think is so simple now, took me fifteen years to do. I started off journaling, talking about it, being okay with it, just accepting it. Everything I was uncomfortable with I became comfortable with. I remember waking up every day thinking I don't want to do this. I hated myself. I hated my life. It was horrible.

Today, most of her energy is directed toward healing herself—treating her depression and ADHD, journaling, talking openly about the roots of her pain, and focusing on sobriety. After fifteen years, she says proudly, she has learned to accept herself for who she is.

The kinds of suffering in intimate relationships that Tori experiences are not unique to her generation. In the 1970s, Lillian Rubin's groundbreaking study of working-class family life uncovered hidden, shameful "worlds of pain"—emotionally distant relationships, neglect and abandonment, grueling financial strain, suffocating gender roles, violent fights, and alcoholism.[11] Mirra Komarovsky's study of working-class marriages in the 1960s poignantly revealed how husbands and wives lived lives of dashed expectations in which they denied their own childhood pain, coped with their lack of fulfillment in work and love with stoic respectability, and quietly winnowed down their expectations of a good life. Komarovsky concludes that working-class family life was not entirely grim, as sticking it out despite their suffering lent a kind of "underlying satisfaction" to "men and women who feel that they have fulfilled honorably their basic roles of provider, mate and parent."[12] But these basic roles, for Tori, have become both unachievable and undesirable. In their absence, as the sociologist Eva Illouz argues, people are on their own to manage the disappointments and disruptions of postindustrial life.[13] Rather than coping quietly like women in previous generations, Tori speaks out openly about sexual trauma, emotional coldness, and intimate violence. Suffering thereby acquires new *meaning* in Tori's life through what Eva Illouz calls "the therapeutic narrative": she tells a story of self-discovery that hinges not on fulfilling traditional gender and family roles, but on liberating herself, vocally, from these very roles. Pain becomes the thread that weaves her life back together in a pivotal narrative of personal redemption and self-growth.

Tori trusts one person in the world: "My dad is my hero. He has a great heart."

Tori has only voted once in her life, for George W. Bush. Her earliest memory of going to the polls was with her father, her hero, by her side. For a brief moment in our conversation, Tori lashes out at "people that just keep having kids to get like subsidized houses and stuff. How the fuck can anyone afford five kids? I can barely afford one. But you know they are not paying for it. At some point the government should step in and sew people right up." Relying only on oneself is a time-honored route to dignity and inclusion in America society, and for a brief moment, she joins the chorus, disparaging these mythical "people" who rely on tax-payer dollars even more than she does.

But Tori also spends most of her free time "couponing." Every week, she waits outside the local newspaper office until they take out the recycling bins. Then, she explains, "I'll sit there and just clip all these coupons. I do a lot of toilet paper, paper towels, toothpaste, toothbrushes. I watch the sales. At night I shop." She then will spend the next few days dropping off free toiletries at the local women's shelter and office supplies at the schools. "It's, like, something for me to do, and I like it. I like the feeling of giving to people that need it," she says shyly. Showing enthusiasm for the first time, she explains:

> Like I get these diapers. We have a pregnancy center here in Coal Brook. I don't know if they get funding from the state. I'm sure they do, but it's not enough, you know? And, like, somebody just called me last night, they just moved here, they're in trouble, they need diapers. I like had the coupon for it, so I could help, you know? I guess it makes you feel good.

On top of antidepressants, therapy, and an unceasing stream of cigarettes, Tori treats her suffering through this solitary weekly ritual of helping others, even as she can barely survive herself. Unlike her parents, she does not even maintain the semblance of political participation. "Like I wish I could, like, stand up and feel like I'm making a difference, you know?" she says wistfully. "I don't know if I am. I feel like bringing, you know, toilet paper and diapers, makes more of a difference, you know what I mean? That's what I feel like." As distrustful as her parents, she says, "Whoever is in power, I don't know how it works on top, but you know whoever is greedy. I mean I think a lot of people like the power, the money, it's addicting, and I think that ruins a lot of people." In 2016, Tori did not vote at all.

Steeling the Soul

Tori's sister, Ellen, spent several years taking college classes in Pittsburgh, but she returned home to help care for Tori's daughter while Tori was in rehab. Describing the young adults in her hometown, Ellen gripes: "They have no dreams, they have no drive. They can't get up every day in the morning, and they would rather just lie on the couch all day and collect their food stamps and housing vouchers." While blaming people for abusing welfare is often a coded way to disparage racial minorities, Ellen is talking about her own sister whose years of addiction have cost her family countless sleepless nights and thousands of dollars.[14] Ellen unveils the dark underbelly of Tori's redemptive journey: the revolving door of abusive boyfriends, in and out of jail, who sold drugs out of Tori's home; the phone call she got late one night from her four-year-old niece who, after stepping gingerly over passed-out bodies, was ravenously munching on a box of stale animal crackers she found on the top shelf of the kitchen cabinets because no one had fed her that day. Ellen recalls coldly that her niece knew how much a brick of heroin cost before she had learned the alphabet.

A group of women in her neighborhood meet every week for wine, cheese, and a "positive thinking" book club. This week, they are reading *Codependent No More*, an enormously popular self-help guide that promises to liberate readers from dysfunctional "helping" relationships:

> I help a lot of people. I'm not looking for a pat on the back. When you have that persona, you got to watch out. When someone's down, I have no problem giving them money but you have to be careful. It's hard to tell the difference between who needs help and who is using you. I'd never ask for help. Especially from my family. Honestly that didn't even cross my mind, to get some kind of government aid. When I was in college, I would have starved before getting help. And there was no way I was coming home. I'd go weeks without eating. My roommate and I would decide, are we going to smoke cigarettes or eat this week? Cigarettes were cheaper and they'd make you feel full.

Ellen calls her father "the master enabler" for bailing Tori out of jail and lending her money. She derives a sense of self-worth from rejecting dependence on others and sacrificing to make it on her own. Like her father, she critiques Democrats who have made it too easy to be dependent on the state: "I think welfare had its purpose when it was implemented and it served its purpose. But it needed to stop then. Instead it just kept going and going and now we have whole generations of that's all they know. That I guess is what the problem is." One evening, as we discuss how emergency responders in the county have started carrying Narcan, a nasal spray for reversing opioid overdose, she confides: "If Tori dies, that's on her, those are her choices. If she was in front of me overdosing, I would let her die. I've had enough. How do you make people live with the consequences of their own choices?"

Applying cognitive science to political reasoning, the linguist and philosopher George Lakoff argues that authoritarian politics are undergirded by the metaphor of a strict father—one who upholds exacting rules of right and wrong, sets firm boundaries, punishes wrongdoing, and demands personal responsibility for failures.[15] In Arlie Hochschild's study of Louisiana Tea Partyers, conservatives express the strict-father code of hard work, sacrifice, and personal responsibility. Janice, one memorable character, declares unapologetically: "If people refuse to work, we should let them starve," echoing Ellen's "let her die" rhetoric. Hochschild argues that this orientation stems from a need for social honor, to feel recognized for one's sacrifice and rewarded for one's own efforts.[16]

But there is a fervent self-righteousness among Arlie Hochschild's Tea Partyers that doesn't quite square with Ellen's experience. When Ellen goes home at the end of a long day, battling depression and the empty feeling that she has already given up on her own life, she practices visualization techniques where she imagines an angel descending from heaven and enveloping her niece in its arms. Next, she imagines the angel embracing her sister, and then—if she can stomach it—she prompts the angel to hug all of her sister's abusive, drug-selling ex-boyfriends. In this exercise, she finds a fleeting sense of peace. The seeming harshness of "letting people die" may steel her soul, at least temporarily, against the heartbreak and disappointment of seeing her sister fall prey, again and again, to addiction and despair. It serves as a flimsy shield against the uncomfortable knowledge that kindness can be manipulated and drained away.

Even more critical than her mother, Ellen believes a president should serve on a volunteer basis: "I think the biggest problem in our country is the lobbyist. If you got rid of that, cause the drug companies and the banks are making the laws by paying off all the officials, the congressmen, they're paying everybody off to make the laws. So if you outlaw all that, it all goes away." She rolls her eyes at Trump's popularity in the coal region, and within her own family, wondering why people who are struggling to make ends meet would vote for a Republican: "It's ironic. Why wouldn't you vote for the one who is giving you the handout? It doesn't make sense to me." When I ask Ellen whom she plans to vote for, she shrugs: "I always have a soft spot for the underdog. I always did and maybe that's why I'm a Democrat. I don't mind paying my taxes. I'm just doing my part." While Ellen relies on the strict-father code to protect herself against the most visceral pain, hardening herself against her sister's relapses, she nonetheless remains faithful to her identity as a person who has always looked out for the underdog.

The Adams Family

When I walk into Roger and Brenda Adams's row home, my eyes burn from the fumes of kitty litter. Roger, a forty-two-year-old white man, and his wife, Brenda, forty-one, keep their doors and windows shut, sealing themselves off from the people around them, armed with just one small fan to combat the oppressive July heat. Roger and Brenda live in constant pain. They report that they have been trying unsuccessfully to get medical assistance for disability for years: him for depression, neuropathy, diabetes, the early stages of congestive heart failure, and obesity; her for scoliosis, hypothyroidism, and PTSD from her troubled, abusive childhood in foster care.[17] "I'm waiting for actually an answer right now for my hearing," Roger informs me. "She has to go for a second hearing."

Roger has been out of work since 2009. He is the grandson of a coal miner. His father, a construction worker, also bootlegged coal to bring in extra money for the family. When he was younger, Roger worked as an EMT and volunteered as a firefighter. "And then we lost our son," he says, recalling Brenda's late-term miscarriage. "Everybody said it wasn't my fault, it was just, he didn't develop properly, but I couldn't get it in my head. I just, you know I couldn't save him. I gave everything up and that's when everything went down, depression set in." Roger accuses his employer of firing him "cuz my health was starting to deteriorate and I was trying to get FMLA [Family and Medical Leave Act] leave to try and maintain my health and try and get it back, but they fired me before I could even get the papers in. So it was like a dirty, dirty trick type of thing." After losing his job, he reports, a plumbing issue resulted in the loss of their older children. "A neighbor complained and called child protective services or something, and they came in, took our kids," Roger describes angrily. "And I was fixing the issues, but I couldn't get it fixed in the proper amount of time and they went and placed them with my mom. And all of a sudden, my wife signed a paper behind my back, and off the kids went." His "evil mother" got full custody. Since then, Roger has been "just trying to make it right. That's why I never pulled out of their lives. I'm just trying to make things right. A man needs to make things right, not pull out of their life. Make things right."

Roger spends his days lying on his recliner with an orange pharmacy bottle on the shelf above his head. He occasionally calls a doctor in town who is infamous for prescribing opiate painkillers. "Like if I have like a cyst or something on my side or a sore, I'll say could you look at it?" he discloses. "Ever since I had my spleen out for my anemia on this side of my body, I've been getting cysts left and right and they've been popping. He does [look at it] but it's five minutes, a five-, ten-minute appointment, out the door I go. And you know what's going on, he'll look at it and go, eh I'll just write you a script, go ahead." Roger explains that they "squeak by" on food stamps and their five-year-old daughter's Social Security Insurance. This daughter was diagnosed with Attention Deficit Disorder (ADD) and Oppositional Defiant Disorder (ODD) when she started school. Roger reflects, "You know, the worst part about it, or the hard parts, is when they struggle with a lot of things like in their life. Like people are always at them or bullying them with like their medical problems at school," he says sadly. "If you ain't popular and have money in that school, you get nowhere. My son was put in for band president, but he didn't have popularity and money and hobnob with the snobs, and he didn't get it."

Brenda has never voted. "I don't vote," she insists, even when her husband urges her, "it's something you have to do to make your freedoms known." A registered Democrat, Roger is not guided by party affiliation or by his parents' voting history, though he maintains his affiliation out of loyalty to his father. He does not espouse the neoliberal mantra of freedom from government intervention, reporting proudly that his dad collected "seven checks" from his pensions and injuries. He voted for Barack Obama in 2008. Roger's criticism of the Democrats is that they do not do enough to sustain people like himself, as they did in the past.

When I ask who he is planning to vote for in 2016, he explains:

> I'm a Democrat, but I hate Hillary. My dad was a Democrat. I'm gonna stay Democrat for him but I'll never vote Democrat again. At one time the Democrats helped our family, they really did, but right now, they are—how is Hillary bringing the Muslims over when JFK banned it?— They don't do enough to help people. They don't do enough to create jobs, to get people back to work, I mean I think they could have gotten me back to work with my health, look where I'm at, I would go back to work. I wrote Donald Trump that! I said, if you help me get my health back, I will go back to work. You can have more than my vote. I'd go work for him. I'd go be on his personal security, just tell him to make me some kind of friggin' bionic man.

A few moments later, tears run down his face as he remembers his father, a Vietnam veteran who passed away three years ago. His father was "my hero, the only person I looked up to, I wanted to be just like him. Since he's been gone it's just like I've been lost."

Roger sees himself and his forebearers as the backbone of America, fighting to protect and preserve his country. "There's an old phrase, a gold catchphrase," he cries. "As the American flag blows in the wind, that wind is the last breath of every soldier that has died, blowing that back and forth for freedom. I don't care how much I hurt, I will always salute it, I will always stand and I will cover my heart."

"I think it's dying," Roger answers when I ask if the American Dream is still alive. "I really do. I mean for some people, I think for the refugees, I think it's alive. I think for anybody living here, it's dying." He angrily recounts the story of a Muslim family who refused to say the Pledge of Allegiance at his daughter's kindergarten play. He continues: "If I had a Confederate flag up outside people would say it was a hate crime, but if I had a gay flag, or an Islam flag, people would celebrate it. Hell, even having an American flag is seen as a hate crime. But that will come down over my dead body."

Historically, people in power have counted on hostility and division within the working class, particularly between African Americans and northeastern ethnic whites or southern white populists, to reduce the possibility of a strong, united working class.[18] The social protections of the mid-twentieth century were carefully crafted to exclude many black and Latino workers from their promise of collective economic justice.[19] Attempts to correct the exclusions built into the New Deal Order—to open up its protections to African Americans, women, and immigrants in the 1970s and beyond—were met with hostility by blue-collar Democrats, who felt that the party was protecting new groups at the expense of their constituents who built it. Gradually, white working-class people who once saw their own interests as aligned with the downwardly redistributive US government came to believe that the government was promoting the interests of less-deserving groups over their own. This resentment sparked a reimagining of society's fault lines: the "real Americans" pitted against undeserving immigrants, racial minorities, and flag-burning, politically correct liberals.[20]

Roger is seething. He declares ominously, "A race war is coming. It will be black against white, Hispanic against white, and we will fight it out in the streets." He tells me candidly that maybe God made him disabled just so he "wouldn't be able to go out into the world and start shooting people." Roger longs to restore the legacy of violence and power that was created by his forebearers. "My family has a dark history too," he boasts. "My family was in the KKK. It goes pretty far back. It goes to my great, I think it's my great uncle or my great grandfather on my dad's side." He fumes: "At the last football home game, we sat down in the seats, the reserved seats that my mom got. Three . . . "—he stops himself. "Black people. I want to be correct. I didn't want to say that word. Three black people stood in front of us. I asked them politely, could you please move. You know, these were the reserved seats we bought, you know, please move so we can watch the game. Very politely. And they purposely just stood right there and made sure we couldn't see nothing."

The sociologist Rory McVeigh traces how the Ku Klux Klan framed the protection of white privilege as an urgent national concern in the twentieth century, depicting immigrants and African Americans as threats to the social fabric.[21] While Roger does not belong to any organized groups, he imagines himself to be part of the lineage of men in his family who were committed to upholding white supremacy through terror. Roger staunchly believes that the government "needs a totally new overhaul. Clear everybody out, start over kind of. Or just put them all down there and put one little bomb on them." Roger summarizes his life: "I very rarely trust anyone because every time I started trusting someone, something happened. Stone Cold Steve Austin said it on wrestling, and he put it in three letters. D.T.A. *Don't trust anyone.*"

Both 2016 presidential candidates Donald Trump and Bernie Sanders put forth a vision of ordinary people rising up against a self-serving, corrupt, "crooked" elite with the end goal of overhauling rather than reforming politics.[22] Roger's political views embody the right-wing populism that triumphed, pitting the employment and health care needs of "the people" against recent immigrants and ethnic minorities. At the end of our conversation, he asks if I have ever played video games like Fallout, Fallen Earth, S.T.A.L.K.E.R—"I think all these games, like on Xbox, you see how it looks like a wasteland? That's how America is gonna look like soon, it's gonna be a civil war, and it's gonna be all real nasty." Sitting in his recliner, imagining scenes of violent annihilation, he dreams of protecting his body, and America, from becoming a wasteland. As he talks, his wife sits quietly on the floor, wringing her hands.

New Beginnings

Just an eight-minute drive from Roger's house, I meet Gabrielle Hunter-Jackson, a forty-four year-old African American woman, for coffee. Gabrielle grew up in Crown Heights, Brooklyn. She was raised by her mother, a postal worker, in a public housing project. Gabrielle's early life was scarred by poverty, instability, and trauma. She describes her neighborhood as a "very bad area, there was drug dealing, a shooting every day. I seen a lot of my friends, a lot of my friends are not alive." She was molested by her father, got pregnant at age sixteen, seventeen, nineteen, and twenty by men who were "not even her boyfriends"; dropped out of high school; and spent six years in an abusive relationship. She explains: "I did a lot of odd jobs. I did something I wasn't proud of. I tried the prostitution, I tried stripping. I tried selling drugs." The worst moment of her life came when her younger son was taken away from her for a year.

Gabrielle's mother had moved from Atlanta, Georgia, to Brooklyn, New York, as a child of the Great Migration. She was part of a mass exodus from 1915 to 1970 of nearly six million African Americans who migrated from South to North, fleeing violence, lynch mobs, and Jim Crow segregation. During this era, African Americans were disenfranchised by grandfather clauses, which restricted the right to vote to people whose ancestors had voted before the Civil War, poll taxes, and fraudulent literacy tests.[23] As the white working class experienced its midcentury "golden age," African Americans were barred from advancement in many working-class jobs. For example, not only could black men not work their way up from firemen to engineers in the railroad companies, but they were also paid less than white firemen who might one day advance to engineers.[24] In boom times in Pennsylvania, such as World War II, black men were hired in mining but would also be the first fired, suffering a disproportionate share of job loss when the economy contracted in the Great Depression.[25]

It was not until the 1970s that black men began to truly share in stable factory work and its financial benefits.[26] But the 1970s also witnessed the closing of factory doors in the Northeast, resulting in catastrophic disinvestment from urban neighborhoods.[27] The loss of jobs spurred higher rates of juvenile delinquency, drug addiction, homicide, and out-of-wedlock births.[28] A devastating crack epidemic in the 1980s and '90s tore urban African American families apart and led to increased neighborhood violence.[29] The government responded by launching the War on Drugs, implementing mandatory minimum sentencing, increased surveillance of poor inner-city neighborhoods, stop-and-frisk policies, and long prison sentences. The resulting mass incarceration of low-educated black and Latino men quadrupled the prison population over four decades.[30] Many of the descendants of African American families who came to northern cities from the South in search of greater opportunities remain trapped in economic and geographical immobility.[31]

Gabrielle describes a pivotal moment that led her to break out of this trap:

[L]et's see about, 2006, I had a wakeup call. My kid was in school and coming home from school and somebody pulled out a gun on him and tried to rob him. And that's when something clicked in my head: I gotta get outta here. And I moved to, I moved to Pennsylvania. It wasn't this part at first, I moved to Lebanon at first. And I was there with my kids and at first life was good. I found a good job. I started working, I worked for American Red Cross. And then I said, lemme go back to school and get my GED. So I did that. And of course I was older than most people. I didn't think I was gonna pass it, but I wanted to and I kept wanting to go. I wanted to keep going. Because so many times it got so hard, I wanted to go back to what I was used to. But I just kept going, kept going, kept going.

Gabrielle married a man who works as a casual laborer in the construction trade. On the advice of his aunt, they moved to Coal Brook, where they bought a home for eight thousand dollars.

Gabrielle enrolled in a for-profit associate's degree program in business. "Oh yes," she affirms, when I ask her if she is in debt. "I took out a lot of loans. I'm like thirty-five thousand in debt. But it gives you, it gives you a sense of self. I feel so happy now. You know, I'm at the happiest place I've ever been. I'm really happy." Gabrielle ponders, "Who would have thought, little old me from Brooklyn, owning a home?"

When I ask Gabrielle if she has experienced racism in her new town, she offers the following measured reply:

> You know a lot of times, even now, you go places and you're the only black person, you know? And it's just hard sometimes. You know, everybody's not gonna accept you for who you are. And we had a lot of that at first here. It's come a long way. I love the small town. It's really community-based and it's really small. And like just to see everybody get along, it's really fun in itself. When I lived in New York, I felt so alone. When you come here people actually speak to me, they say hi to me. Yeah, when you go places people know you by name, and you go and order something and someone already knows your order because you've been there before. Things like that matter.

In stark contrast to the white residents of Coal Brook, who describe it as a wasteland, Gabrielle emphasizes racial progress, painting Coal Brook as a fun, friendly place where everyone knows her name, and she no longer feels alone.

Gabrielle has voted once in her life—"I always register, just never vote. I voted for Obama. That was it. Only once. That was my first time voting, and my last time." In many states, targeted demobilization of minorities and African Americans continues to operate through photo identification and proof of citizenships requirements, registration restrictions, absentee ballot voting restrictions, and reductions in early voting.[32] Gabrielle, though, demobilizes herself, maintaining her optimistic stance by ignoring the impending election: "Yeah, I like to avoid the news. It's so depressing. The election gets me laughing, I love the election. I try to stay out of it."

When I press her, insisting that she choose a candidate, she rattles off: "I think Donald's a good businessman. And I think as far as money-wise he'd be good in the White House. He knows his money. And America needs that. But everything else, no. So I guess Hillary. But there's something about her, it's not good. I don't get good vibes from her." She perks up: "But her husband, you know, I liked Bill. Well, then when I think about it, I think you know, maybe he'll give her some pointers and maybe she'll be good in office!" Projecting a comical yet deliberate distance, Gabrielle laughs deeply, and it is clear she will not be going to the polls this year.[33]

When we discuss Black Lives Matter, she focuses on themes of personal happiness, innate goodness, and self-fulfillment, rather than on the movement's concern with police brutality and mass incarceration:

> Everybody matters. It shouldn't be about black lives. Everybody matters. If I walk down the street and I see a white person laying around

and they needed help, I wouldn't stop and say no I'm not gonna do that. I would help them. If I see a black person, I would help them too. No matter who it is, I would help. And that's what I think matters. Everybody matters. There is too much hate. There's a lot of hate in this country. If everybody would just be happy, do something to make them happy, I think there'd be a lot more love in the country. And I think that everyone should, everyone should experience living around a certain amount of different people. Get to know people.

Gabrielle, in this way, chooses to believe the best of individual people, rather than seeing systemic inequalities and divisions between groups of people. "Everybody doing something that makes them happy" becomes a solution to racism. Her optimistic narrative of self-growth and resilience seems to bolster her belief that the future will be better than the past. Gabrielle Hunter has built her own American Dream of a home, marriage, and community in a new place. She embraces a language of personal redemption, rather than one of resentment or anger, deflecting conversation about racism and politics.[34] Like Tori Lorino, Gabrielle embodies the kind of therapeutic self that protects her psychologically even as it is politically lifeless.[35]

The Limits of Optimism

While Gabrielle describes Coal Brook as the best thing that's ever happened to her, her twenty-four-year-old son, Aydrian, calls it "the worst mistake my mother ever made." At age thirteen, Aydrian was excited to move out of New York, looking forward to living with his family in a quiet ("there was no gunshots") and safe neighborhood. It did not take long for his enthusiasm to turn to dread:

I got suspended my first day in school. My first time ever getting in trouble in school. I used to love school until I went out there. I got suspended for, cuz I used to like rapping, so I had a rap book and I'd write my raps in it. And I guess I took it to school one day, my first day of school, and I meant to put it in my locker, it probably fell out my locker. Somebody found it, took it to the principal and said they felt threatened. I'm like how you feel threatened? I don't know you, you don't know me. And it's a piece of paper. It don't even got their name on it, just raps.

Aydrian describes being constantly under surveillance by the local police:

The cops came to the school one day for me and my brother. They, a detective. They said that we fit the description of a old lady getting robbed, robbing the old lady's purse. And it was confusing. I'm like what time did this happen? It was like they said a time, I'm like well we was in school, y'all just got us from school. They're like well y'all fit the description and it was in this area after school so we coming straight to y'all. I'm like that don't even make no sense. We in school, how we gonna do a robbery?

Aydrian dropped out of school. "I just felt like it wasn't for me like they, they stop you for no reason. If I'm walking outside like I'll walk, my pants be sagging, cuz that's how I wear my pants. So they might stop me. They stop you for where you come from, a lot of things." By fourteen, he was stealing cars, buying and selling marijuana, and going on joy rides late at night with his friends. By fifteen, "I wound up doing other stuff like I met somebody that gave me some crack to sell. So I started selling crack for a little bit."

Aydrian and his older brother were arrested for stealing cars. In a "crazy" ending, he explains, "the judge, my P.O., and my mother came up with a solution that we just, they told her if she pack her things up and go back to New York and don't come back, they'd let us out. Once they confirmed that she wasn't in the house no more in P.A. they let her drive back out to P.A. to pick us up to take us back to New York." To keep the boys safe, the family returned to New York, this time to one of East Brooklyn's most dangerous neighborhoods, and moved into his grandmother's cramped one-bedroom apartment. Aydrian was furious when his mother and stepfather moved to North Carolina a few months later, leaving him and his brother on his own. At first, he sold "metro cards and weed," getting "locked up" here and there. It took him a while to realize that he could make more money by going back to selling crack cocaine: "Cuz when I first got introduced to selling crack in P.A., I was selling to white people. So I come to New York and then I's like damn, there ain't no white people out here, who am I gonna sell crack to? Not knowing that black people do crack too," he adds drily.

Soon after, he was selling crack again, in a neighborhood besieged by gun violence and constant police raids: "So I started selling drugs again. That's the only thing I know how to do. But we gotta worry about people that, we gotta worry about people trying to shoot us, and we gotta worry about the cops." Aydrian headed back to Pennsylvania, this time to live with old friends, and resumed selling crack, making $600 a week plus money for meals without the constant fear of being shot. He says flatly: "I gotta have money to support myself. Cuz now I'm realizing like, nobody gonna do nothing for you. Like you gotta go do something for yourself."

Aydrian eventually found a legal job, earning $11.75 an hour pulling twelve-hour shifts at a shipping and receiving facility: "It was a good job. So I stopped selling crack. I didn't tell nobody I stopped, I just stopped."

Before I stopped selling crack, I had already sold to a undercover. Like he had called me, I wouldn't answer no more. I wasn't answering nobody, cuz I'm not selling crack no more, what are you calling me for? So I guess the undercover was looking like damn, where this guy at? Like, we gotta get him. It was around Thanksgiving. I went back home for Thanksgiving because I wanted to be around the people I grew up with. And then when I came back to P.A. one of the people I was selling crack with, they wound up getting locked up. So they wound up getting locked up for like, they wound up getting locked up for crack, some guns, they got caught with crack, gun on him, and weed. So they, they got five years for that. I didn't even, I didn't know the person that locked him up was the undercover that I sold to too. So I wound up going to New York for Thanksgiving [and that] messed my job up. Cuz I took more days off than what I was supposed to. So when I came back, of course I don't got a job no more. So now I'm just like, now I'm looking for a job, I'm looking for another job, but it's not that easy. So of course I started selling crack again. And the first person that caught me, first person, was the undercover. Went to him, they locked me up right away. Now that, that ruined my life cuz now I got a felony.

He spent seven months in prison. When I ask Gabrielle about him, she says wistfully: "I wish I could've afforded a lawyer for him." She beams: "My third son, my youngest son, is nineteen. And right now he's doing so good. Just got his new job. He works at McDonald's here, he seems to be on the right track." Aydrian has been out for under a week, living with his mother and looking for jobs, when we meet. "I filled out applications for McDonalds, I mean for Dunkin' Donuts too. I did the application at the temp agency," he tallies, counting on his fingers. "Cuz like I could easily like sell drugs out here cuz I'm pretty sure like, people, when people look at me, even walking down the street, like, people associate black people that look good selling drugs."

When I ask Gabrielle about her children, she sighs, "Oh boy." Aydrian's older brother, she says reluctantly, has been in prison for robbery for the past five years. Taking a deep breath, she muses, "I look at my kids and I see a reflection of myself. And sometimes I wish I could pull them back and say no, no. I tried to tell them no along the way, but it's hard. Because sometimes you have to let them learn from experience and it's so hard. I'm hoping that he gets on the right path." Just as Gabrielle sees her own traumatic past as the catalyst for her journey of self-transformation, she believes that being arrested and going to prison were necessary consequences for her sons to face in order to get "on the right path." Putting their fates entirely in their own hands, she hopes they will draw willpower from their painful experiences and transform themselves as she did.

When Aydrian and I meet, the presidential election is just a week away. It means nothing to him.[36] He believes that having a Democrat in office is likely better for his own personal well-being—"I mean I definitely, I would rather Hillary Clinton be president than Donald Trump, of course." But Aydrian refuses to vote: he has no faith that life could ever improve for him or that either political party has his best interest at heart: "Either way like I grew up poor, like I'm still poor. Nothing gonna change for me. Either they gonna make it better for rich people or make it harder for poor people." He believes that the American Dream and all of our institutions have been corrupted to such an extent that fairness, justice, and opportunity no longer exist: "Everything's about money. So American Dream, where it's like no racism or people not judging you, I think that's just people living in their own fantasy world. If you got money, people judge you based on your money. They look at you different depending if you got money or not though. You got money, you do whatever you want. You go, you go kill somebody and beat the charge if you got money."

It could be argued that Aydrian expresses a healthy skepticism, especially about issues of racial justice, as being naïve in an era of racialized surveillance could literally endanger his life.[37] Then Aydrian goes even further, summoning conspiracy theories of a government determined to decimate its own citizens:

> I think the government is, what is it? New world order? I think the government is really, I think the government really is gonna kill people off to control the population. I really believe that. I believe that. I think they wanna control the population so they can control everything else. You control the population, you control what's going on. So you don't got that many people, you don't got that much stuff to worry about. Or you have more government-issued officers than you got regular people so it's easier to control. I think they're gonna try to do that.[38]

As Aydrian hones in on the government as a secretly murderous force, his belief in the possibility of his own political efficacy understandably wanes.[39]

Both Gabrielle and Aydrian reject existing channels of political change. Gabrielle mindfully focuses on her home and her happiness; Aydrian decides that the government is his enemy, leaving them both completely disengaged. If we are moving toward a new understanding of democratic participation, in which people engage based on loyalties, identities, and attachments to others, then we have to ask why disadvantaged people refuse to connect to others in the first place. In Gabrielle and Aydrian's accounts, disengaging from the outside world is not a simple manifestation of apathy, ignorance, or complacency. Their rejection of collective action serves as a practical strategy to get through another day, turn suffering into learning experiences, and protect themselves from despair.

From Pain to Politics

The people we have met—the Lorino family, Roger and Brenda Adams, and Gabrielle Hunter-Jackson and her son Aydrian—occupy different generational cohorts, occupational spheres, and racial and gender identities. They have all become acutely distrustful of the institutions that could connect their individual problems up to collective action. And they all accept unequivocally that politicians are not working for them. In response, each family struggles to come to terms, on their own, with the tumultuous economic and cultural transformations that have rocked their basic sense of trust in the world. Their efforts to manage their pain—to understand the roots of their suffering, and to hold someone accountable for it—convince many of them that the politics they were raised on are inadequate at best.

Antonio and Joyce turn to outsider candidates as a last-ditch effort to stem the tide of corruption that looms over their children's futures. They are fiercely critical of corporations that put their desire for profit over working-class people's well-being. However, as they agonize over the unraveling of their own family, they zero in on government safety nets as the source of their problems, not a solution to them. They blame politicians for offering government "handouts" to gain votes, shielding their own daughter from the growing pains that would have made her stronger. According to this logic, only an outsider candidate who does not need votes to stay in power could possibly break the cycle. Unconvinced, their daughter Ellen grudgingly votes for the "underdog," even while she resigns herself to feeling taken advantage of.

Roger Adams knows that he has failed as a worker and a father. While Roger insists that "a man needs to make things right," he cannot live up to his own ideals of masculine provision and protection. He fantasizes about violent white supremacy to restore his family legacy. He is livid that his own mental and physical pain are not recognized as legitimate and casts himself as more deserving of government aid than others by claiming that he is a true patriot. Proud of his family's dark history, Roger no longer wants to work within the existing political system. He wants to destroy it completely, fighting a race war in the streets.

Others turn inward, away from politics altogether. As they reconceive unjust, painful, and traumatic events in their pasts as learning opportunities, Tori and Gabrielle transcend the concerns of the outside world, turning safety and happiness into matters of perception, rather than of social change. These women claim a sense of dignity forged from their own suffering and redemption in a world that continually lets them down. They frame suffering as a test of character, leading to self-growth and awareness on the one hand, or addiction, despair, and crime, on the other. While Gabrielle tries to remove their struggles with poverty, unemployment, and racism from the realm of the political through positive thinking, her son Aydrian, unemployed and desperate, learns only that "nothing gonna change for me."

From chapter 2 to chapter 5, I continue to explore these strategies of managing pain, looking more closely at how different groups within the working class narrate their suffering and imagine strategies for healing. In chapter 6, "Democracy Denied," I examine what unites working-class people across race and gender: an utter lack of faith in democracy, and the self-help mantras and conspiracy theories that they embrace in its place. In the conclusion, an urgent question emerges: Could working-class people harness their stories of pain to collectively demand a response?

2

Forgotten Men

On Friday nights in Coal Brook, high school football games draw teeming crowds of thousands, the yellow-and-green trucks of the volunteer fire companies leading the parade down Main Street. Mothers take shifts selling hot dogs, ice cream, and "Make Coal Brook Football Great Again!" T-shirts. Fans tailgate in the drugstore parking lot or turn their garages into speakeasies, selling plastic cups of warm beer and pretzels as they cheer boisterously for their home team. As we stand together under the bright lights of the football stadium, putting our hands over our hearts for the national anthem, it feels like we are briefly transported back to a simpler time, before coal miners, whose labor formed the bedrock of the mining communities, were made obsolete.

The white men in Coal Brook express their suffering through their fleeting attempts to sustain the masculine legacy of provision, protection, and courage that they inherited. In this chapter I explore how these men remake their political alliances in creative yet sometimes disturbing ways. Some white men struggling to provide for their families put dignity, fairness, and economic justice for workers at the center of their politics, criticizing politicians who have failed to fight for workers' rights. These men feel frustrated by the lack of social recognition for their persistent struggle, personal integrity, and generosity toward others. To compensate, they exclude racial minorities, immigrants, refugees, and nonworkers from their vision of collective bounty. Among other working-class men, particularly those who have never known a social contract between labor and business, hard work and self-sacrifice remain at the center of their identities. Although they identify proudly as *a* worker, they do not see themselves as *workers* with a shared economic fate. Instead, they readily assent to the reality that no one owes them anything that they do not break their very own bodies to get. Glorifying their own suffering, their harshest scorn is reserved for those who succumb to dependence. A few men attempt to redefine what it means to live a worthy life, detaching masculinity from wage-earning, stoicism, and aggressiveness. This process of detachment also entails cutting themselves off from the political traditions they were raised in.

Dignity and Exclusion

Ed Fessner, a fifty-eight-year-old white construction worker with a high school diploma, has lived in Coal Brook his entire life, like his father before him. His wife, Dorothy, just retired from her job at a flower shop. "Growing up," Ed remembers, "there was a bar on every corner. And there was like a family store at every other corner. You had the milkman. You had different bakers, they came to the door, you know what I mean?" In the first few minutes of our conversation, Ed shares that his "father was a coal miner, that's what eventually killed him, the black lung." Back then, the factories employed thousands of workers. "Now," Ed says, "the corporations killed everything. Everything went to pot. It's bad all over. You used to be able to go to bed when I was a kid and not lock your doors. God forbid you do that nowadays. I'll tell you what: I never had a loaded gun in my house. But I do now."

Ed is proud of his long career, his personal integrity, and the security he can provide for his family. "I have a pension going. I have real good insurance, she'll tell you that," he looks, proudly, to his wife. "Sure, guys can go and work non-union and make a little more money, but they have nothing in retirement. It took me twenty-five years to get it, but I didn't kiss no rear end to get there." Since the 2008 housing crash, there has been very little construction work. Ed can't retire because he still needs his health insurance, especially since he was diagnosed with Type 2 diabetes last year. To support his family, Ed drives three hours every Monday morning, leaving at 3:30 a.m., and spends the week sleeping in a shared motel room and working on a natural gas field: "We run the pipe from the wells to the big pipes or to the valves and we do the pipelines. That gas line was a life-saver. Heck, I took this job last October, and I'm there all winter." Even at twenty degrees below zero outside, Ed is grateful, "though it's kinda hard on us because I haven't had to live away in twenty-four years."

Ed and Dorothy passionately agree that the government should redistribute wealth to benefit the common good, investing in job creation, infrastructure, and education. "I blame the politicians," Ed explains. "Cuz they could've had good industry years ago in the area. They didn't want people making good money. They wanna hold the people down. And the problem with our area now is there's nowhere to work. There's no industry, there's nothing." Ed connects this problem up to a national scale: "I think the problem is they, they import too much. They don't make nothin' in this country anymore. It's crazy, like the pipe we use, comes from overseas for God's sake. You know?" Ed and Dorothy are also frustrated by low tax rates on corporations. Ed zeroes in on the endless, unproductive quibbling between Democratic and Republican politicians: "He [the governor] wants to put a tariff on the gas. And they won't let him. Why are we the only state that does not have an extraction tax for natural gas? Even West Virginia has one for God's sake." He bristles: "It's just another example of companies buying the politicians off. They just won't go with a tax. It'd pay a lot of bills, 500 million dollars. He could improve the schools. They're having trouble with the schools and all that, you know, the roads, the bridges, and that money could go toward schools."

Ed asserts that politicians have a duty to provide work that can sustain a family. He acknowledges a need to tame greed through higher taxes on the wealthy and investments in a broader sense of "we"—public goods like schools, roads, and bridges. His unionized job has given him a strong distrust for politicians who advocate for cutting spending: "When Republicans are in, we don't have the work." Ed and Dorothy are lifelong Democrats—"oh, we never go Republican cuz it's rich people." They are certainly not against government assistance for people who need it—"I'll be honest with you, we got WIC when I was laid off in the winters." They mention how angry they were when Bush defeated Gore in 2000—"I even got money back from Bush. I didn't want it. He inherited a surplus. And he blew it. It's a shame who they get to run for president, know what I mean?"

But their sense of "we" is carefully limited to those who are perceived as deserving. For example, Ed is not yet old enough to qualify for Social Security, which leaves him resentful: he believes, "They're giving it to people who didn't put a nickel in it. I mean that's why it's going broke." Like the Tea Partiers in Arlie Hochschild's *Strangers in their Own Land*, Ed resents the "line-cutters" who appear to have stolen the American Dream for which Ed has worked so hard and sacrificed so much. In this vein, Ed argues, the United States cares about the wrong people. Tracing his family history, Ed begins: "[M]y grandparents came over from there, and they spoke Polish. But they learned English. These people, these, they don't wanna learn it. From Mexico or wherever they're from. You know, that's wrong. And I buy something now, it's written in Spanish to benefit them. That shouldn't be! Learn the language or get outta here."

His own father "went through heck in World War II":

He died eight years ago at eighty-three and last couple years of his life he told me things that he wouldn't tell me when I was younger. Like he wanted to get off his chest. It was amazing. I was like whoa, ok. You know. He was in the, he was in war. He killed a lot of people, and like he said, it's either me or them. What are you gonna do, you know? And he told me they took prisoners in Germany. But if they were SS, two shots, not one. They wouldn't take SS prisoners. They were the bad guys.

Through this story of his family legacy, Ed honors men who were willing to risk their lives, make unyielding, violent life-or-death choices between good and evil for the sake of their country, and stoically endure. Ed is visibly moved at how much his ancestors were willing to sacrifice to be American. Feeling like he has been demoted from the center of the country's priorities to the fringes, as Justin Gest puts it, he invalidates the struggles of other groups who did not go "through heck" to build America.[1]

Today, he believes that "[the immigrants] don't wanna work for it."

E: I think it's wrong. I think like hospitalization, it's out of hand. I don't know. If you don't have insurance, you go have a baby, you're gonna have a fifty-thousand-dollar bill, you know what I mean? But yet they'll deliver a foreigner's baby for free.

D: Or like even like people on relief. I think it's for each child, so they just keep having children, they keep getting more.

E: I'll tell ya, to get into medical school, it's all foreigners. *What's wrong with like, people like us?* What kinda grades do you need? I mean it's all foreign. You go to the hospital, you can't understand these people. I told a telemarketer, I said when you understand how to speak English better, call me back and I hung up. And I hung up cuz you couldn't understand him! You know, but that kinda irks me.

Taking an uncharacteristically bold stance, Dorothy adds: "If you wanna become a citizen you need to do it right. If not, they shouldn't be here if they're illegal. They should round them up, ship them out!" Like the white "working-class heroes" in Maria Kefalas's study of a changing Chicago neighborhood, Ed and Dorothy also fear that the newly arrived racial minorities in town pose a threat to their precarious stability and time-honored, respectable way of living.[2]

And even if there were jobs, Ed and Dorothy worry that the young people "wouldn't wanna work." Even the football players they cheer on every Friday night "just don't have that oomph anymore. No matter who you get as a coach you're not gonna have a state championship team."

Ed and Dorothy believe that parents have destroyed this generation's moral character by devaluing hard work and self-sacrifice. Parents today, they observe, teach their children that complaining, putting yourself ahead of the team, and doing whatever you can to win is what leads to success. They offer this example from their son's baseball days:

E: When they played little league, I'll tell you something. You had a coach that if the parents would bitch, their kid would play. They'd put my son in, he'd hit a double, knock into it, next thing you know he's on the bench. Cuz someone else . . . we never bitched at the coach. And I should have probably because people would look at me, say, why'd they take your kid out? But we, the coach is like, I wish all the parents were like you.

D: If you didn't scream, your kid wouldn't get in the game. But we wouldn't do that. We wouldn't fight or cause a ruckus.

E: Everyone just wants their own instead of caring about the team in a way, you know what I mean? And if I had to do it again, I'd bitch like them.

As Michele Lamont found in her seminal study of blue-collar workers, white men were once able to achieve a sense of dignity by performing the *disciplined self*: hard work, stoicism, the integrity to make hard choices, solidarity with other workers over personal ambition, and sacrifice for one's family and country. But Ed believes that these qualities are now longer valued or appreciated. The lesson is clear: if you are a good person, and if you put others first, then you get nothing but the scraps.

As the economy grows more predatory, and his trust in others wanes, Ed desperately wishes to restore himself, and his family legacy, to their former place of pride—throwing illegal immigrants out, making the United States an English-speaking-only country, and cutting benefits to people who do not work as hard as he does. Fierce distrust in politicians leads them away from the Democratic Party and toward outsider candidates who offer one last hope at putting their own problems back to the center of the nation's priorities. In August 2015, even though they have never voted Republican, Ed and Dorothy find themselves drawn to Donald Trump. "I think the man is speaking the truth," Ed informs me. "I mean, Hillary's a Democrat, but I think she's a phony. I'm sorry. Cuz [Trump] talks about like Hillary Clinton, he says, I gave her money, so she'd go to my wedding." He ponders: "Why do we have to have parties anyway? They're all bought off. It's so sad you gotta be a bazillionaire to run for president. It's sad." Dorothy raises fears about the loss of male authority: "[P]eople respect the male in that high position more. They'd be more afraid of him. We need somebody forceful to get things accomplished." In their model of the world, it is time to take back America from those who hijacked it. Trump symbolizes a new beginning, a washing-away of the moral pollution that has rotted the foundations of the America for which his father fought so hard and gave up so much.

"Just Waiting, We're Prepared"

At first glance, Brian Reczak, a thirty-one-year-old metal factory worker, seems mild-mannered and chivalrous, projecting a rugged masculinity in a flannel shirt and bushy beard. But inside, Brian is quietly preparing for war. After finding heroin needles in the park, he recounts, he recently organized a two-hour evening march of "forty vigilantes openly carrying guns," ready to "take back our town." "We are kind of a form of militia," he explains calmly. "You know, if Black Lives Matter takes to the streets, we are trained and prepared to treat it accordingly. If we need to defend ourselves, our families, or our area, that's what we're there for. Kind of like a praying mantis. Sitting aside, not doing anything wrong, just waiting, we're prepared."

Brian idealizes men who are steadfast protectors and providers. Brian descends from a long line of veterans. His own father was stationed overseas, then worked as a state prison guard until a riot left him unable to work: "Like when he was in the service there was no such thing as PTSD, people didn't know what it was. At the time my old man was just diagnosed with anxiety and didn't realize the repercussions of getting out of the service and going into a job like that." Following in his father's footsteps, Brian enlisted right out of high school. He spent seven months in combat in Iraq. Since returning, he has worked as a pizza deliveryman, a seasonal Walmart cashier, and a carpenter. His girlfriend, the mother of his two children, is uneasy about the prospect of marriage because of their constant fighting about paying the bills. He is currently training for a factory job two hours away, where "the benefits are terrific. Like I start off at twenty-two dollars an hour. There's so much room for us to move up." Moving away, Brian hopes, might give them a fresh start at a good life.

Brian describes his father as emotionally distant, a heavy drinker who rarely left the house. His father's only source of social connection was his white nationalist biker gang: "I grew up around biker types, grew up around radical white groups. I was friends with a lot of those skinhead guys from childhood," Brian recalls. Brian claims to reject the "derogatory language"[3] of his father's generation while he steadfastly maintains whiteness as a meaningful identity: "I don't want my kids thinking that the KKK is okay, you know what I mean? But I don't want them to think all white groups are bad just because they're a white group, you know? Pride in everything. You know, my family, who I am. I am who I am because of the way my family was made. My whole family's been all white, all the way up."[4]

Brian belongs to a militia in which "you have to be of white nationality to be a member."

> We consider ourselves the white gentleman of what we do. You know, like I said before, you know, we hold doors for everybody, we say hi to everybody. You know, we support a lot of other groups, like the Latin kings. We support them. They're pretty much the same thing we are. They're for preservation and advancement of their own race. A lot of them believe in racial purity like we do. So I kinda believe in that. Family,

faith, and folk. You know, like a lot to do with our heritage, traditions, like I said before they're very important to us. Like I grew up saying the national anthem, I turned out fine. You know it's not like we're going out trying to stop anyone doing what they're doing. If the gay community can have pride day, we should be allowed to have pride too.

Anxiety over boundary maintenance is central to contemporary white nationalist thought, from the genetic purity of individuals, to women's sexuality, to the security of our national borders.[5] Brian roots himself in a community of "white gentlemen," seeking pride and recognition "for my family, who I am."

Masculinity must be continuously demonstrated, differentiated from the feminine, publicly affirmed, and privately validated.[6] Previous studies have shown how the threat of shame and humiliation coerced working-class white men into performing exploitative labor.[7] In his study of working-class young men working in manual labor jobs, for example, Paul Willis found that working-class adolescent boys accepted demeaning jobs because they viewed manual labor as an expression of masculine dominance over women.[8] Confining men of color to the most menial and dirty jobs also shored up feelings of superiority among them. For Brian, who cannot anchor his identity in paid labor or in authority over his family, only whiteness remains appealing as the source of "who I am."

Brian is angry that the United States has fallen from the most powerful country in the world to a laughing stock, below "even Canada":

I don't wanna necessarily use the word ashamed but I'm a little, not as proud as I used to be to say that I'm a vet. And it's not, it's not really because of like the stigma some vets get, cuz I could care less what other people think, realistically. It's just what we've become as a country and it really doesn't have anything to do with our leaders. Like we've allowed ourselves to become very sensitive, we've allowed ourselves to become very weak. I believe that we are the laughing stock of other countries. Like when I was younger, before I joined the service, I thought that Canada was weak. And a lower country than us. And now that I'm older and I see everything, I'm like, huh, Canada's not weak because they don't have an army, Canada don't need an army. Cuz they're not sticking their nose where it doesn't belong.

Brian does not particularly like Donald Trump: he thinks he acts like "an arrogant jerk" and does not speak with dignity: "You have to hold yourself up to a standard. Like look at Putin. There's no dirt on him. There's not a bad picture of him, there's nothing." However, Brian still empathizes with Trump: he calls him a "man's man," out of place in the feminized, sensitive, and weak country that

America has become. He argues that "Trump was created by basically our new America. Like we created him":

> Like we created men like that with his beliefs. Like look at the 1950s, it's only 70 something years away. And back then you know, it was okay to be racist. It was okay to use you know derogatory terms toward women, the gay community, people of color. And here we are, seventy years later, and it's not that it's not okay to be against that stuff, but it's like, the people who are against it are like, oh Trump should be killed for his beliefs. How does that make you any better, trying to bring violence on somebody over your thoughts? Like this is a free country. Like it was founded on free speech. You should be able to support Hillary without any backlash, you should be able to support Bernie without any backlash, you should be able to support Trump. Like if you look at Obama, Obama was the first and biggest controversy our country's ever seen. Personally, do I think he was a good president? I think he could've done better. Did I vote for him? No. And I do feel there was a lot of reverse racism? I feel a lot of people voted for him and supported him because he was black and they didn't wanna feel racist for not supporting him.

By this logic, the true United States, protected and sacrificed for by real Americans like Brian and his father, has been stolen from the "man's man" by the politically correct, weak, and sensitive. The Tea Party Republicans studied by Arlie Hochschild in Louisiana expressed a similar resentment of liberal rules that policed how they should feel—whether "happy for the gay newlywed, sad at the plight of the Syrian refugee, unresentful about paying taxes."[9] Brian restores a sense of pride and purpose to his life by openly celebrating his identity and power as a white man, insisting on the right to not feel racist in the process.

Unlike the Tea Party Republicans, if Brian could have chosen anyone for president, it would have been "Bernie's demeanor with Trump's thoughts of what he wants to do." Even though "Bernie's a little bit more on the communist side," he admits, "there are some good things about communism that could benefit people. I think his heart and his head is in the right place. This country is an entity and it's a machine and everybody has a spot to fill in. Some people should make more than others, but there should be an absolute bottom rate. No American should be hungry. No American should be homeless." Brian believes that the government should not merely exist to protect individual freedom but also to ensure that every person has a "spot to fill." He calls attention to the shame of treating workers as "expendable" and believes that the "entity," or the whole, is greater than the sum of its individual parts.

Brian reflects on his own history: "My ancestors, a lot of Irishmen coming to the coal mines were murdered. A lot of the people that were illegal were considered expendable and that's how they used them. There's a lot of ghosts in this country that a lot of people just don't see. You know, we've been against illegal refugees and immigrants since the dawn of this country." He pivots to invalidate the suffering of black Americans, equating the experience of coming to America as an Irish immigrant with being enslaved and forced to leave their home: "And I understand that the black community has been oppressed and held down. You know, the Asians, whites, blacks, you name it. They've been oppressed and held down. And it seems like everyone has kind of either moved past it or made themselves better. And now you have the BLM protesters and it just kinda makes you think like, did they ever move past it?"[10] Even as Brian finds himself drawn to "Bernie's heart," the exalted whiteness that sustains his sense of dignity, purpose, and family pride deals a fatal blow to his vision of class-based solidarity. And the push for racial justice by Black Lives Matter turns Brian into an armed vigilante taking to the streets to defend his home: "I feel like it is more of a smoke and mirrors as to what they're really trying to do. Now we see that they're more militarized, that, we see a lot of the power behind it. We've seen nothing but violence coming from it. To me it's the same thing as the KKK."

Brian did not vote for any candidate. Brian credits Trump with not caring about winning votes like typical politicians do—"You know, he didn't care about any backlash from anybody, you know, he just told the truth and that's the one thing I like in him. She's [Hillary's] way too wishy-washy. You know thirty years ago she said one thing, now she's saying another. I feel like she was kind of like the unpopular person in school and now she'll say anything to get people to agree with her." When we meet for lunch the day following the 2016 election, both numb with shock, he cannot believe that the government allowed Trump to win: "Yeah, I watched the polls all night. Like I saw a lot of the stuff, like the shady things that were going on. Like all the polls were changing people's votes for a little bit, like that was happening in PA, especially locally around here. Like I really believed up until like the hour after it happened that Hillary was still gonna win."

Like many working-class men, he cannot shake the feeling that the America he wants to believe in is a sham. "I'm not really one to buy into the whole government's trying to hide stuff. But now that I see a lot more things going on, it's like, maybe they *are* trying to hide things." Considering the attacks on September 11, he muses: "I don't really buy into the whole government planned it. But you know I've seen the videos. It is what it is. Maybe the government *did* plan it." There is uncertainty lurking underneath his armor: he wants to proudly believe in the integrity of his country, but he cannot will himself to do so wholeheartedly.

A Worker, Not Workers

Jacob Kobs, twenty-seven, meets me on the day he files for divorce from his wife. Jacob and I meet at the fire company where he volunteers, which raises much of its needed funds through the attached bar. There are more fire companies in town than are actually needed for fighting fires, but the vibe is friendly and the beer is cheap.[11] At three o'clock in the afternoon, the air is thick, almost blue with cigarette smoke, and the senior-citizen crowd is beginning their daily pub crawl from the Shamrock Fire Company, to the American Legion, and then down to the Knights of Columbus. Jacob orders us both Yuenglings, two dollars each, and finds a quiet back room in the pub where we can talk. He tells me upfront that his wife cheated on him.

Jacob's arms are covered in ink. I ask him to tell me about each of his tattoos. "That one is the firefighter definition of courage," he points out. "And that one is Japanese for courage. I have eleven tattoos. I think eight of them are courage-related. Courage, brotherhood, honor." Jacob has tried out several different occupations that require self-discipline, physical strength, and sacrifice, the hallmarks of the industrial working class. He first enlisted in the Navy but had to drop out of basic training because he had "two bad knees, from breaking my body working and in football." He continues: "I tried my hardest, then I tried joining the Reserves. It was three years ago, then I developed a heart problem which actually made me drop out of the police academy." He also enrolled in a two-year program to train as a foreman in construction and engineering, but failed out of trigonometry.

Jacob's father works in a paper factory, and his stepmother works as a merchandise receiver at a discount retail store. Jacob identifies all of his family members as "laborers": "My dad, he's a laborer. Just like myself, my brother, my step-mom." Jacob refers to himself as a "self-employed contractor," which means he and his cousin travel around the state doing welding and construction on a contract-by-contract basis. The pay can be good—"$20 some an hour and you have to bust your ass to do it"—but the work is erratic. He has no health insurance. "I think last time I priced it, I did it for health insurance with $300,000 coverage, it was about $100, $145, $160 a month. So now I pay the penalty, $196 a year on my taxes. Granted if I get hurt, the hospital can't do nothing. They'll stabilize you and . . . but I've been through a lot." Over and over again, Jacob projects fearlessness, emphasizing his willingness to take risks and live with the consequences.

Coupled with his individualistic, stoic masculinity is a love of community, a yearning to sacrifice for the collective, and a desire to preserve his heritage. "I'm proud of where I'm from. If it wasn't for this town . . . this town built me," he says earnestly. "So when I came back and became a firefighter, I wanted to give back to the community that made me who I am now." In his vision of a good life, it is the honorable character of tightly knit people that ensures self-sacrifice and taking care of one's own; he yearns to feel embedded in relations of mutual obligation and reciprocity: "Like you said, you're from Boston, you had the bombing, now the community came together, they did, the city came together. But if something like that around here, it would actually blow your mind about how many people you just see in a small area just come out of nowhere to help that one person." Indeed, when a volunteer firefighter in a nearby town was killed in 2002, the funeral procession stretched over five miles.[12]

Like Ed Fessner, Jacob feels that the integrity he grew up with does not serve him well in this self-interested world. He has slowly learned that doing the right thing is only for the "young and dumb":

> When I was twenty-two, a certain someone I knew stole a . . . something. I was interviewed for it, I knew who did it. But I didn't tell them who did it. I was born and raised not to tell on people. So I didn't tell 'em. I was young, dumb. I was actually, I was incarcerated for about a week. Nowadays, yeah I would tell you who it was. It cost me a lot of money. You won't get that around here anymore.

Jacob does not blame the police for his false arrest; he blames himself. He reasons: "The person who arrested me is a good friend of mine to this day. But I mean, they did their job. So I would have to say the legal system's fine. They're going to push for a confession, but in my circumstance I should have told 'em who did it. But I didn't. They did what they had to do. And obviously I was getting in the way of an investigation. So I got charges. Everyone's trying to criticize cops for doing their job."

Jacob does not understand why fast-food workers have captured the public's sympathy: "Like this whole McDonalds thing for $15 an hour, no. No, I'm not a big fan of that. I mean I can see upping it, but not to $15 an hour. I was literally breaking myself to make $15 for the longest time and you want to flip a hamburger and make the same thing I was doing? I couldn't see that." He is particularly angry that American veterans come home from war and are simply forgotten about. He envisions a battle over whose suffering deserves recognition from the government:

> Honestly, I'd close the borders in a heartbeat. Like I just said, I worry more about our own people. I'd be trying to . . . countless people, thousands of people go hungry every day, families, kids, that'd be a big thing for me. I know several people that are low-income and they fight for food. I have a friend personally that I take out once a week,

I take him out for lunch. Bringing the refugees and not probably screening 'em. And you're housing them. But if you have millions, thousands actually, several thousands of American veterans that are homeless and you're bringing in all these refugees? No, you should worry about your own first. No, that's not very American. You're going to bring in these refugees, how about you worry about your home first. You have all these military veterans that are homeless, sleeping on the streets, that serve their country, and the government's not doing shit for them.

Viewing government provision as a zero-sum game, he insists: "You worry about your home first."

Jacob's code of individual merit prevents him from engaging in racial scapegoating. For example, when I ask Jacob about the racial conflicts in town, he says in a measured tone: "It's definitely in the area, there's a lot of tension, especially with the drugs and everything coming in. And a lot of them being of a different ethnic background. But you know, I can't say it's putting two and two together cuz there are a lot of Caucasian people that do it too." Unlike Brian, his ethos of individualism prevents him from lashing out against other races as a group. On the other hand, seeing only individuals makes it impossible for him to consider how race systematically shapes individual life chances.

I ask Jacob, "If someone said to you the American Dream is dead, what would you say to them?" His reply wholly encapsulates his mantra of no-excuses personal responsibility: "That person is just not trying hard enough." He has tried, and repeatedly failed, to build a masculine self in the most time-honored ways we have in American society: as a worker, a soldier, a husband. Jacob instead tattoos his values onto his body, finding strength in his narrative of self-sacrifice and self-reliance. He is unenthusiastic about the coming election and plans to abstain from voting: "Every president that has ever gone in office screws us in some way, shape, or form," he shrugs. "But what if I forced you into the ballot box and made you vote today [July 2016], who would you pick?" I press him. His reply converges on an acceptance of market logic and distrust of the prevailing establishment: "Trump. He'd run the country like a business. The way it should be."

"I Have More Chances of Dying at My Job Than They Do at Theirs"

Joe Flynn, thirty-two, comes from a long line of unionized welders. He has worked manual laborer jobs in the natural gas and coal industries his entire adult

life. He worries that his current career in the gas field, moving rigs and equip-
ment, hauling water away, and fracking sand, is "declining rapidly":

> I thought it was going to be pretty good. My wife's uncle is the one who
> actually told me to get into it, because it was doing really well, and I get
> into it, and then now it's declining rapidly. Actually they just closed
> down our facility where we're working from—now we have to go from
> Ohio, about a seven-hour drive from here. And it's kind of like they call
> you when they need you, but you never know. It's hard to get a con-
> sistent paycheck with not working. I need something that I know that's
> going to stay steady, that's not going to just all of a sudden drop, and
> with the energy, the coal even, everything, it just fluctuates.

He is currently applying for a job as a correctional officer at a state prison because, "If I get a prison job, there's always going to be prisoners." The last job he
was rejected from, he shares, received 250 applicants for eleven slots.

Joe supports his wife, Denise, and their two small daughters, on $13.50 an
hour. Denise, who has Type 2 diabetes and a form of muscular dystrophy that
makes it difficult for her to walk, struggles to take care of the children while Joe is
away: "She gets disability, and it's just bare minimum for everything." They currently have about $15,000 in debt. Joe quickly takes responsibility for "messing
up" their lives:

> Right now is when we're actually hitting it, and we're realizing, yeah, we
> kind of messed up a lot in the past. We bought two cars almost a year or
> two apart. That pretty much did it. I ended up getting laid off. We ended
> up paying the one, and we ended up talking to them, and they let us
> return the other one, but even since we returned it, it still went back to
> repo on it. Messed us up. What made me mad is the car that we chose
> to keep paying on, I only owed $1,200 on it, and then I got into an acci-
> dent and it totaled, so I would have owned it in less than a year. I think
> we're right about $12,000 to $15,000 now. It was a lot worse before.

Joe's father purchased their $23,000 row home because their credit score was too
low to apply for a mortgage. Luckily, his father is forgiving when they fall behind
on their monthly payments. Joe and Denise have applied for food stamps in the
past, but Joe says "they always kept declining us, because they'd say, well, you
make too much, or you're right on the line. We kind of just gave up on trying that."

Living on the brink of poverty, Joe's dependence on gas and oil makes him
fearful of environmental regulation. In July 2016, he worried, "If Bernie or
Hillary get in, it won't be around at all anymore, because they're pretty much

100 percent against it. What are they going to use for energy? Everything's going to be solar-powered?" As he speaks, he grows incensed: "Do you realize how much more panels you need to produce the energy compared to burning coal and gas? A lot more, and those things actually are very hazardous if broken, the chemicals inside of it. The chemicals inside those are very, very toxic if broken, and wind turbines, it takes a lot more of those even than solar power. Where are you going to put them?" Joe tells me about his brother-in-law, a liberal Democrat who has "honestly had a problem with every job that I've ever done. He's against coal. He's against gas. I told him, if I get a prison job, are you going to be against those?"

Joe shows me his Facebook wall on his phone, where he posts frequently throughout the day: "I know Facebook's not always reliable, but if I have more inquiries, I'll actually search it online or whatever and look into it. Usually I'll just Google it and find out, read some of these articles, because I know a lot of news sources can be just one-sided too. You can't always trust news." He views "the internet" as the only space where he can dig up the truth because mainstream news sources lie. He also relies on Facebook memes to provide pithy evidence for his beliefs: "I don't care about global warming," he says nonchalantly. "I keep seeing that one meme on Facebook. It's about what Al Gore was saying about global warming, and now there's more icecaps than ever. It's like, wow, gee. That kind of stuff doesn't overly bother me. I've lived by the coal creek here for years. It doesn't affect me."

What does "bother" Joe is his suspicion that some people in town are living off welfare checks while he works hours away from his family, risking his life, to barely make ends meet—"If I go to Walmart and I have just enough money to buy a couple of things, groceries, and then the people behind me have two carts full, and then they get into this brand new car . . . I'm not saying that they're necessarily on the welfare, but it just kind of feels that way." He continues:

> Here's a good example. My wife and I were driving to—I think we were taking her car over to get inspected, where we got it, and right there on the highway, there's a brand-new red Corvette sitting there, and I said to her, who would park a brand-new red Corvette right there on the highway? Who even has the money in this area? The houses are broken down, rundown, everything like that. Who has that kind of money? It's a brand-new 2016. I always ask my wife, well, how do we just live off of the system too? But I'd just feel like kind of a dirt bag then.

In many of the interviews with white residents, descriptions of these "dirt bags" took on an almost apocryphal flare. I heard the same story again and again—of watching helplessly as people piled bags and bags of frozen crab or lobster in their shopping carts or casually bought expensive steaks with their food stamps to feed to their dog. For Joe, who lives in debt, the Corvette story allows him to make a virtue out of his daily struggle, taking pride in his ability to endure rather than succumb to his pain. Fearful of falling down the economic ladder, Joe is quick to apply the "dirt bag" label to people who do not strive for self-reliance and instead "live off the system."

Although Joe's father is a Democrat, Joe has registered as an Independent since he was twenty-two and "just recently switched to Republican. The current Republican candidate [at the state level] is talking about bringing back more jobs. He's for coal, for gas, and that's all things that I've done in the past." But he continues: "I'll tell you who my favorite candidate is. He's not even running this year now: Ron Paul. I've always voted for Ron Paul. I always just write him in." Joe puts individual rights and lack of state interference at the center of his political engagement: "If the government's going to force me to do something, then it's basically not a free country anymore. It's not your free choice." This concern extends to social issues: for example, he says it is "ridiculous" that people use the Bible to justify laws prohibiting gay marriage, as "the Bible also says you can't wear clothes from two different kinds of cloth or work on Sundays and no one listens to that. People should be happy."

Joe fully embraces his identity as an uneducated, hard-working man—in opposition to hypocritical, educated elites and the unemployed. He particularly likes the memes on Facebook from a source called "Liberals are hypocrites": "I'm tired of the media saying uneducated white men. Next time their car breaks down they can fix it." But Joe does not want any kind of class-based labor rights, either. Like Jacob, he is outraged that people who work less demanding and less dangerous jobs would demand fifteen dollars an hour when he only makes $13.50. He is willing to fulfill his side of the bargain by taking on monotonous, dirty, and dangerous work, but he wants to be recognized and rewarded for it:

> I go into these fast-food places if I'm on rotation or whatever, and they can't even remember to get my order correct, so they want $15 an hour to do that, and I can't even get $15 an hour for doing a job that's probably ten times harder than theirs. I have more chances of dying at my job than they do at theirs. There are so many things in my job field right now that could probably just kill you instantly, and you wouldn't even know something happened.

Joe does not suggest policy changes like increasing regulations to make his job safer, his hours more regular, or his wages higher. On the contrary, he is proud that he could die on the job. In return, Joe wants validation that his sacrifice is appreciated more than that of someone "flipping burgers." He wants, above all, to make his pain feel worthwhile, and that requires invalidating other people's claims to economic sustenance.

"I am definitely not a liberal," he reiterates. "People that are just crazy trying to take everything away, control. They don't want us to have—I know the whole gun issue is one thing. I just went and got my permit to carry and everything like that. I'm planning on eventually getting something." Like many of the working-class white men I interviewed, owning a gun and defending his home were central parts of how he understood his role in his family. "Only a couple of months ago, right out back of my house, right in front of my car, somebody was exchanging [drugs and money]. I'm like, really? I'm like, are you guys kidding me, right out in front of my house?" he recalls. He shows me another one of his favorite Facebook memes: "Somebody broke into my house and all he took was one of my bullets." In fact, several white men in this survey informed me that they carry their handguns everywhere—high school football games, the grocery store, the sub shop across the street—projecting an image of living in constant danger and being always ready for battle. Perhaps protecting others from harm becomes even more vital when the other cornerstones of industrial masculinity—earning a living wage, keeping one's family together—falter.

Dissolving Industrial Working-Class Masculinity

So far, the men we have met have displayed anger and resentment, aggressively policing their homes and neighbors. But beneath the veneer of fearlessness, we can see hints of pain in the stories of these men—in the isolation and unspoken trauma lived by Brian's father when he came home from war, in the loneliness as Jacob drinks every afternoon he has off. A few men I met were in the process of detaching themselves, at least partially, from older models of masculinity. The new sense of purpose and meaning they forge rejects victimhood, yet also explicitly focuses on spiritual healing rather than economic justice.[13]

Giving Voice to Trauma

Glen Allen, a forty-four-year-old veteran, and I sit on the bleachers of a public baseball field as he coaches his adult football league for the upcoming playoffs. It is Tuesday, November 8, 2016, and he plans to head to the polls right after practice. Keeping a close eye on his team, calling out occasional corrections and accolades, Glen tries to blink back the tears from his eyes. "If it wasn't for my children, I probably would have committed suicide from my PTSD," he states matter-of-factly. "'Cuz there was several times I was up on the mountain with my

.45 in my mouth ready to do it. The only thing that stopped me was my children. I didn't want to hurt my children like that."

Glen came to the coal region by way of Pittsburgh: his father was a steelworker in the 1970s until "a lot of the steel went over to Japan and China and that's what killed it. And the union couldn't really do anything because the company kind of folded so I mean, what are you going to do? It was the start of foreign trade at that period for steel because that really, that impacted the entire country, not just Pittsburgh." When his father "went from making $15 an hour at the steel mill to $3.10 an hour" at a gas station, his parents started fighting. They divorced when he was nine. His mother moved into a housing project and his father moved in with Glen's grandmother. His memories of childhood, and his parents' downward spiral, are marked by pain:

> My mom physically abused me, I was beat with extension cords, I was hit in the head with a 2 x 4 when I was eight, knocked me unconscious. I wasn't a bad kid, I was a good kid. My mom was drinking and was mad at my dad and would take it out on me. It was really horrible. But my mother now, she's like oh I never did that, [and I say] yes you did, you were drunk and don't remember. But I love my mother, I do, I love her.

Glen found solace in playing baseball, but he otherwise struggled in high school—he was constantly arguing with the administration for "picking and choosing who followed the rules" and fighting other boys: "I was the antagonizing one . . . I had a lot of pent-up aggression from my parents. I held it in, held it in, held it in, and I finally let it out."

When he was brought before a judge, he describes:

> The judge told me I'm going to give you two options. You could either go to prison for eighteen to thirty-six months or you can go into the military. I said. Your Honor, I have college scholarships for baseball. He said, "Sucks to be you, doesn't it?" He said, "Make your decision." I'm eighteen years old, I don't want to go to jail so I'll go in the military. I joined the Navy.

Glen is fiercely patriotic, but his service proved "definitely traumatic and intense. Everywhere I went all I'd seen was death and sadness. Anybody who says that doesn't affect them, they're either a cold-hearted monster or they're a sociopath. There was an incident where a woman and a small boy got killed, and it was because of me. It was directly my fault and that's why I got the PTSD." He explains that part of the trauma was not being able to talk about "things that you need to talk about."

Glen shies away from describing exactly how he was discharged, merely explaining, "There was some stuff that happened with our unit and we did what we were ordered to do, but we got in trouble for it because what we did we shouldn't have done and of course higher-ups aren't going to take the blame, so shit rolls downhill." He "signed away benefits or the judge was going to send us to jail," which meant he has no pension or medical care. His military service left him distrustful of mainstream media—"the news is lying to the American people. I can tell you, I was there and everything they reported was opposite of what happened, what we did, what we were doing there."

He suffers from acute posttraumatic stress disorder: "It made me verbally abusive towards people, violent towards other people, one guy cut me off at a red light down there and I tried to run him off the road." His wife asked him to leave after ten years of marriage, but he is still clinging to the possibility of getting back together: "I see her all the time, every day. I give her rides to work. I don't want to be separated. I was the one who was an asshole so she kicked me out. It was the PTSD, I was verbally abusive." Although his doctor has prescribed antidepressants over the years, he does not currently have health insurance and thinks "the medications just make me worse." His children just lost access to government medical assistance, he explains, because his teenage son's part-time job increased his wife's household income over the limit, "even though he doesn't provide any money toward the household whatsoever."

Glen currently works as a butcher but is hopeful about being hired as a guard at a state juvenile detention center where he would earn "sixteen bucks an hour, full benefits." He believes in giving kids a second chance, especially since one was denied to him: "What I want to do is help these kids before they make the wrong decisions and go to prison. You're still a juvenile, until you're twenty-one, even though you're locked up you can change your life and not go to real jail." Glen says urgently, "I got to get in [the juvenile detention center job] so I can get them [his family] health insurance."

Glen is the victim of multiple traumatic events, beginning with his father's job loss and his mother's physical abuse, to the horrors of combat, to feeling like he was simply thrown away by the military to protect his corrupt leaders. He cannot fulfill his role as a provider for his family and hopes that his wife will let him back into her life, even though he admits to victimizing her. Glen puts no trust in religion to help him heal—"they're [religious people] out sinning six days a week, now they're righteous and asking for forgiveness and come Monday they're committing the same damn sins over again"—nor does he trust judges, doctors, or the media. He is eager for the state to legalize medical marijuana, the only outlet he has for easing his daily pain: "It's one of the things that actually keeps me calm. These politicians, they don't know what it's like to feel the way we feel, veterans feel."

Despite his intense distrust of American democracy, Glen still identifies as an American soldier. His acknowledgement of his own past traumas fortifies his belief in protecting the weak: "I joined the military and fought for people who couldn't fight for themselves." This logic gives him an openness to helping others that separates him from his peers, as he ponders, "Let me tell you what, I don't care how many refugees they bring from other countries. I don't care if they're Muslim, I don't care, it don't bother me whatsoever. Our constitution covers everybody who steps foot on this soil, doesn't matter if you're a citizen or not." He is also critical of the legal system and believes that most incarcerated people are there because "the federal government closed down all the mental institutions. Now we got a huge problem there that they need to take care of. That would solve a lot of social issues if they would bring back mental health and the government pay for it."

While he was a registered Democrat like his father for most of his life, Glen now believes that *no* party wants to help America: "People think, oh, the Democrats are for the poor, no, they're not. They're for controlling the poor with welfare, free cell phones, free housing, free cars. And they have you under their thumb." Like several others in this book, Glen wants to see more investment in poor people so they can build better lives for themselves: "The Republicans they say, oh, they're for the people. No, they're not. They're for their own agenda. They're only for their own rich constituents." When he leaves our interview, Glen heads to the polls to vote for Donald Trump. Disenchanted with politicians, he is drawn to Trump's perceived sacrifice for the American people: "For like the past year he's being ridiculed, under a microscope, why would anybody do that unless he's really trying to fix the country? Why would he go through all that?" With eerie prescience, he observes, "You're listening to the news saying, oh, the polls have her [Clinton] ahead. Meanwhile you look at the Trump rallies and there's thousands of people. You look at the Hillary Clinton rallies and there's maybe a hundred. But Hillary Clinton is probably going to get put into power because of who her family is and the political influence she has."

It's All about Yourself

Joshua Meier, twenty-eight, and his father Steven, sixty-two, live in an old farmhouse that has been in their family for three generations. The house feels warm and inviting, with thick green carpets, glass hutches full of porcelain dolls, bubblegum pink bathroom tiles, and jars of homemade pickles lining the cellar. Joshua describes his childhood as simple and untroubled. "As far as money goes, there's no college degrees in our family, you know just hard working," he elaborates. "My grandma worked in a fishing factory. When she wasn't doing that she was working on the farm. My father worked here as a janitor. My mom works in banking, customer service. So yeah, you know kind of paycheck to paycheck. Saving up."

Joshua remembers his first time trying pills in high school. "That was like, 'Oh I can take a pill and feel like this. Okay! This feels warm, this feels nice.' I remember taking them and walking around the hallways at school just like free, flowing. Fearless. Heroin just sounded exciting." Joshua liked the way pills quelled his nervous energy and dulled his mind, and he spent the next ten years of his life trying to get high, working on and off in service jobs to support his addiction. Joshua notes wryly that the close social ties of his rural, small community facilitated buying and selling drugs: "The protection of each other is so easy. We're not going to have a lot of people around here that are going to tattletale, if you tattletale on a person you end up not being able to get your spot."

After years of anxiety and acrimonious debates that tore his family apart, Joshua was finally arrested. That moment, he explains, his spiritual journey began:

> My spiritual journey began in jail. My addiction was fighting, it was tough cuz the urges and cravings where there. I detoxed in jail. So, basically what happened was, I did four months in there, and within that four months it allowed me to let go of . . . to go from victim, hold myself accountable, and reflect, and then had a lot of love and support from my family who didn't bail me out. So the time I was in jail, I started to look inward, started working out, doing fitness, and I started to be grateful. So I started bringing in the loving quality of gratitude for the small things. So I went from a negative mind-state to a positive place.

Since then, Joshua has lived with his parents. He has devoted his energy to developing and cultivating a completely new kind of self, beginning with the "boot camp" structure of court-mandated rehab. He was able to "break that cycle of thinking, that pattern of behavior that makes you do what you want to do all the time, or get your way all the time." Now, Joshua spends his days organizing activities like cleaning trash and graffiti off the streets and running car washes to raise money for cancer. He is trying to launch an athletic-wear company, printing inspirational recovery messages—"Surrender," "Rise Up," "Together We Become Stronger"—on T-shirts and running shorts.

Joshua has thoroughly rejected a life built on earning money, or "just accumulating." He believes that finding meaning in external sources like "the trophy on the wall, the fancy car, the clothing, the status, how many friends, the girlfriend" leads to emptiness and resentment. In stark contrast to the other men chronicled in this chapter, Joshua wills himself to expect nothing from life.

In the past, he confesses, he was guilty of believing that he was a victim. He now attributes these feelings to "negative energies" that he must relentlessly flush out:

> What has to go, negative thinking, negative thoughts, victim status, all this resentment, self-hatred, all these like negative thoughts, negative energies. Just that, I thought I was a victim of everything. So I had resentment towards people, or situations, or life in general, or just society, or whatever it may be. You fill yourself up with this hate that everything else, everything that happened to you is a result of something else. So when I let go of that, well what's the opposite of all this stuff? What's the opposite of resentment? Forgiveness. Forgiveness, forgiving myself, accepting myself for who I am, accepting others for their flaws. Gratitude, just being grateful for every fucking thing.

Joshua reconceives of failure as a foundation for growth through which people "are humbled and that is good for them."

He loosely ties his outlook on life to Christianity: "When you talk about how Jesus died on the cross for us, for our sins, I think if we live with a fearless approach to life with unconditional love, then we can be the stillness in the chaos, we can endure." Joshua was raised Protestant and attended church frequently as a child, but now believes (like Glen Allen) that organized religion is a veil for hypocrisy: "I have an aunt and uncle who are so willing to go to church every Sunday, but they are like the most horrible people I know." For Joshua, there is no church that exists beyond his individual self. He uses spiritual language to anchor himself, define his own purpose, and dramatize his own self-growth.[14] Through his recovery, he becomes the "stillness in the chaos."

Joshua's father, Steven, reminisces about his own childhood, a simpler time where "we never had any money." Steven worked in the fields before and after school, and a Friday night out entailed his mother "taking me to the firehouse for the firehouse dance." He fears that his own desire to give his children an easier life has created a generation of young people who cannot cope with the hardships of everyday life: "They don't know what it's like to have a little bit of a struggle. It's our fault too. We spoil them." Steven valorizes hard work, sacrifice, and self-discipline, believing that suffering is essential to growth.

But Steven does not appear genuinely angry. Mostly, he just seems tired. When I watch Steven and Joshua Meier interact with each other, it is clear that this hard-working, tough, manual-laborer father does not quite understand his son, but he is nonetheless achingly grateful that he is alive. Steven wants to live peacefully in his rural town with his healthy family, far away from the violent crime and crowdedness of the cities, with no one telling him what to do and a pile of assault rifles in the barn just in case.

Joshua and his father engage in a fraught conversation in the kitchen:

JOSHUA: What do you think was missing in my childhood that might have prevented me from becoming an addict?

STEVEN: Not a clue, Joshua! Not a clue. I wouldn't be able to answer that. We asked ourselves the same thing. What could we have done?

JOSHUA: I know what you could have done.

STEVEN (OUTRAGED): Oh, you have the answer? You should have thought about that about twenty years ago.

JOSHUA: Instead of just taking me to church, actually sitting down and teaching me why I'm at church. The spiritual part of life. Through application. It's practical. Practical exercises and real-life scenarios to teach spirituality. Going out and helping homeless people, going out and lending a hand in our community. Creating projects and programs and getting involved. We're in the middle of a spiritual crisis, but it's so easily overlooked because we, it's not comfortable to look at the hard, it's not comfortable to want to get out of our comfort zone.

STEVEN: Well, I ain't blaming myself cuz you turned out the way you did.

With heart-wrenching sincerity, Steven tells me that his son, over the last four years of his sobriety, has become his hero: "He could be my hero for the last four years. Five years. He changed my life back to normal. Or better than normal. Oh yes. [*Chuckles.*]" Joshua also instructs his father to be more open-minded about gay marriage. "Nobody can take your right to love another person," he insists. "That's true. It's not up to me to judge that, even if I don't like it," his father agrees. Steven adds: "He enlightens us continuously. It's great. He really is."

With this encouragement, Joshua enthusiastically chronicles his transformation from a life of purposelessness to one of fulfilling a higher calling. He reconceives his past failures as opportunities for redemption. Joshua yearns for a collective, moral awakening that restores a "why" to people's lives:

It's like you got to think about drug dealers, you think about their "why." And what it's based around. Even if they can sell the most drugs out of any drug dealer, what is their reason? What are they doing with the money that they're getting from their drug? They're buying things of no real spiritual value. They're buying houses, TVs, and cars and jewelry and whatever. So it's always about the why. Even if every drug dealer could get rich, they're still not gaining, they're still not growing anywhere in life. And so how do you inspire them that there's more value in actually appreciating life and doing positive things? How do you do that? It seems like an impossible thing to do. It's not gonna be easy. It

takes a literal *timed rising*, and not just one day. Like everybody has to
rise up all at once and sit and make a plan and follow through with it. You
know what I mean, everybody coming together in this one big sweep.

Rather than fight for economic opportunity, whether individually or collectively,
Joshua proclaims, "Money has no real value." The "timed rising" he envisions
reflects a yearning for solidarity that we also see in Brian, the white supremacist;
Jacob, the volunteer firefighter; and Ed, who puts the good of his son's baseball
team over his son's individual success.

The end goal of Joshua's "timed rising" is personal salvation for all, completely detached from everyday material needs and desires. In this way, Joshua
constructs money as outside the sphere of justice. "I don't think it's even about
really rich people paying more taxes," he muses. "I think it's about inspiring really rich people and showing them the pure value of them contributing their
money. In other words, not taking it from them but inspiring them to give it. By
creating programs and projects that they feel they want to give to."

Joshua puts forth a new vision of the self, one that is devoid of any kind of social contract and instead entirely contained within himself. He urgently believes
that spiritual contamination—negativity, hatefulness, resentment, judgment
of others—leads, punitively, to emptiness and death. Everything, he explains,
comes from inside the self. "Now they have a new study that shows your outlook
and your spiritual, basically your outlook on life, your attitude and everything
like that actually has the ability to prevent disease and it changes your genetics,"
he says excitedly. "So if you're hateful and judgmental, uncompassionate, a
selfish person, and you're laying in the hospital bed with maybe some crazy form
of cancer, what could I have done different to not be here? I could have just loved
instead of hated. I could have just been compassionate instead of judgmental.
And science is showing it now. It's not about the people you're hating or judging
or discriminating against. It's about yourself."

Because he views hardship as an important foundation for self-growth,
Joshua worries about what will happen "if we continuously give handouts and
people don't know how to appreciate and take what they're given and understand that it's in place for them to grow. So like if you've been given the opportunity, you're living on assistance, everything's paid for, your bills or whatever,
and all you do is sit around and watch TV, that's not, that's taking advantage."
The definition of hard work is expanded beyond getting a job to include
improving the self: "What it really comes down to is how you inspire people to
want to, maybe not, not so much getting a job or whatever but maybe inspiring
them to better themselves." He gears personal salvation toward a remaking of
what it means to be a good person that both emulates and rejects the disciplined self. He wants to save souls, not reform politics, freeing himself of the

longing for social recognition and economic fairness that torments the other men in this chapter.

Steven and Joshua agree that politicians are corrupt. "All politicians are bought off. Once they get thrown into the machine they become puppets like all the rest," Joshua reflects. "I'm not a fan of either of them [Trump or Clinton]. It's like choose shit or a shit sandwich. Either way . . . " His father interjects, laughing: "No matter who wins it's going to stink!" Steven and his wife are longtime Republicans who voted for Donald Trump in the Pennsylvania primary: "I think he's the best candidate I've seen in the Republican Party ever," he declares, smiling. "Oh, he got us rednecks!" he adds, embracing the derogatory term. "Though Bernie Sanders, he ain't a bad guy," Steven follows up. "I'd vote for Bernie." Joshua agrees. While Steven will vote, simply because he believes that "somebody has to vote somebody in," Joshua relegates voting to unimportant, distracting "matters of the flesh, form, physical. We forget that, sometimes we just got to remember where we came from. All I know is that the thing that trumps it all, not Donald Trump . . . is love, unconditional love and acceptance."

Piecing the Self Back Together

Across the middle decades of the twentieth century, white working-class men organized against corporate power, redefining freedom as more than a lack of barriers and also as a bedrock of economic security. The white blue-collar man of the coal mine, the steel mill, or the assembly line seemed to be wrapped up in the nation's collective sense of its own destiny, sustained by American dominance over manufacturing across the world.[15] Despite the persistence of lively church festivals, rowdy fire-company block parties, and packed Friday-night football games, the white working-class men in Coal Brook today give voice to isolation, purposelessness, and resentment. All of them are only tentatively attached to the political sphere, struggling to convince themselves that "America" stands for something larger than individual greed. In this era of uncertainty, they take it upon themselves to rearrange, exalt, or dissolve the lingering pieces of industrial working-class masculinity.

Some men, like Ed and Brian, hold onto visions of collective economic justice for workers. For Ed, the scarcity of resources like health care and jobs leads him to angrily defend the deserving, hardworking, selfless Americans over outsiders who "didn't put a nickel in it." For Brian, who is stuck in a series of dead-end jobs and a floundering relationship, preserving whiteness—even by violence— becomes the stable, enduring foundation on which he builds his life. Other men let go of the connection to social class as an identity altogether, glorifying back-breaking labor and staunchly rejecting the idea that they deserve fairness or justice. In a few instances, white men take a reprieve from the stoicism they were raised on, choosing to vocalize their suffering, rather than hide it, and thus liberate themselves from shame. For Glen, the veteran with PTSD, this freedom allows him to widen his sphere of compassion—yet his own history of betrayal and disappointment with social institutions also leads him to reject existing political channels for change. Finally, Joshua believes that living a good life is not about collective action, mutual obligation, or economic justice—"It's all about your *self.*" In the next chapter, we turn to the lives of working-class white women, examining how they encounter the massive transformations in gender, work, and family that have ripped open these men's lives and left them scrambling to put them back together.

|| 3 ||

The Coal Miner's Granddaughter

The white women in the coal region use words like "shame" and "sickens" and "trash" to describe themselves. Living on the edge of poverty, struggling to afford heat, housing, health care, and food for their children, white women mourn the loss of their subordinate roles as wives and mothers even as they are victimized in them. For some, enduring their suffering, and "sticking it out" despite infidelity, violence, and trauma, lends a sense of moral worth. Combating shame, other women create an identity based on breaking free from controlling men and refusing to stay silent about the abuse they have suffered at the hands of their families and partners. Still others numb their feelings of disappointment and despair by splitting their Zoloft in half, turning to food or cigarettes or heroin, or asking God to take them out of life.

In their solitary searches for explanations to their suffering, white working-class women wage their political battles within the context of the fragile and aggrieved working-class family. Some women squarely reject the social safety net in the belief that suffering is good for the soul. Condemning their own family members for their inability to rise above pain serves as a way to feel validated, in control, and safe. Some women cut themselves off from family members who have hurt them by deciding that dependence makes them vulnerable and isolation is the safest way to survive. They offer half-hearted support for forthright, "brutally honest" male politicians who resonate with the harsh world they live in. For others, the impossibility of personal trust in the family simply renders impersonal trust in democracy unimaginable.[1]

The Best System for Growth in Life Is Stress

Shelly Moore, thirty-three, laughs when I walk her through the ethical procedures of consent before our interview. "What are you gonna do, kill me with your smile?" she scoffs. Shelly is a coal miner's granddaughter. He was "born in 1916 and was an old angry Polish and Irish man, just very mean," and most of her family has lived in the coal region for generations. Her mother was just thirteen when Shelly was born, and her father was twenty-one. Their shotgun marriage lasted only a few months. Shelly grew up in a trailer with her mother and stepfather, Curtis, an "angry truck driver," and four younger siblings.

One of her earliest memories involves watching her stepfather rape her mother's close friend, Pam:

> Curtis, my stepdad was pouring the drinks, and the next thing you know I was peeking through the door and Curt had Pam by the neck and slammed her down on the bed and hit her. Then after that I remember my mom's jaw being wired shut. And I remember the conversation about that when my mom's friend was like, "He raped me, why are you going to stay with him and he broke your jaw," and my mom looked over her shoulder and seen me sitting there playing and my mom said, "little pigs have big ears," and Pam was like, "I don't care. How are you going to let him do this?" My mom screamed really loud, "You can get the fuck out of my house." But after that my mom said we are not to speak of it ever again.

Curtis began sexually abusing Shelly when she was four. Shelly told her mother, who did not believe her. At age eight, she "testified in my own rape case" when school officials uncovered the abuse. Shelly moved in with her biological father and stepmother—"the evil stepmom, Cinderella story, that exists, that is real." The nightmare of abuse spiraled:

> And I knew she [the stepmother] was cheating on my dad, and she wanted to make sure I never told my dad. She used to do things like when I was thirteen she would give me money to go downtown and hang out with my friends and be like, "Can you get me a bag of weed?" She goes and calls my dad and says that I stole money out of her purse for drugs and cigarettes and that she had proof. Then she pulled her pipe out and told my dad it was mine and that she found it in my stuff. So what do you think happened? Dad's head popped off. That was the first time Dad made me get on my hands and knees and he beat me with the guitar strap.

As she entered her teens, Shelly was taken away from her parents and put into a group home for girls.

The first chance Shelly got, she married her high-school sweetheart, who was enlisting in the army. They moved to an army base where she gave birth to a daughter. Shelly decided to make a trip home for the first time in more than a decade so that her own mother could meet her new granddaughter. During their reunion, she remembers: "My mom looked at [my stepfather], and my mom looked at me, and she just started crying cuz that was the moment she realized her husband had been having sex with her four-year-old daughter. I took my kid, I packed up all her stuff, I ran out the door. I drove off and I never spoke to my mom again."

Then, six years later, "I got a phone call saying mom died." Shelly explains:

> And when I walked away from her, she spiraled completely out of control and I never went back and she was always waiting for that phone call. She was always waiting. And my mom's friends told me, "You know your mom used to sit all day long as soon as her cell phone would go dead she'd freak out, Michelle's gonna call me one day." I never called. Never called. . . . That is when I spiraled into my addiction, that's when I didn't care anymore. That's when life said, "We're gonna catch up with you. You didn't kill these people, you called them out, you forgave them, but now you're gonna punish yourself." And I did. I ripped my whole life apart, because I didn't know how to cope with what I did.

Shelly developed a raging heroin addiction, which she hid from her husband and two children while living on the army base. Meanwhile, she discovered her husband was cheating on her and descended further into despair—"I'd find his burner phone and I would see the messages and I would see the pictures and instead of talking to him about it, I would shut down, I would use drugs, I would go shopping, I would have promiscuous sex with people." Finally, after her young daughter saw her crawling up the steps one day, high on heroin, Shelly locked herself in a hotel for five days. She "started sweating and shaking and puking and crying" until she had detoxed herself. Afterwards, she confessed everything to her husband, who "couldn't handle it. He needed perfect." He got full custody in the divorce "because I was high around my child."

Today, Shelly lives with a new boyfriend. She rarely leaves the house and does not work. When I ask her what she does for money, she shrugs: "I mean, granted now I could probably get full disability. I have PTSD and severe anxiety and all that other kind of stuff, and I could be hopped up on all kinds of medication according to Pennsylvania." She launches into a thoughtful discussion of how she has made the shattered trust, pain, and betrayals of her young life meaningful:

> There's a doctor on YouTube, he was talking about how he'd seen a magazine and the article was "How Do Lobsters Grow." And it says that lobsters are soft mushy creatures that live inside a tough rigid shell. And what happens when the lobster starts to grow, the shell doesn't expand,

the lobster does, so the lobster starts to swell and starts to feel tight, starts to feel uncomfortable, starts to feel under stress. So the lobster goes off, sheds the shell, grows a little bit, produces a new shell, goes out into the world and deals with life. He says that if lobsters had doctors they would never grow, cuz the moment the lobster would start to feel uncomfortable, the lobster would go to the doctor, prescribe it this, pre-scribe it that, and the lobster would never experience what true growth is. So the trigger for growth in a lobster is feeling uncomfortable, so what is the difference between people?

In other words, Shelly decides that suffering is a positive experience—even for children trapped in situations that are not "positive"—because stress is a catalyst for growth. Avoiding pain leaves one vulnerable and unprepared for life's inevi-table traumas:

So you take these kids out of these stressful situations where it may not be a positive thing, but they're growing, and you seclude them and you medicate them and you put them in these little isolated bubbles and you don't allow their brains to learn how to deal with misfiring and mishaps, they don't learn how to naturally cope with and deal with the things that are happening with their bodies.

She continues heatedly: "And then you're blaming society, why? You need to be stressed out. I'm a recovering addict, heroin addict. I didn't take medicine to get off of the drug, I didn't take anything to get off the drug. I sat my happy little ass in that bedroom and I sweated it out, and I suffered it out, I stressed it out. Because I am not ever going to feel that way again. The best system for growth in life is stress." In this account, avoiding suffering, blaming others for one's misfor-tune, and evading responsibility will only make you more vulnerable in the end. Resilience takes the form of a celebration of pain.

Growing up, Shelly learned in excruciatingly painful ways that trusting others is dangerous. She registered as a Democrat when she turned eighteen, just like her parents and grandparents. But she now abstains from voting as a way to dis-tance herself from her family past, linking their dependence on government benefits to the chaos and cruelty she was raised on: "My family is so fucked up on drugs and they live off the state. I want my hands out of this shit show." Shelly describes herself as "more worried about survival than the shit show of politics." The two realms—survival and politics—are completely distinct in her mind. She ends our discussion by connecting her distrust to politics on the following humorous yet unnerving note: "Am I gonna put my life or my child's life in the hands of somebody that can't keep their stories straight? I'm not, and I'm not going to put my life or my child's life in the hands of somebody that uses that much orange spray tan."

Confronting Shame

Danielle, a twenty-eight-year-old white woman, grounds her identity in acknowledging her suffering and choosing to grow from it. She draws strong boundaries against people who try to escape their pain rather than face it head on. Danielle found her current apartment a few months ago when she and her husband, Nathan, were briefly separated. "A few years ago, he was dealing drugs out of the house," she recalls. "I worked the seven-to-seven nightshift. He had my daughter with him. And then one day I was off work, one of his friends came, and they didn't know I knew nothing about it, and they said something. I was like, are you kidding me?" She shrugs: "So instead of confronting him I went and cheated on him." Over the past year, as Danielle "was going through anxiety," acting like "a raging lunatic," "he took it as I was treating him unfairly so then he went to someone else and then they had their own little thing. I could kill that teeny bopper. And then we were split up for about three weeks in August last year." Danielle moved out. "For a while there I was just sleeping out of my car, at my mom's house," she describes. "I was only working part-time; he was working full-time. Had all my crap in my car."

Mercifully, the pastor from her family's church offered her their current apartment for $500 a month and no security deposit. Danielle and Nathan eventually reconciled: "We've been through so much," Danielle reflects. "His parents were all about drugs and going to prison and alcohol. He was abused as a child. We've been through the wringer," she confides. "But it just makes us that much stronger, like we just, we're able to take on what most people can't." Danielle has forged a sense of pride out of their ability to withstand suffering and emerge even stronger.

As Danielle tells her story, she spins a web of connections between economic decline, family fragility, trauma, and politics. Her grandfather was a coal miner, and her parents worked in a garment factory until they retired with disability in their fifties. "My mom, oh my gosh, she has so much stuff," Danielle explains. "She's a little heavier so she has like diabetes. She had neuropathy, blood pressure, all kinds of stuff. And my dad, I know it has something to do with his back." In the beginning of our interview, I ask her to describe what it was like growing up in the coal region. "It wasn't bad. I was spoiled rotten. I was the only one out of all the kids that got a Power Wheel when I was four," she boasts. Scarcely pausing for breath, she adds quietly: "My dad actually sexually abused me when I was a kid. From twelve to sixteen. My mom didn't know. Nobody knew."

For years, Danielle kept silent, suffering from sudden and unpredictable moments of debilitating fear:

> But then I was at work and I had an anxiety attack, I've had them for years. But then in one week I had like six of them. Over half of them landed me in the ER cuz I could not get myself to come out of it. The last one, I actually fell unconscious. It was just that bad, it was just, my body just said, "Well, we're done." And I dropped to the floor. So I went to go see a psychiatrist and a therapist and everybody and then one of the questions came up and they were like, "Were you ever sexually abused as a child or abused in general?" And for years, I've been saying, "No, no, no, I'm fine." And for some reason my mind just told me just say yes. So I did. For the first time in twelve years, I spoke up about it. And I thought, "Okay, maybe this is why everything's going on, maybe this is why all the anxiety attacks are happening. It's my body's way of saying something's happening, you gotta speak up."

Danielle "expected that after I spoke up that it would go away, all the emotions, all the anxiety, everything would just disappear. And it was the complete opposite. Oh my God. It was so much anger, resentment. I was crying nonstop."[2]

Danielle had been working at a local grocery store for three years, beginning as a cashier making minimum wage and steadily working her way up to supervisor "in just four months." Since she has started talking openly about her abuse, she has been unable to finish a shift. "The last time was only a four-hour day. And I felt my chest going, I felt my hands getting sweaty. I go in the back room, I'm just gonna take a breather. I was back there for ten, fifteen minutes. I felt better, I said, 'Okay I'm gonna go back out,'" she remembers. "I'm out there for not even two minutes and it was just, bam! In my face panic." For the next week, she sat at home in a chair, not moving or speaking except to tell her oldest daughter to "go make some mac and cheese, go make some hot dogs." By the end of the week, "I couldn't even get off this chair. Even opening my eyes, everything was just spinning, because I hadn't eaten in five days. And I'm 130 pounds." Danielle takes a deep breath. "My life did a complete 180 within months."

Danielle chronicles the disturbing experiences that have led her to this breaking point. She got pregnant during her junior year of high school. Her mother, who had a shotgun marriage when she was just fifteen, "told me not to have sex. I told her I was having all these feelings. My dad was very, a no-go when it comes to birth control." After a year of having sex with her boyfriend, Danielle found out she was pregnant when "my mom said, 'You're taking a test. I was like, 'Why?' And she was like, 'Well, you missed your period for two months.' And

I was like, 'I did not.' So then she went out to the store, came back with a test, and then I thought nothing of it, nonchalantly peed on a stick, went upstairs, changed out of my school clothes, came down and she was crying in the bathroom. I was like, 'Oh shit.'" Her mother "made me sit in front of her for like an hour, on my knees, and just lectured me. As she told me about the birds and the bees and how I shouldn't have done it, how I shouldn't be like her. My dad was like, 'Oh she got what she wanted.'" Danielle suspects her father knew she was sexually active and used "it kinda as blackmail against me. Because I think he knew that I was having sex with my boyfriend. And he was like, 'Oh well, if you do this, I'll let you go see him.'"

Danielle's mother insisted that she graduate from high school. Soon after, she moved in with her boyfriend, who has a GED and works in a variety of auto mechanic and factory jobs. They put off getting married until her second daughter asked, "'Mom, why do you have a different last name than me and Daddy?' Cuz we weren't married at that point. And I said to him, 'I feel bad.' And so we got married." Despite the fact that her "own family wasn't so stable," Danielle believed that marriage "would kinda give that structure." Danielle takes pride in the fact that she married the first man she had sex with and that all of her children share one father.

> Half my friends that have kids, I would say most of my best friends had kids when they were fifteen, sixteen, seventeen, and none of them are with their original fathers. Most of them, I think all of them, have either a second or third child to another person. And it, it kinda feels good that I can put on any paperwork that we have, whether it be school or doctors or anything, all of us have the same last name. Where my friends, they have their name and their kid's last name and the next one, ironically, all of them, their second kid has their last name. The first and the third have the dad's last name. So they have all different last names. And that would just kill me, I think.

She draws self-worth from the performance of moral rectitude, even as adultery, violence, and abuse lurk beneath the surface.

For a while, the family was doing well: "I was bringing home seven hundred every two weeks, he was bringing home eight hundred every two weeks. So we were making decent money," she recalls. "Like we almost had his car paid off." But just "when you think you get ahead, something always happens, every single time." Danielle's husband injured himself at work and "was leaking brain fluid," and she had to quit her job because of her incessant panic attacks. They have not paid their rent for four months—but "the pastor said the other day, don't worry about any of it. I was blown away because this is the church's income."

Plunging from "almost low middle class" to "just stuck," Danielle obtained medical assistance for workers with disability for her panic attacks for $36 a month. They qualified for nearly $600 a month in food stamps. She admits that she has changed the way she thinks about food stamps since her days as a cashier at the grocery store: "So there's so many people that judge people on food stamps. And I do sometimes, like the one lady came through and bought meat for her dog. And I thought, 'You're buying meat for your dog, and it's [supposed to be] for a human? I have to struggle to put food on my table and you're buying meat for your dog.'" But she also advocates empathy: "But like it's hard for someone on the outside that's never gotten the help or seen what could happen to understand. And I'm living it, to be honest. I mean I hated it, but you have no choice."

Danielle began seeing a psychiatrist, who referred her to a women's recovery group. She finally told her mother about her father's sexual abuse: "I let it all out. And it was hard to watch her be hurt, you know. Like, she kept asking, 'Did I miss something?' Cuz she had an inkling, but I must've said it a thousand times you know, 'Nothing's happening, everything's fine.'" Soon after Danielle told her, her mother got into a debilitating car accident, and Danielle stepped in to take care of her disabled adult brothers. Pretending that nothing ever happened in front of her father became a necessity of survival in small-town life:

Cuz my biggest fear was what if he left my mom? Because now it's, it's all on me. He'd leave. I have three handicapped brothers. I'd be the one that's running around, doctor's appointments, paying the bills, this, that, and the other. So I'd pay the consequences anyways. Plus everybody, the whole town, the doctors, they know my mom, they know my family. They would know everything that's going on, it's a small town.

Until her mother gets back on her feet, Danielle cannot risk her mother and brothers' well-being, especially since her father is an "alcoholic" and "volatile."

"How do you do it?" I ask her. "How do you just deal with everything?" Danielle replies:

You don't have a choice. Either that or you're six feet under, because it just gets to you. That's how I feel. If you don't take it head-on and just deal with it, you're going to the loony bin. You're gonna kill yourself. Pick one. That's just how I see it. Either you deal with it or you don't. And if you don't deal with it, you're gonna end up doing drugs, alcohol, or you're gonna end up in the loony bin or dead. And I get why people do heroin. I get it. It's so much easier [to say], not gonna deal with reality. But it's what you gotta do to stay alive. When you have kids, you don't have a choice. And that's what pushes me.

Danielle grounds her identity in facing her harsh reality head-on and pushing forward, in contrast to taking the "easier" route—drugs, alcohol, suicide.

A few hours into our interview, Danielle's cousin Kristin stops by to drive her to visit her mother in the hospital. I ask them about their political views, and they staunchly assert that they are not "political." When I ask if any candidate appeals to them, Danielle names Donald Trump, because he "is so in your face, like eff you, I don't give a crap what you think of me. I think he belongs in this area because that's what we are. We're honest, we don't give a crap and that's what this country needs. I mean I don't agree with everything he says, but I think he'll actually push to do something." Her cousin nods in agreement: "Yes, his mouth is overboard and stuff, but I think he's brutally honest. And people don't know how to handle it."

Danielle is drawn to a strong candidate who is aggressively "in your face." She connects her respect for Donald Trump to "what we are," who could represent a community that is forthright, "brutally honest," and does not "give a crap" about maintaining a false, polished image. Danielle is drawn to unapologetic honesty. The ability to stare reality in the face, acknowledge its brutality, and nonetheless persevere—no matter how unpleasant or unsettling—resonates deeply with her own experiences.

Both Danielle and Kristin agree that "we should tax people more to help people like us." Kristin recalls:

> Like when I left my husband, I needed a place to stay. I applied for housing. All these years, I mean I was making twenty dollars an hour, doing this, doing that. Like I busted my ass working since I been twelve years old. I had to take care of my family, do all that kinda stuff. I applied for HUD and was gonna be homeless with my kids. You know what they told me? "There's a waiting list. 250 people are ahead of you." But somebody that might be, this is the best, somebody that may be worse off than you will have, will be bumped up on the list. I said how can somebody be more worse off than I? So what did I do? I had to sit there and bust my ass and not see my kids for almost three weeks to make sure I got the money. I pooled everything I had in order to get a place to live.

However, just a few minutes later, they lash out against their own families:

> Kristin: Last year was the first year I went down to the Salvation Army for help for Christmas and I got, the kids each got two toys a piece and a bike. The toys were literally, listen, I'm grateful, I don't wanna sound like I'm not. But then my mom went to the same place, my sisters got

iPods. She knew all the ladies by names. And I'm thinking, you know what? My first time ever asking for help for Christmas, my first time. And I actually don't have nothing. And then I see my mom getting all that shit.

　　　Danielle: Her mom is the one that gets pills from crooked doctors and sells them for income for the house. Her parents are the prime example of corrupt. They pop children out just to get more money from welfare and they get whatever they want while people like us suffer.

Their progressive political impulses are stymied when they take a stand against the personal—when they connect their disdain for their own family members to their ideas about social-welfare abuse. Disparaging women in her family who "pop children out just to get more money from welfare," Danielle underscores her own commitment to a stable family structure where her children all share the same last name, even as it puts her "through the wringer." Forging a sense of dignity from her hard-won victories, Danielle seeks validation for the "people like us" who withstand their pain.

Danielle has never voted, and Kristin thinks she might have "voted one time once." Neither of them plan to vote this year. "We're too busy during the day!" Kristin insists. Danielle adds: "I think it's all corrupt. Whoever they want to win is gonna win and it's all a matter of who has more money. Whoever's gonna win, they already set up. And that's how it like, in this area, you know somebody. That's how you're getting in, if you know somebody. I think it's like that everywhere."

From Self-Loathing to Self-Help

When I meet thirty-three-year-old Lucy Ladowski, half the walls in her row home have been stripped of wallpaper from her husband's bath-salt induced rages.[3] A construction worker who is the father of her youngest daughter, he has spent the last nine months in a mandatory drug and alcohol rehab program two hours away. Lucy is currently torn between two visions of how she should live her life—she fights to hold onto a nuclear family structure while also developing a keen awareness of the dangers of staying with someone who is angry, unfaithful, and violent. Two books sit prominently on her rickety wicker bookshelf: *Codependent No More* and *All I Need Is Jesus and a Good Pair of Jeans*. "I have books all over the place so I'm like halfway through all of them," Lucy says eagerly. "Like I'm learning now . . . how do I word this? You're treated how you teach somebody to treat you." Lucy chronicles a long, arduous journey of self-acceptance, letting go of the shame of not living up to traditional feminine virtues, and finally speaking out about her suffering instead of silently medicating it away.

She takes me back through several generations of family history, providing her own moral interpretations along the way. "My dad's father was a coal miner. He was a very, very mean, angry alcoholic," she explains. "My grandmother who was married to him stayed with him the entire time and was a saint as far as I'm concerned. I don't know how else you'd put up with all that." Lucy's father, one of seven children, spent several months in jail for robbery when she was young. Her mother married her father at just seventeen. Lucy continues: "My father got what we call 'saved' in jail. He's a laborer. He drives a concrete truck. Very hard worker ever since he accepted the Lord and changed his life and stopped stealing. The one verse that he always said to us that stuck out to him was 'you need to work with your hands and make your own money.'"

When she was growing up, Lucy's family went to church three times a week and rejected "secular things"—"no smoking. No dancing. I couldn't wear bathing suits. I couldn't cheer lead." Her mother, a homemaker, kept the house "OCD clean" and always had "a hot supper when my dad came home." Lucy remembers feeling worried all the time growing up but did not know how to describe her feelings or ask for help: "I had major anxiety and self-esteem issues but I didn't know what anxiety was. I think if I would've gotten on like some kind of medication or something, I could've so excelled."

Like Danielle Muller, Lucy "never got the talk" and "didn't even know what sex was. My mom never told me I would get my period, what it was. It took me like two years to know how to put a tampon in." She met her first boyfriend in church youth group when she was fifteen and they "had sex in the parking lot at church" until she got pregnant her senior year of high school. "He wanted me to have an abortion. He did not want to be a father. He didn't wanna get married. And eventually I was just like, 'Okay, forget it. I'm done with you,'" she explains. Lucy got a job working in a distribution center, raising her child at home with her parents, and entering into a long battle with self-loathing and shame: "I felt horrible about myself. Not only because my parents made me that way, but my religion made me feel that too. I mean I was unwed and a mother. The only thing I ever saw was my parents. Being a housewife, that was my thing. I wanted to stay home, take care of kids, be a mom, and have my husband go to work."

Lucy had struggled to even get out of bed: "The whole depression thing, I didn't even know I had that but it hit like . . . like my parents just didn't get it. It's not like 'Well, just get up and do what you have to do.' And it's like, don't you think I want to do that? You think I want to feel bad or feel like I want to die? Who would ever wanna feel that way?" Only getting drunk or high temporarily alleviated her depression. She met her current husband at a bar and they "did drugs together. His drug of choice is methamphetamine or any kind of speed or upper. And I guess that I was medicating. It did take that kind of pain away."

As their relationship progressed, Chris asked Lucy to go camping for the weekend before his impending thirty-day stint in jail for a DUI. Lucy seized the opportunity to push for marriage: "Going away was a no-go for my dad because we weren't married. I wanted a commitment, you know, I wanted a family." They were married in her parents' backyard and purchased the house across the street at her mother's insistence. As soon as they got married, "he wanted me to quit my job and I was like, that's what I wanna do, too! I wanted to be a stay-at-home mom, he would go get a good job and that's how it was gonna be." But Chris was in and out of jail, racking up DUIs, and could not hold down a job: "He was taking the money and buying drugs with it. He wasn't paying our bills. Like we would get our income tax back and I would pay all the back bills, all the credit card bills with the income tax. I would get it put right into my account. That's how I would live." She has relied on food stamps and medical assistance, which adds to her shame: "It sickens me and I hate to be on it. It's shameful. It's embarrassing. It sucks to have to use an access card in Walmart."

During our interview, Lucy repeatedly refers to herself as "fat"—even when I ask her about her general health, she quickly replies, almost as if she is anticipating judgment, "Well, I need to lose weight. I know that. It's obvious." She is disgusted by her weight, which she believes ballooned because of her mother feeding her "crazy portions" at home. At five feet four inches, Lucy reached 260 pounds: "I was on medical assistance at the time and I said listen, I need to lose weight. I need to lose weight and it's not working, nothing's working. So they sent me to a nutritionist who told me 2,000 calories a day. OK thanks, that's not gonna help," she says, defeated. Lucy instead flew to Mexico for Lap-Band surgery: "And so I don't know how the heck I did it, but I figured it all out and I put it on a credit card. I went to Juarez, Mexico. Yeah, me and my husband. Now later I found out, he was high out of his mind." Lucy had to have her lap band drained back in the US when she had stomach flu and was unable to have it filled again because "they closed all of the fill centers. So I have this lap band and I can't get it filled anywhere, it was very shady!" Complications from the surgery have left her in chronic pain.

When Lucy's marriage became abusive, she had nowhere to go:

> Yeah. I think this is my third PFA [protection from abuse order] I have on him. We got in a fight, probably something ridiculous. I don't even remember. But he hurt me pretty bad. And then I would fight back because that's just who I am. I was a lot thinner and smaller. He's pretty big. He choked me. I had like huge bruises and stuff on my neck. I mean I was bleeding like and stuff. My friend said "You need to call your dad

right now" and I said, "No, I can't! All he's gonna do is say we shouldn't be drinking, this is what you get," and she called him and that's exactly what he told her. I deserved it. And if I'm gonna stay here with him then that's what I deserve. They still feel that way.[4]

She reports that the local police share this view: "They don't wanna be bothered. They don't wanna help you. I feel like there was a stigma, like, 'Well if you had a PFA and you took your husband back, then you deserve it so stop calling us, this is not our problem.' I don't feel like it is that way, it *is* that way, actually, that's really what they said."

While Lucy felt that religion was forced on her growing up, God was her only guide and comfort during this time. Lucy feared divorcing her husband, as "the Bible says God hates divorce." So she prayed every night that he would commit adultery, which would give her a legitimate reason for leaving him. She says incredulously:

> I prayed and I just wasn't feeling good for a long time. I had an STD for a very long time and didn't even know it. I went to a local clinic to get checked. And of course I've never slept with anyone but my husband, I mean since I've been married to him. And she [the doctor] didn't di-agnose it at first. And I was still having a problem and I went back a second time and she said you have, I can't remember. But thank God it's curable and it's not like herpes or HIV or something. But there it was!

Lucy did not even broach the topic of her husband's affairs and sexually transmitted disease: "But you see, he had to be treated too. So I came home with these pills and I said, 'I have to take these pills to get rid of my infection and you have to take these pills.' And we didn't even discuss it cuz at the time I was scared, I just didn't wanna deal with it. But he took the pills, I made him take them, and he didn't even question it because he knew. He knew. He knew that I wasn't un-faithful." Lucy stayed with her husband. "God answered my prayer. And I still couldn't do it," she says helplessly.

In the following years, she developed severe depression and social anxiety. As she explains, "I just felt horrible. I didn't realize how much my husband played a part in how bad I was feeling. I just didn't . . . I was like, 'Well why can't I just get up and do what I have to do?' I wanted to die." When Lucy confessed these feelings to a counselor at church, "she had really never dealt with this before. I don't know if she was a seasoned counselor or not, I don't think she was. So she said, 'Would you wanna go to the hospital?' and I said 'I guess, I don't know.' And they checked me into the mental . . . the psych ward." Lucy shares this harrowing experience, which further deprived her of autonomy and self-worth:

I didn't wanna live anymore. I've never ever had a plan for suicide or ever wanted to commit suicide because it's against everything, religiously, I believe. So that . . . I just wanted God to take me out of life. And they asked me a bunch of questions. It was the most humiliating thing. They strip you down naked. You know, and take everything from you. You don't have anything but like a hospital gown, a sheet. Nothing. And then when I got there I realized . . . like nobody told me like, "OK this is a voluntary check-in, but you can't voluntarily check yourself out." Well nobody told me that. And I'm like, "Wait a minute! What do you mean I can't leave?" That same night, I guess I was calming down, and I was like, "Wait a minute. I want to leave." And they're like "no honey, it doesn't work that way." I was scared to death. That was not the right fit for me at the time. Although I can't blame the counselor. I mean she didn't know what to do. I guess she thought I was gonna kill myself, although I didn't ever say that to anyone there. I just said I want God to take me and I don't have . . . you know. And it was just the worst experience of my life.

As Lucy's husband completes his third rehab, Lucy is learning to focus on her own healing: "But I'm in such a better spot with going to meetings for the families of addicts every Monday, and my codependency book, and my own therapy, I go once a week. I feel really, really strong. I've been a single mom this, almost the entire time we've been married. I've been financially taking care of us almost the entire time we've been married." As she continues to see her counselor through the church and to attend weekly services, she reflects: "But what I also know now is that God does not want you to be abused or treated in a way that is unacceptable, for any spouse." Now, Lucy vows, "This is the last time I will do this."

Lucy recently reached out to an organization that provides free support services to survivors of domestic violence. With their help, she has made peace with the idea of needing help: "There was this one time I was going to try and get cash assistance. But the lady was just, she was an asshole. She was just an asshole. She treated me like trash. Like they're better than me," she recounts heatedly. But Lucy refused to be cowed: "I brought this lady from my counseling with me, and she said, 'Listen, they cannot treat you like trash. You're not trash.' And she kinda like talked me up and I thought, you know, you're right. I'm going through a really hard time right now. I'm really hard on myself and I forget all this crap that I'm going through. Whether I bring it on myself, or however, it's still valid and it's still really tough stuff." It has taken her a long time to see herself as good enough on her own, capable of surviving, and deserving of some help, even as she still blames herself for her plight.

When her food stamps did not cover the cost of laundry detergent and shampoo, asking her parents was not an option: "I hate taking help. Especially from my parents, oh my gosh. Because I feel like then I owe them. And I know that I can't pay it back, at least not right now or anything." Instead, Lucy turned to a woman from her church: "But I did go to her at one point and we were getting food stamps, but we didn't have like toiletries. Like shampoo, that kind of stuff. Toilet paper. She actually brought me down to the store and bought me tons of toilet paper. Just everything I needed. Laundry detergent, all that stuff," she says with wonder. When we talk about the economy, she is reluctant to talk "about the money stuff." She believes that the wealthy should be taxed more, "at least tax them, what they're not being taxed?" she asks me tentatively. But even using food stamps is described as a process of self-acceptance and empowerment by Lucy. She casts herself as worthy of aid based on her moral restraint ("I do not abuse it, and I work hard") rather than on a foundation of economic justice.

Lucy does not think about politics very much, even in the weeks before the November 2016 election. Her parents are passionate Republicans and fans of *Fox News*: "My dad will sit there and yell at the television. My girls watch it with him and they have that, like at the beginning it says something about, '*this is the spin-free zone*,' and they have it memorized." Lucy has been a registered Republican for most of her adult life: "One time my friend's dad took us to work the polls," she laughs, and "he was a Democrat, so I registered Democrat. And then as soon as I told my dad that he's like, 'What are you doing? You have to change that!' So I just went and changed it. Either way it didn't really matter to me. I mean I wanted to vote, and I guess I trusted my dad's views on things." When she was younger, Lucy never thought of herself as someone who could have valid policy preferences of her own.

"I think every politician is a liar," she shrugs. "I don't trust politicians and I don't trust cops." I ask her whom she does trust: "The only person right now that I can trust is God. I've never trusted anyone I think, in my life really. I don't trust anyone. I don't trust my parents. Honestly. That sounds really sad though, doesn't it? That's sad." In 2016, Lucy voted for Trump, but not because she trusted her father to choose for her. This year, she made up her own mind: "I think that Trump's, that he would be more, he's against abortion, right? Abortion is a no-go for me," she says hesitantly. When Lucy votes based on her loyalty to her church, she is not choosing cultural issues over economic ones. She is staking a claim to her own identity and interests—out of allegiance to a God and to a church that drove her to the grocery store, bought her toilet paper with no strings attached, and remains the only source of trust in her life.

One Day at a Time

Other women are weary from years of relationship-churning and the problems of addiction, infidelity, poverty, and violence that have exploded in their lifetimes. Mary Ann Wilson, fifty-one, and her daughter Vivian, thirty-two, live in lonely desperation, linking the decline of trust and commitment in their families to an unshakeable feeling that their town is slowly poisoning them and everyone around them. Their rejection of men brings a knife-edged clarity to their politics, but their lack of belief in the possibility of a better future narrows their concerns to their own daily survival.

Mary Ann and Vivian live in Mary Ann's small row house—three rooms upstairs, three rooms downstairs—with Vivian's fifteen-year-old son Clyde. Vivian, cuddling her ten-year-old pit bull named Stella, walks me through the household bills: "We pay $167 a month mortgage. We don't have cable. We don't have Internet. We pay one bill this month, and a bill the next. Whatever that month is saying they're going to shut off if you don't pay it, we pay that one first. I get food stamps for my son. I get $357 a month for me and my son, and that's it, and we both have insurance through the welfare." The attached house next door has been vacant for years, which makes it even harder to heat their home during the long, cold winters: "I'm on a budget plan with my electric bill, because I let the bill go real high, because I couldn't afford to pay it, so that's $200 a month."

Mary Ann's grandparents worked in a silk mill that has since been demolished, and her own father held three factory jobs "to keep my mom home so he could pay for seven of us." Her parents were both registered Democrats and members of the Moose Club. Her mother always had "a hot meal ready when the children walked through the door." Mary Ann speaks with a kind of wistfulness about the simplicity of her childhood: "We had what we needed. We had one vehicle, a station wagon, and when it got wintertime, one door wouldn't shut. He'd shut it with a clothesline."

Mary Ann went to work in a factory at age seventeen, dropping out of high school one credit shy of graduating: "If your parents couldn't afford college, you were going to the factory to work. I mean, this is what they did, so I guess I'll probably be doing the same," she reasoned. Mary Ann divorced Vivian's father, a bootleg coal miner whom she describes as a serious alcoholic, when Vivian was seven. Vivian muses, "For my generation, I just feel like love's not what it used to be. There's no loyalty. I think that's why relationships lasted so long back then. Once you were committed to your relationship, that was it. And nowadays it's not like that. If it don't work, you just move on, and I think that's why everything's just a mess the way it is now." Her mother agrees: "Everybody's just quick to say, 'I quit.'" Sticking it out earns the highest praise, yet neither of the Wilsons have been able to stomach it.

Mary Ann has worked in factories all her life, and is "still banging my head against the wall," earning $10 an hour doing metalwork that "is very hard on your hands." She has no health insurance: "Well, they offer it, but when you do the math and see what your bills are, and then see what you have left, what do you do? Do you feed your family, or do you get health insurance? I'm betting the odds, because now they fine you for not having health insurance, so I figure right now I'm still ahead. Well, this year it'll be $600." Mary Ann is not against the principle of mandatory health insurance, but argues that if the government is going to require it, then factories "should pay the employees more to cover that." Vivian chimes in: "Yeah, I would like to see them live on $10 an hour and maneuver monies. You know what I'm saying?"[5]

Recently, Mary Ann's boyfriend died at the age of forty-six: "He had a mass in his lung. He was a welder, so we think all the chemicals that he breathed in . . . and he was a smoker. We're all smokers." They share a creeping sensation that everyone around them is dying—that "everybody is getting cancer." Mary Ann recalls how the undertaker told her, "You can't imagine how many people that I've gotten have passed away from cancer in the last six months in this area. He said it was like mass quantities of people. Everybody had the same exact issue, cause of death. Lung cancer."

Vivian shudders: "There's something in the air. I don't know if it's when they were digging up the coal or if something was coming up through the air, if it was from welding, the chemicals, the smelting. I don't know if they're bringing something here and burying stuff in our mountains. I mean, in reality, we don't know that. I mean, trucks come from New York, you name it, and they put it in the landfill." Her mother replies with a mix of resignation and bewilderment: "I don't know if it's the coal or if it's something that they dug up that stirred stuff, but it is weird, because everybody is getting cancer, everybody. Everybody just keeps getting cancer."

At age thirty-two, Vivian already has chronic bronchitis. "Every time I get sick it settles in my lungs. I'm a smoker. I always end up with bronchitis." She was recently hospitalized for "bronchitis and pneumonia in my left lower lobe of my lung, so I was on antibiotics, steroids, pain medicine, and back to the hospital three times after that for more treatment." She describes how the doctor disdainfully asked her about smoking: "I'm like, yes. It's so hard. It is very hard. They don't realize it, and unless you're a smoker, you don't realize how difficult it really is. It's part of your life, routine." Her mother, lighting up across the room, adds, "Especially when you're stressed out. I feel like everything is on my shoulders."

Mary Ann and Vivian's fear of pervasive pollution and their sense of helplessness—that everyone around them is dying, that the air and water and soil are killing them, and that there is nothing they can do about it—is mirrored in their conviction that the town has become unrecognizable. The bonds that once held people together have withered away and died:

> Growing up, it didn't matter where we went. Everybody knew everybody. It is not like that anymore. I had people come right in, steal stained-glass windows off my back porch. Originally, before the new windows were in, there was an old-fashioned stained-glass window at the top. You'll see in the older houses that have that. They came right in, sawed it right out of my back side porch, and took it and cashed it in. And now you have people with drug and alcohol problems that are quite severe, and everybody's just worried about themselves and how they can take care of this and that, and nobody's looking out for the neighbor.

Vivian is not simply a bystander in this social unraveling: she is a main character in it. She has three children with three different fathers and has been married and divorced twice. She describes: "My daughter's father was very, very abusive. He was much older than me, and he was very nasty." Thinking back on her dating history, she elaborates: "Well, most of the men around here, they don't work. They're all alcoholics. They have nothing going for them. My daughter's dad is forty-seven, and he still has no job, still lives at his mom's. My son's dad's the same, in and out of jail, doesn't work, lives with his mom."

When her marriage to her daughter's father fell apart, she explains,

> I think I was searching for something. I didn't know what I was looking for. I got myself caught up in alcohol, drugs, the whole nine. I went to prison for four years. Yeah, because I had a lot of prior stupid stuff, and it kind of adds up. It spirals, so after you get a charge and a charge and a charge, you can't just keep getting them, and then they keep slapping your hand. The group of people that I hung out with, we were all kind of wild and crazy, and it kind of just spiraled, and almost everybody of that group that I was with, if they're not dead right now, they're already in prison. I've buried so many of my friends. I was a drinker. They picked up the drug. That's not my thing, and it's killed them. It's killed most of them.

Rampant alcoholism and drug addiction among her peers solidifies her suspicion that everyone around her is dying. She says bleakly: "You can never get out, it's like you get stuck if you don't have a skill and education to get a better job."[6]

When Vivian was released from jail, she got a job at a factory making $8.65 an hour and quickly got married again. This marriage also imploded: "My ex-husband's very sick. He's addicted to heroin. He needs two kidneys and a pancreas, and he's been a diabetic since he was twelve, so he's on dialysis right now. He's thirty-five." She gave birth to a son, who is now two, and lives with her mother-in-law. She describes this woman as controlling, making her feel like she could never do anything right—"I was all stressed out. I was starting to miss work, because I was getting sick from my nerves. It was just way too much." Vivian was laid off and has since been looking for jobs. Her criminal record makes it hard to get a job—"I've probably put in, in the last two months, probably sixty applications, and everything is, 'You don't qualify.' That's a nice way of saying, 'Your background stinks, so sorry.'"

Yet Vivian has no resentment about her plight. "I know what I did was wrong, so I feel like whatever consequence I got was what I got. I did it to myself, so I can't be mad at somebody else now, because you won't hire me, because I was a jackass. Do you see what I'm saying?" She finds other ways to prove her virtue and distinguish herself from less worthy others, demonstrating self-reliance, thrift, and humility: "I know a lady that has six kids, never worked a day in her life, gets welfare for every single one of them; owns her home. You have fake boobs, fake hair, fake nails. I can pay thirty-five cents for a can of vegetables, and then I'll go over across town to the meat market, and I get hamburger, chicken, and I just separate it all and freeze it for meals for the month." She also stakes a claim to dignity in a time-honored American way—taking responsibility for herself and disparaging those who cannot survive on their own.

One stark difference between the Wilsons and the women who are still endeavoring to uphold the traditional family is the way in which they talk about white men. Vivian and Mary Ann condemn the aggressive masculinity and virulent racism of the men around them. It is obvious to them that many young white men use race as an easy scapegoat to prop up their own self-worth. Vivian was enraged when a group of white men in a neighboring town held a "take back our streets" rally, marching for hours carrying guns. "Why were they allowed to carry a rifle on the street?" she demands. "I was heated, pissed, that the police allowed that to happen. They walked the streets with guns on their shoulders. No blacks, all whites. They walked with their children, strollers and all." Vivian scoffs at the idea that these men were protecting their town: "The same exact people that were walking the streets with guns sell their prescription medication to these people that are buying the drugs. And they put them in the newspaper like they were saving the town, walking around with guns!"

Vivian watches helplessly as her own teenage son espouses hateful speech that he learns from his peers: "As soon as they realize they're black, they're a [n-word]. My brother is included. We drive down the street, and he's like, 'Fucking [n-word]s.' My son will tell you, 'I hate [n-word]s.' I did not raise him that way." She puts forward a vision of class solidarity and interdependence that she dismisses just as quickly as a pipe dream: "If we as the people could all come together and be a whole, we would be an amazing team, because we're all a majority uneducated, unskilled. And instead of saying, 'Look, I don't know what I'm doing, maybe you can show me,' we're going to say, 'We can't, because you're black. You can't teach me anything, because you're black, or you're Spanish, or you're Mexican.' It's just so stupid." Mary Ann, weary of violence and death, fears that Trump will send "us right to war. He doesn't think that families and children are somebody's son, daughter, wife, husband. Just get them to defend our country, and who cares about what's going on with you. I think that he's going to be selfish in that aspect and not think about the consequences for other people's lives except for his."

Mary Ann and Vivian dream of the "uneducated, unskilled" people joining together into an "amazing team." But they both opt not to vote. Mary Ann urges her daughter to instead stay focused on *today*—to think about the good things in her life, to stay sober, and not give up hope: "Just when you think you have it the worst, you might look outside and somebody has it so much worse. Life's like a rollercoaster ride. Sometimes you're here, sometimes you're down there." But Vivian is unmoved. "Yeah?" she laughs drily. "Well, our tram's at the bottom. Our tram is stuck at the bottom." She has ceased to believe that she can change her life for the better.

No Hell Worse Than This

Women who have endured violence and turmoil within intimate relationships may learn to survive without their role as a wife or girlfriend, like the Wilsons do. But they get little joy from their independence, just a lurking sense that something is missing. Women who express distrust in intimate relationships, like Mary Ann and Vivian, explicitly seek withdrawal from the public sphere for the sake of self-protection. Living on the brink of despair, they turn to food, drugs, and self-care strategies to ease the pain brought on by a lifetime of trauma. They frame their distrust in politics as an adaptive response to trauma, as their memories of betrayal and abuse make putting their faith in politicians feel terrifying.

Ashley Jones, a twenty-eight-year-old white woman, is unloading her car full of plastic grocery bags into the small mobile home she shares with her mother, Megan, and daughter, Paisley, when I pull up. Paisley, who just turned three and does not yet talk, immediately climbs into my lap; "She probably thinks you're a teacher from Head Start," her grandmother Megan jokes. As she unpacks plastic bags of groceries, Ashley tells me how her mother's "emotional meltdown" in-spired her shopping trip:

> I was like in the grocery store and then she waited in the car and I don't know why I had this feeling, but I had a feeling that she needed a parfait. Well, when I got it out to the car I took one look at her and she's like all puffy and I'm like, "What's going on?" She's like, "Well, I was just crying." I said, "Eat your emotions," and I handed her the parfait. I guess she said she was watching couples walk out of the grocery carts with their arms around each other and she doesn't have that. So I went and got stuff to make lasagna. And I got a cake and ice cream and all that fun stuff. She was just having an emotional meltdown.

As we talk, Ashley fixes a snack for herself and Paisley: two Eggo waffles each, toasted, smeared generously with white frosting and topped with rainbow sprinkles, washed down with a tall glass of red Mountain Dew. Paisley munches on red, white, and blue gummy bears, on sale after the Fourth of July last week. Eating their feelings, as Ashley quips, offers respite from a life that she describes otherwise as pure hell: "Some days I feel like there's no hell, that this is hell. And you can only go, there's nothing worse than this. Like if there's something worse than this, then I definitely don't wanna go there."

Ashley tries to cheer up her mother, a petite, mild-mannered woman in her fifties who, shame-faced, tries to hide her missing front teeth. "You have your own place, your own car, a really good job," Ashley tells her mother. "You did it all without a man. That's more than a lot of people can say for themselves. I can't say that. You should be proud of yourself, not hard on yourself." Ashley turns to me: "We don't have a man around the house, ever. Some days she's my hero because a pipe is broken in the hot water heater and she goes in and fixes it and I can take a shower." Her mother finally reluctantly cracks a smile. "Okay, I don't need a man, but I want one!"

Megan's grandfather worked in a shirt factory, and her father was a construc-tion worker. Her mother spent months at a time in a state mental institution. Eager to escape home, Megan married Ashley's father when she was just sixteen and had two children. Megan worked ten hours a day, six days a week, as a bar-tender. Her husband never held a steady job. They describe some of their early, most vicious memories:

Ashley: My little brother would be crying and she would get up in the night with him and he'd [her husband] say, "If you get up one more time

I'm going to bust your face." And then he [her brother] would cry, she would get up and he [her husband] would bust her in the face. Smashed her face with a flashlight. Just real . . . he would go on drug binges and not come home for days or a week or a couple weeks.

Megan: All I had to do was say, "Where have you been?" He'd say, "It's none of your business," and then he would flip out on me.

Megan left her husband. Ashley remembers court-ordered visits with her dad as "pretty bad. Like finding needles in the couch, one time he overdosed and he was blue and I remember that." Megan then quickly married another man and moved the family across the country to be with him in Las Vegas.

Violence against women and children is linked with chronic poverty, limited employment and educational opportunities, and more conservative attitudes toward gender roles. The sociologists Mary Patrice Erdmans and Timothy Black conceptualize interpersonal violence as "an expression of power and domination" that serves to restore the hierarchy of men over women and keep women in their place.[7] Ashley and Megan minimize the violence they suffered at the hands of the men in their lives, idealizing love and commitment in any form. Ashley describes her father: "Now, like later in life, he has apologized and said he regretted the way he acted and he still to this day says that my mom is his love, his one love that he lost. He regrets it." She still praises her mother's second husband: "He was abusive towards her a lot. Sometimes physically. But to get with a woman with two kids and be with her for ten years and help raise 'em, I give him credit for that." Nonetheless, after this man stopped coming home, Megan left him and the family returned to Pennsylvania.

After high school, Ashley was licensed as a certified nursing assistant and worked at a home for the elderly. Although she wishes she could keep working, "Bad backs run on my dad's side of the family. And I mean lifting people, everyone always called on me cuz I was stronger and they wouldn't help me, so I was always running around picking people up." Ashley and her boyfriend began experimenting with painkillers, which quickly led them to heroin. "Well I think it was pain mostly. I think that's when either the disks ruptured or that's when it was really like, that's when things started like really getting bad."

Soon, Ashley and her boyfriend were driving thirty minutes each way for heroin deals, five or six times a day. "If you purchased bags of heroin, down in this area, you were spending anywhere from fifteen to twenty-five dollars on one bag. But up there, they're only like maybe ten, like you could usually get ten bags for like eighty bucks or ninety bucks, like you get a deal you know." She quit her job and sold heroin full time. She clarifies: "When I was selling drugs, yes I shouldn't have been doing that, but I was only selling drugs to feed my habit." A few weeks later, she suspected she was pregnant—her friend, who is now dead ("she didn't die from an overdose, but she died from something that happens if you use. She got endocarditis, it's like a bacterial infection of your heart") brought her a pregnancy test. Throughout the pregnancy, she was uncertain about Paisley's paternity: "'Cuz at first I didn't know if he was the dad or not cuz there was a little situation. But I was like, 'If she's black, she's definitely yours, cuz you're the only black person I was with.'" When she confirmed that this man was indeed the father, he eventually visited, violating his probation by spending the night away. The mother of his other child "called his P.O. and said he was up here because she got mad and jealous of me because I have a kid with him."[8] Ashley shrugs: "Yeah, so now he's in jail until Paisley's like five."

When she was pregnant, Ashley checked herself into rehab—her biggest fear was to "go to jail and be sick in jail from not having my drugs." Graduating from her rehab program with "two certificates, at like the highest level you can graduate," Ashley now understands heroin use as a dangerous form of coping: "The only way I was taking care of myself was like, 'Oh I have a minute, I can get high.' Like instead of taking a couple hours out of the day to paint my nails or pluck my eyebrows or put my makeup on, or something to make me feel good for me."

Megan fell very ill. Ashley explains, "The first two days she had like diarrhea and the next two days she was vomiting and then she couldn't move. She said her head hurt. She kept saying she had the flu and I said the flu isn't like this long. The flu don't make it so you can't move." Megan finally went to the emergency room, where she was diagnosed with a brain tumor and had intensive surgery: "I had to sit in a chair and get my head shaved and they cut my head open from here to here. Then they pulled it apart and cut a square in my skull out and was going down through, when this doctor said, 'I can't finish this.' So they flew a neurosurgeon in while my head was open and he finished my surgery."

Days after her surgery, Megan was "working when she wasn't supposed to because she needed money," Ashley frowns. Her mother protests: "I couldn't quit, I had the kids to feed. I applied for disability. But I couldn't keep a job. I couldn't remember . . . it's my short-term memory that's really bad. At first, I could not feed myself. I talked like someone who was mentally retarded. I had to go to speech therapy, occupational therapy, physical therapy." After losing her health insurance, Megan relied on a local doctor who saw patients for cash. Ashley explains: "He shouldn't even be a doctor. She would go to him and it would cost like $35 for a doctor's appointment, he would just stand there like, 'Mmmhmmm.' When you walked into his office, it was like you were walking into 1960. Even the ultrasound machine that was in one room looked like it was from 1960. But I guess when you don't have insurance you don't have many choices."

Megan grew depressed. Ashley explains, "She was just a mess. I've never seen her like that. She still didn't have insurance, but I was getting Zoloft for my depression so I would give her half of my medicine just to try to make her feel better." "It helped!" her mother affirms gratefully. Megan finally qualified for state health insurance and disability payments and now takes 100 milligrams of her own Zoloft. Ashley was diagnosed with fibromyalgia and prescribed muscle relaxers, "morning, noon, and night." Ashley, her mother explains, "applied for disability. And they denied her. And then she applied again and had to go to a hearing. And they denied her again. How would they expect her to work when she can't open her eyes and she's in so much pain? Why don't they spend a day with her?"

Neither Megan nor Ashley connects their struggles to survive to the political realm. The traumas that Ashley has endured leave her wary of politics—why put her faith in a politician who would ultimately betray her trust?

> I just don't feel like I can put the whole country in their hands. It just scares me, I think more than anything, cuz putting your faith in one person is a lot. I have such bad trust issues. People have really messed with my trust, like just saying, one of my biggest pet peeves is saying like that you're gonna do something and you don't do it. Because so many people have done that to me in my life. I can't even put my faith in certain people that are in my family that I should be able to. [Shrugs] They're gonna pick a president anyway.

She provides a brief analysis of the two candidates, most of which she learns from Facebook: "I hate Trump. Like yeah, he has the money to make things happen and the gumption, but I think he's rude and ignorant and racist and I just don't like that. And then Hillary, I think she's a mess. Like with that email thing, I don't like that. Like what else, what else was she capable of screwing up? Like if she screwed up something like that, you know, is she gonna accidentally like hit us with an atomic bomb or something?" But Ashley is not registered to vote, and she has never voted before. Megan, on the other hand, is a registered Democrat like her own parents were—"I still have my voter registration card in my purse." She liked President Obama: "I think that he actually did a lot for us." But "good Lord," she does not like any of the candidates running in 2016: although she approves of Bernie Sanders's ideas, especially about health care, she does not like his image: "I don't think he's all that professional. Look at his wife. I know you're not supposed to go by appearances, but dear God. Jesus." Although Megan laughs, how a candidate's wife presents herself casually becomes a legitimate way to evaluate a candidate, reinforcing the constrictive gender ideals that, despite their best efforts, they cannot seem to escape.

You Just Can't Help Someone Who Doesn't Want to Be Helped

Finally, the relationship between pain and politics among working-class white women unfolds through fierce moral battles within their tumultuous intimate relationships. When I meet the Amatas—twenty-three-year-old Natalie and her forty-five-year-old mother Marcy—they are barely on speaking terms. Natalie is living with her father, a police officer, and working at a nail salon. She pays her own cell-phone bill, car payment, and student loan payments. She owes about $16,000 from her one-year program in cosmetology. Natalie is trying to save up for her own apartment as she cannot tolerate living with her father much longer: he does not allow her to have her boyfriend at his house, nor does he allow her to spend the night away. He also has a rule against locking any of the doors in the home, even the bathroom, which leaves her feeling uneasy about her utter lack of privacy or bodily autonomy. For Natalie, much of her story of who she is centers on her vulnerability and powerlessness in the past, the unwillingness of her family to protect her, and her own willful insistence on surviving trauma and emerging independent and strong.

Marcy, who left Natalie's father ten years ago, attests to his controlling nature: "I think his job changed him." When Marcy got a part-time job when the children entered their teens, she explains:

> He didn't want me to work. I only worked part-time, you know, three days a week. He just like didn't trust me. I don't know, like started accusing me of like not being at work. The house was still managed, you know, his clothes were still ironed. His shirts were still ironed. The house was immaculate, you know, dinner was in the crockpot. The kids were taken care of, they didn't mind that I was gone three days. He just was, I think he wanted his dinner on the table the minute he came home.

Marcy felt trapped. She had no money of her own, and her husband repeatedly reminded her that "the courts would never give me custody of the kids because I didn't work." She continues: "I always felt like he was the warden in our house. And the kids and I secretly like called him the Warden. Like he would go outside, and he would like lock us in the house, you know? Like just, yeah, I don't know, like against us or other people coming in. It was just really, really weird." When he became abusive toward the children, Marcy told him he had to leave.

Natalie lived with her mother and siblings until she graduated from high school. "I mean it's tough . . . you have that perfect image of your parents always being together and now they're not, but it is what it is," she says flatly, displaying no emotion. But she found that she could not tolerate living with her mother. Her younger sister, Ella, "has been addicted to drugs pretty much since the divorce," which disrupted the household. Marcy elaborates:

> She's been in and out of the house. She's been in and out of rehab as well. I think she's still using. She's been in trouble. She got in trouble for theft at Walmart, you know. Stealing DVDs to get money to feed her habit. She took my diamond ring. She totaled my car. Almost killed herself in the middle of the night at like 3 o'clock in the morning. She was on drugs. So she's got in trouble for that as well. She broke her neck at the c2 level. Ended up, crawled up out of the car, and out of the embankment, and you know, called 911.

Distraught, Marcy shakes her head: "I don't understand it. I don't understand how that could make somebody feel that good. And I was to the point like, you know, you can't keep doing this. Like I'm scared to death, you know, that something's gonna happen. I've had my tires slashed on my car, eggs thrown at my house, by people she owes money to." Marcy admits that "people say I should just let her go to jail," but she continues to provide her daughter with a place to live and to pay her bills.

This is because Marcy is the only person who knows the full extent of what Ella has survived. A few years ago, the police called Marcy and Ella's father in the middle of the night after they found Ella sobbing in the Burger King parking lot. Her blood alcohol level was .35, on the edge of death, "and she kept saying stuff to her dad, this is really bad, but she said, 'He kept trying to put his penis in me.' I'm like, 'What are you talking about?' Here, we found out that this kid had raped her. She was over here at her friend's house, and Ella had to go in and go to the bathroom. So this kid had taken her in there, well then, he took her into his bedroom and the kid's mom walked in and didn't even stop it."

Last year, Ella confided in her mother that she was pregnant, and Marcy urged her to have an abortion "because I had taken her to the doctor, and here she was positive for drugs again." Crying openly, Marcy remembers, "The thing that breaks my heart about Ella too, with this pregnancy, is that the baby was due on my birthday. But we had an abortion, which I have not told anybody. Especially her father." Stressing the "we," Marcy reveals her commitment to protecting her daughter, and keeping her secret safe, even as she deeply mourns the loss of a potential grandchild.

Marcy, the daughter of a coal miner, was raised to believe that "the Republicans, I've always said, are just big bullies. Trump is a bully. People should, you know, get support and stuff like that. Not be taking advantage of it, but support." In opposition to her mother, when Natalie describes her mother's perceived weaknesses in continuing to support Ella, she becomes infuriated. She emphasizes Ella's lack of willpower and seeming choice to stay miserable, rather than face the harsh realities of life and triumph over them:

> I mean Ella, she's twenty now, she doesn't have anything for herself. She has no vehicle, no education, no job, no money, no nothing, but she's made her decisions and . . . we've all tried to help her. My whole family has tried to help her. I mean we all went through the same divorce. It was tough on everyone. She had different means of handling it and expressing her feelings about it and got in with the wrong group of people and got into what she got into. You just can't help someone who doesn't want to be helped. If you want something bad enough you work for it.

Natalie connects her sister's dependence on her mother—"She has no income so she's dependent on my parents"—with the taxes that are taken out of her own paycheck every month: "It makes me mad that I'm busting my ass and I get like how many hundreds of dollars taken out of my paycheck a month for people who don't want to better themselves?" she asks.

The other, even more pressing reason why Natalie moved out of her mother's house was her disgust for her mother's new boyfriend, Paul. He does not work, drained Marcy's savings, and tries to control her every move. Marcy doesn't disagree with her daughter's description; she admits cheerfully, "On the truck, [he] actually has a system on this truck. And it's on his cell phone so he can see wherever his truck is. To know where I am all the time. I'm to the point where I just ignore it." Marcy coolly normalizes her lack of bodily autonomy and her boyfriend's control and restriction over her whereabouts. In fact, compared to her last marriage, she feels free: "I just feel like I'm independent. When I was married, I didn't have money, I didn't have anything. I don't wanna have to go through that again. My boyfriend, if he gets mad, he can leave, you know? It's my house."

When Natalie looks at her mother—at her parenting, her romantic relationships, how she lets men debase her and her own daughter steal from her—she sees someone who is weak, who enables other people to be weak, and whose sympathy is a liability. She also sees a mother who failed to protect her. When Natalie was fifteen, her mother's brother demanded she make him a sandwich. When Natalie refused, he called her a "cunt." Natalie dissolved into hysterical sobbing—"no woman should ever be called that. But my uncle, my mom, my mom's boyfriend, they just laughed." Natalie feels like she has been humiliated, betrayed by her family, and taught the lesson that her body is not her own.

Natalie's boyfriend is her refuge. She adopts his political leanings, attending a "Blue Lives Matter" 5K event and coyly sporting a red "Make America Great Again" cap. Natalie rolls her eyes when telling me about her mother's vote for the Democratic candidate. "Pushover," she sneers. She views Democrats as too focused on helping victims: "Like if someone is perfectly capable of bettering themselves and doing things for themselves and putting themselves in a better situation then I don't feel like you should just hold your hand out. Do something for yourself." Natalie actively rejects her mother's political affiliations, just as she criticizes her mother's life choices and condemns her moral flaws. As Natalie's boyfriend has become her lifeline, his interests have truly become her interests. Voting for Trump, and against the weaknesses and betrayals of her own family, allows her to feel accomplished and free.

Shifting Perspectives

The first half of this book documents the hopelessness, distrust, and disengagement of the white working-class residents of Coal Brook. In this chapter, white women fight to hold on to their subordinate, feminine roles of wives and mothers even as they are victimized in them. There are moments of reprieve in these women's narratives—of churches, therapists, support groups—that buffer the loneliness that has come with economic decline and family disruption. But they are scarce. The white women in this chapter resist the pull of alcohol and heroin, stay out of "the loony bin," and will themselves to face another day by retreating inward, framing their suffering as moral quest, and convincing themselves that trauma makes them stronger.[9]

White women's distrust within the family reverberates into larger visions of a political arena where putting one's faith in a politician is just asking for betrayal. Shelly Moore and Ashley Jones, two recovering heroin addicts, explain how their experiences of early childhood trauma and violence become a rationale for disavowing voting and rejecting the social safety net. Natalie Amata, whose anger toward her own sister—whose ten-year heroin addiction continues to tear their family apart—leads Natalie to scorn her Democrat "pushover" mother and defiantly wears a "Make America Great Again" baseball cap. Mary Ann and Vivian Wilson, a mother and daughter pair, partially stave off despair by willing themselves to focus myopically on just getting through today—they have no hope for tomorrow.

But as the coal region, like other rural areas across the United States, becomes a new destination for racial and ethnic minorities in search of jobs, safety, and affordable housing, some newly arrived families contest the idea that Coal Brook is a wasteland of despair.[10] In the next two chapters, I uncover conflicts over the meaning of place that divide the longtime white working-class residents from the newcomers. Recasting the coal region as a place where their own shameful pasts can become their children's bright futures, the newcomers magnify the positive effects of pain in their lives and stake a claim to social inclusion and self-worth. These new collisions of race and place open up the possibility of new kinds of selves, relationships, and politics.

4

In Search of Redemption

Chapters 4 and 5 give voice to the "newcomers"—often labeled "welfare migrants," drug dealers, and criminals—who have moved to the coal region and disrupted the urban-rural racial divide.[1] In this chapter, I focus on black and Latino men, who consciously defy the expectations of deviance that await their arrival. (Chapter 5 will chronicle the lives of black and Latina women.) These men critique the poverty and racism that scaffold their lives with a sharp, unforgiving clarity. However, they portray Coal Brook as a place where they can tirelessly transform their own shameful pasts—selling drugs, going to prison, perpetrating violence, being hurt or vulnerable—into their children's redeemed futures. These men exaggerate the positive consequences of pain, leveraging their experiences of trauma as pivotal moments of self-growth.[2] They demand their fair share of respect and social inclusion based on their hard work, tenacity, and will power. Paradoxically, even as they assume control over their own futures, they speak of a malevolent "they" making political decisions beyond their control, leaving their powerful political critiques unspoken.

Competing Realities

Edwin Acosta, a thirty-one-year-old Puerto Rican construction worker, rolls his eyes while gesturing toward the "Silent Majority Stands with Trump" sign on the weathered front porch across the street. "If they had any fuckin' sense they'd be more with Hillary, you know what I mean?" he demands. "Cuz let Trump get the seat, half of you motherfuckers are going outta here. You broke bastards, you lazy sons of bitches, you're all gone. All you guys that like to sit around and just wait for your check, you're outta here, you know what I mean?"

Edwin's parents moved to New York from Puerto Rico when they were teenagers.[3] They raised Edwin and his six siblings in Newark, New Jersey. His father, who is now deceased, worked as a security guard in a hospital. His mother still works as a bus driver. "There were some hungry nights. We never had the best of stuff, but you know, it could've been worse," he recalls. When I asked him about his childhood neighborhood, he explains: "Nothing's safe about it. I wouldn't want to raise my kids over there. Drugs, violence, crackheads running around and all kinds of shit going on." His mother fell off the bus one day and was prescribed Percocet for pain, and "she grew pretty addicted to it for a while. It took her a while to get off of it."

When Edwin was a teenager, his parents moved the family to Pennsylvania, into the northern counties of the coal region, to "get us out of the city." They continued to commute to work every day: "My parents were out of the house at four o'clock in the morning." Edwin graduated from high school and pursued several different educational trajectories. He borrowed $12,000 for a pharmaceutical degree program at a for-profit college. Unfortunately, he did not know that "I could've went to junior college and got the same degree for a thousand." Edwin left the program because he "didn't see myself crouched behind a counter." Moving back in with his mother, he took a two-week training course in construction. Edwin fell behind on his college-loan payments in the meantime. He says ruefully, "Yeah, my credit's like 300 something because of it."

Edwin has a daughter with his longtime girlfriend who still lives in the northern part of the coal region, but they are "always having problems." Comparing himself to his own parents, who were married until his dad died, he reflects: "Nobody wants to go through any bad times, everybody just wants everything to be good all the time." Edwin was elated when an old friend of his father's asked him to help renovate several dilapidated houses he bought in Coal Brook after the housing market crash in 2008: "It's not that I wanted to leave, but there wasn't nothing there anymore." Edwin was able to live in the houses as he restored them. He currently works in construction and paving, dangerous work that pays twenty-four dollars an hour: "I get paid every week, I get winters off." Although his fellow workers are mostly white, "a buncha meatheads," he assures me that "we get the watermelon jokes and shit like that, but that shit doesn't even matter over there."

When Edwin is off the job, though, it is better to "just stay in the house." He explains, "I've been called a [n-word] several times out here. Yeah you can just tell, you know, you just feel the tension in the air. Everybody gets real quiet and you know, fathers are hugging their daughters all extra tight for some reason. It's like there's a high beam over your head when you're walking through here." A keen observer, he continues: "Just little stupid subliminal shit. Like you walk down [the main street] during one of those street fairs with me, and you'll see, here lemme put my arm around you and walk down there and see how you feel."[4] Edwin feels most vulnerable when he is around white women, as every move he makes comes under scrutiny.

Edwin makes a point of telling me that he has never "grabbed a crack pipe or stuck a needle in my arm or swallowed a bottle of pills." While driving through the coal region one day, he reports being pulled over at a random checkpoint because the police "said they saw a nub or something." He was taken into custody for five hours, then let go. Edwin has no faith in the criminal justice system and believes that "the cops and judges went to school with each other, they all know each other." His experiences have left him critical of the relationship between power and money: "I learned coming out of high school, that you could actually own prisons. Like prisons and stuff are owned by, yeah, like they're privately owned. Like that's fuckin' nuts. So you gotta think about stuff like that."

Edwin becomes especially frustrated when talking about how the longtime residents accuse the newcomers of abusing welfare. By his own reasoning, it is *poverty*—the lack of affordable housing, a dearth of decent jobs, the incessant violence—that has pushed him and the other newcomers out of urban economies and neighborhoods and into small towns. He seethes:

> Who the fuck wants to live here in Section 8? Do you know the homes you could get for Section 8? Do they understand that Section 8 pays like 90 percent of your fuckin' rent? Who the, if I could get 90 percent of my rent paid, why would I wanna live in one of these shit houses? Ok no, they're coming out here because they're not on Section 8. They don't have welfare and this is the cheapest fuckin' place in America to live right now. This is literally, it was just on the news. It's like in the top five cheap places in America to live right now. That's out of every little crack and crevice, every little bit of woods and little town and valley in America right now. This is one of the cheapest places to live, why wouldn't people migrate here?

According to Edwin, the newcomers migrate to the coal region for the same reason that many of the longtime residents stay: the inability to survive anywhere else.[5]

Edwin casts a different light on the accusations surrounding Section 8. He suspects that poor, frustrated white people console themselves for their own failures by deflecting blame onto the newcomers. He comments: "They just want to throw a jab at other people. This is why everybody's so miserable here." Edwin sees many similarities between his own life and the poor white people's lives in town, emphasizing how "America" blocks everyone from escaping poverty: "White people aren't no better, you know what I mean? You guys are just like anybody else. They're [the newcomers] here for the same reason you broke mothafuckas is here, because they can't afford to live anywhere else. And unfortunately America's not making it possible, you know what I'm saying?"

Edwin moved to the coal region for job opportunities and rent he could afford. He also brings with him a drastically different interpretation of the world around him. Edwin exhibits critical awareness and a paradoxical interplay of nonexistent expectations and dogged persistence. "I gotta be around my kid and stuff. I don't wanna be around her with this look of hopelessness on my face because you know we went through another whole day of trying to achieve a goal that's gonna take forever to achieve," he shrugs. He reports that by the time Obama ran for office, he had already completely given up on societal change and did not even vote. "Driving myself crazy with situations that I have no control over, is just brain-fucking yourself. I don't set myself up for disappointment. When it comes to something that isn't about me or my immediate family, just leave me out of it." Thinking about his own life, he muses, "I've had times where I thought to myself like you know, if some big ass rock from the sky just came and landed on the town right now and just ended this shit, I would not be mad. But nothing that would make me like, ever felt like I'm gonna kill myself."

Demanding Our Place

Andres, a thirty-two-year-old Puerto Rican from North Philadelphia, claims a sense of belonging based on his American citizenship and his ability to earn money through his hard work. The day after Trump was elected, Andres, who works in inventory at Walmart for eleven dollars an hour, reports feeling especially targeted. "I was leaving to work and some guy stuck his middle finger up at me and I was like, are you freaking serious? Like I just came out my door this morning and somebody want to come out and stick their middle finger out at me? In a situation like that I felt like I was behind enemy lines because of the fact that we're Puerto Rican and the majority up here is white."

"I'm going to defend myself to the fullest. I was born and raised in America," he asserts. "We feel like we're outsiders but we're United States citizens and we demand our place here because we pay our bills." His life story hinges on self-transformation in the coal region, where he finally got his GED and even took a few community college classes. "I went from living in the ghetto all my life . . . people say it's what, who you're around or it's just all in your mind but I think in Philadelphia I felt as though I was distracted by others too much. I just needed a way out."

When Andres and his girlfriend arrived in the coal region, they "got a house in a housing complex" in town and began attending "the welfare program they put us in." Andres earned his GED. "To be able to get benefits you had to get a job," he remembers. "Do mock interviews and stuff like that." In a surprising turn of events, Andres "got so good at it that I was giving out the interviews myself. I was giving them the interviews and stuff like that." He has been working in inventory at Walmart for nearly five years now. "Like at first, when I first started at Walmart, oh my gosh it was stereotyping like crazy. I'm Puerto Rican but they think I'm Mexican," he explains. He asserts his moral worth, based on his work ethic: "Now I'm at Walmart, I'm like the best worker there, like they know me. Go to Walmart and say Andres, the name rings a bell 'cause the work that I do, I show them that you don't have to like me but I'm going to make you like me. I know I'm not doing nothing bad but earning my respect, you know what I mean?" He turns to individual achievement and sheer willfulness to prove to himself and others that he warrants social inclusion and respect. Andres reports that his boss, who is white, is helping him to "get as much opportunity as possible. Especially with people teaching you how to invest and when to sell, when not to sell. My boss is helping me out with that."

Andres pushes back against the coal region stereotypes of drug-dealers that surround all people of color: "I'm not a piece of shit like other people are, bringing poison up here. It's not for us. They say it's the colored people that's bringing it up and doing stuff, and no it's not. Different colors bring it up. Blame it on the colored people, but it's not only the colored people 'cause the white people do stuff too." He points out that the "drugs up here are like far more like crazy. You go to Philadelphia and ask for some crystal meth they look at you like, what is that? Up here, they got that like moonshine." Despite his personal stance of resistance, coupled with his keen social analysis of discrimination, Andres does not bother with politics and has never voted. "The presidents are selected not elected," he shrugs. He focuses instead on his positive narrative of self-improvement and upward mobility for his family, which in his worldview negates the necessity of politics: "No matter how we put, no matter how you put it, we're still doing way better than we was before. I could be a bum in the streets living outside and I'll still doing better than I was."

"It's about the Effort You Put into It"

Young men frame Coal Brook as a clean slate, one that allows them to pursue better opportunities—safety, jobs, and housing they can afford—as long as they are willing to make heavy sacrifices to achieve them. They create a new identity that minimizes past traumas and present setbacks, underscoring their own self-efficacy and drawing dignity from persistence. Malcolm Wilkerson, for example, is a twenty-four-year-old black man who grew up in West Philadelphia. His parents moved him around frequently when he was in high school to try to keep him out of fights: "But really, you can't really outrun any trouble in Philly. It's everywhere. Everywhere you go there's going to be something. That's what it is in Philly, somebody just got something to prove to someone. I got to be the biggest, baddest, toughest dude out here."

Malcolm, whose father was a carpenter and whose mother stayed home with their nine children, explains that "sometimes the lights got turned off" in their rented home. He hastens to add that they always got a present for Christmas. During his senior year of high school, he recalls, "one of my best friends got shot in front of my block. Got killed right in front of my block. And it happened to be someone who shot him was two years younger than us. Dude had to be like fifteen years old. We were seventeen years old." After experiencing this shock so close to home, Malcolm decided: "I was like, I got to do something with my life. I can't be stuck here."

Malcolm has since moved around from one small coal region town to another with his friends—not as a "welfare migrant" but rather in search of affordable housing and factory jobs that pay above minimum wage in order to build a new foundation for his life. He explains: "I'm out here trying to get my life together. I feel like being out here is probably the best way to do it because the cost of living is so cheap and there's good paying jobs. I couldn't find no fourteen-dollar-an-hour paying job in Philly. Couldn't find it."

Sharing a four-bedroom home with his three friends, their "total expenses for the month with electric, water, cable, gas, food" totals to "no more than $275 a month." His portion is just $75. The house is in dire straits: the basement is flooded and you have to hop over puddles of muddy water to reach the bathroom, where the door is falling off the hinges. The oven does not turn on. Only one burner on the stove heats up, making it difficult to heat the bag of frozen potatoes and bag of frozen spicy buffalo wings they share among six of them for lunch. But Malcolm is determined to "get my own car, get my own place." He says, "That's what I plan on doing. It's like, a month-and-a-half-long plan that would probably take me four or five months if I was back in the city."

So far, his plans have not panned out. He was recently fired from a ware-house job. "I mean granted, I could have been white and went through the same problem, but I feel like they didn't really care because I was black," he says flatly. He continues:

> The car broke down. I end up going my second day there, ended up being half an hour late. Called them and everything, let 'em know I was going to be late, let 'em know I was having car trouble. They was like that's alright, it's fine, just come in. I come in, they see who we are, they're like oh well you're half an hour late on your second day, we can't,

this is unacceptable. Which is understandable but it's not like we didn't show up or didn't call or anything.

Malcolm is now searching for a new job.[6]

The coal region has not wholeheartedly welcomed or embraced him, and it would be difficult to describe his blighted housing as adequate. Yet he downplays the negative aspects of his life and looks toward his future. He takes a calm approach to racism, arguing that people in town were never taught tolerance or acceptance, judging them as uneducated rather than malicious: "I mean, I was never called the n-word in Philly but you have people that just didn't like black people. That's the way they were brought up, that's the way they learned. So I really don't blame anyone who actually feels that way, but people, I feel like whoever brought them up in the world really just didn't teach them any better." He manages his own response to the racism by choosing not to blame racist white people for their beliefs but also opting not to engage with them.[7]

Malcolm hails from a long line of registered Democrats. "My mom used to have this line like, just vote all Democrat. You don't know who to vote for, just vote all Democrat." He voted for Obama in 2012 but has little to say about the upcoming election, partially because he does not feel prepared or knowledgeable. "We didn't have no class for that in school. Like to sit there and teach us exactly what a Democrat is, and what the purpose of all that is, we never had that in school," he shakes his head. "I don't really know too much about that as far as what's going on and all that. If you don't know anything, it's hard. It's hard to get into it." He chose not to vote in 2016.

When I ask him if he feels patriotic, he shrugs, "Not really." He explains further: "I respect any veteran that put their time in the service. Me personally, I can't do it cuz I don't even know what the hell we fighting for. So I'm not going to go to be able to kill people that I have no problem with." He muses, "I feel like *they* brainwashed them [the soldiers] to believe that they [the enemies] are the bad guys." Wary and cynical, he pulls himself back from all things political: "It's hard to get into. When you just don't like either one of them." Instead, Malcolm focuses on his personal goals of stability, hard work, and upward mobility: "I just try to be the best person I can be." His heroes, he reflects, include "anybody that became the best at what they do and decided to make money from it. They just show me how much hard work can get you. Especially if it's something you love and something you really care for. It's about the effort you put into it. Anybody that's done anything positive in their life I look up to." He attributes positive change to his own passions, drive, and hard work, drawing motivation to move forward from the traumas he has witnessed. Meanwhile, he distances himself from what "they" do in the political sphere.

"I Ain't Got No Quit Button"

For George, a twenty-six-year-old black man, suffering crystallizes his identity and makes him even stronger. George asks me to give him the pseudonym of "Mr. Steal Your Girl." When I protest that such a name might be distracting to the reader, he settles for George—as in, "George Clooney." After just a few minutes of conversation, George observes that I smile often, and he demands: "How you do sociology and you so happy? Hearing everybody else's problems?" I shrug, explaining that it is just my personality. "You know what I call that?" he retorts. "White girl spirit!"

George grew up in Springfield, Massachusetts, where "for a young black youth growing up in the area I did, it was serious, no jokes." His mother, a certified nursing assistant, was not home much. George recalls an incident when, "I was like thirteen. Something had happened and some guys came through shooting. And me, not even having nothing to do with it, almost got shot." George explains that he was constantly "getting into little situations," "getting into trouble," from the time he was thirteen. He stopped going to school in ninth grade—"I didn't get expelled, I really just stopped going. Like I just got fed up, and my mom was really, she was always at work so it was like, who was gonna stop me from not going to school?"

George was placed in a juvenile detention center from age thirteen to seventeen, which he reports "was not at all for my best interest." His life spiraled into more and more surveillance: "The situations that I was placed in got me in more trouble. Like every time I got into a fight or something like, and that's not even, it's beyond my control at certain points, you know what I'm saying? After that it's like, I'm getting more time, doing more time in here." He recalls his release at age seventeen, and how woefully unprepared and unsupported he felt to transition to adulthood:

> What do you want me to do now? I didn't even grow up on the streets. So it's just really like alright, y'all want me to come out here and be this upstanding citizen, but what do I know? How do I know to be, to be that citizen? I mean they had school in there, they had school in there. But the teachers, all the teachers that did come in to teach, they were all voluntary. So basically like some days we didn't have school, know what I mean?

George's experiences under state control left him deeply distrustful of institutions. "Growing up where I grew up at, I've seen some real snakes in the grass," he recollects. "I don't like the government really. As a child, you know they placed me in the system, know what I mean? So I really was like, y'all are placing me in all these different places, and then none of y'all is really helping me, know what I mean? So it was really just like putting my life on pause." But George abruptly shifts his tone to one of more optimism, as if consciously managing his feelings to tell a story of progress rather than of decline. "I mean it was a life experience, it is what it is. It made me the person I am today, I ain't mad at it. Know what I mean? Can't stress it. Like dirt off your shoulder, know what I mean? It happened, but nothing really traumatic happened to me while I was in there neither. Know what I mean? Just fighting and shit." He points to a mentoring relationship he developed with an older boy in juvie that helped him change his perspective on his future:

> I met a lotta good people, a lotta good kids that was older than me who was telling me to do better, you know what I'm saying? Even met this one kid, he was eighteen, seventeen turning eighteen. He was doing a life bid, know what I mean? He was going to the, to upstate. So he always used to tell me like, yo, don't throw your life away like I did. And it took me, took me a little while to even figure that out, you know what I mean? That's what made me change after a little bit. I never wanted to be, I never wanted to be in that situation.

Soon after leaving juvenile detention, George met his current girlfriend, whose family in Philadelphia was already moving to the coal region. George earned his GED, and the pair decided to follow suit in search of "a clean start, a clean slate. Nobody looking at me wrong. New and better friends. Go somewhere else, try something new, know what I mean?"

He states boldly, "A lotta people scared of change. I'm not. Especially when the change is definitely gonna benefit me, I ain't worried about it." George and his girlfriend emphasize how safe they feel in the coal region, as opposed to the white residents who anxiously lock their doors and windows: "They ain't been nowhere!" he scoffs. "I leave my front door open, unlocked." His girlfriend got a job at a bill collections agency, but George has been trapped in a series of dead-end, temporary jobs at warehouses and factories. "These jobs out here, they really don't get good till you get higher into the company and then you don't get hired on. If you going through a temp agency, you don't get hired on until after ninety days." He describes how local companies hire him through the temp agency, but then fire him before "you get close to your ninety days. The company would fire you so they wouldn't have to hire you on." These companies could thus maintain a flexible workforce without paying raises and benefits. In one job, George describes:

> It was a lotta heavy lifting, stacking boxes on trucks. You never really know what you're gonna pick up, what's the weight gonna be like. So

I went to grab something and I pulled like a muscle in my chest. That's like the worst place, cuz now that's like all my lifting power, everything. So like I started slowing down, it was just like yo, you gotta catch up. But I had went to them earlier and told them like nah, I just messed up my whole chest, I can't really do it. So really what I did was, I didn't really get fired, I quit, per se. I was just like you know what, I can't do it, I'm gonna leave. He was like you know you leave, you're terminated bro. I'm out, know what I mean?

George and his girlfriend have a two-year-old son, and the one public benefit she receives is food stamps. She applied for a housing voucher and was rejected. They rent an apartment together, and George takes care of their son during the day while she works. "I wouldn't say I'm so worried about the money, I mean don't get me wrong, I want the money, who don't want the money? But I got enough money to pay my bills, and I'm living how I want to in my own house," he considers.

In chapter 3, Vivian and Mary Ann Wilson, a white mother-and-daughter pair, likened the American Dream to a rollercoaster ride. Vivian suspected that her rollercoaster tram had become stuck at the bottom of the slope. George uses similar metaphors to describe his financial situation: "I know how it feels to wake up broke, I've been there before. I been at the bottom. Like the bottom of the totem pole, like I ain't have a dollar to my name. And I was going like this [gestures to his pockets], pulling out lint in my pockets, you know what I mean?" Yet George narrates his life, and his own sense of control over his destiny, in a markedly different way: "I never really felt like I'm gonna give up and quit and just stop. Never been a coward. I ain't got no quit button."

When I ask him if he believes the American Dream is still alive, he insists on it:

My American dream was just to make it out the hood, man. I'm out the hood, I'm living good, I could be living better, but I'm good. I'm living my dream. I'm living the black man's dream, know what I mean? I think, I think we got it a lot better than a lotta people realize, even with a lotta shit that goes on out here. Know what I mean? And with all the racial tension and everything like, we still got it a lot better than a lotta other countries do.

Rather than compare himself to memories of a better past, George casts the future as something he can control, frames his negative experiences as learning opportunities, and affirms his worthy status as someone who does not quit.

George, who voted for Obama once, has long since given up on politics. I ask him about his views on wages and health care and taxes, about the 2016 election, about Black Lives Matter, all with little response. "I don't give a damn," he finally responds. "I just smoke weed. If it's about some weed, we can talk." He avoids the desperation that haunts many of the downwardly mobile white families in this book through an unrelenting projection of self-determination and forward progress. To opt out—to admit to not "giving a damn" as George states—allows him to focus solely on his own narrative of recovery and self-improvement, to leave the world and its baggage behind for a fresh start. His critiques of the forces that shapes his life go unvoiced.

No Longer on the Run

Many of the men who moved to the coal region encountered drugs, gangs, and violence in their youth. Although the white people in town are not incorrect in their assessment that some of the newcomers have criminal records, these newcomers report coming to Coal Brook to give themselves a chance to "stop running" and "walk a straight line." Some of these men even move to Coal Brook to escape the obligations of troubled kin—a brother who is still dealing drugs and in trouble with the law, a mother who is still getting high. Turning inward, and winnowing down their ties to others, they protect themselves by narrowing the scope of whom they care for and on whose behalf they fight.

Jeffrey Wilder, age thirty-seven, is a black man from North Philly. He begins our conversation by reflecting on how "I could write a book about my life. I've been through so much and for me to go through so much and came out to be a good person." Jeffrey was raised in Philadelphia in the 1980s, when the crack epidemic was exploding. His father, a line cook, "wound up slipping," his sister was taken in by a neighbor, and his older brother "ran off and started selling drugs at the age of fifteen." Jeffrey's earliest memories feature his mother getting high: "I'm like six years old, watching my mom. I got to go to my friend's house to get like food and pretty much give it to my mom, like we got something to eat. I was going to school and it was like the same clothes every day. I pretty much learned how to take care of myself at an early age because my mom was so high all the time. I had to wash my own clothes by hand at an early age." His mother would "open my pocket and take my little change I had." Over the next few years, Jeffrey was first sent to live with an older cousin and was then "bounced around" to different foster families.

For a short time, during his middle school years, Jeffrey landed in a "really nice" Christian, white foster family where he flourished, going to church several times a week, singing in the choir and playing the drums, and even earning As and Bs at school. "It was a big change," he explains, but it did not last long. Bullying at school left him self-conscious about his bargain-brand clothes, and he relied on fighting to maintain his sense of self-respect. His foster mother "couldn't deal with it. It's just like I'm getting picked on, I'm trying to defend myself the best way I can so then I'm fighting. So they got me kicked out cuz she couldn't deal with it. She was like, 'You know what, it's too much for me, you got to send him to a boys group home.'"

Jeffrey moved again, this time to a group home where he could take classes in cooking and cosmetology. At the home, he reports, "they had staff that would work on certain kids' weakness and strengths and stuff like that so I had a staff member that was there for me, helping me out when I needed help." This staff member, Keith, quickly became his best friend—but was also, unbeknownst to Jeffrey, "a bad guy, a real bad guy." One day,

> Keith was like "Listen, you want to make some extra money?" I'm like "How?" He was like, "I know you know people in your school that smoke weed." I'm like, "I don't know." So he was like, "Listen why don't you find out?" A lot of people like, "Yeah I smoke pot, you got some?" I'm like, "no," so I go back and I tell him and he's like, "Oh okay here take this." He showed me how to sell it. He said, "If you do it like this this is how much money you'll make." I wound up going through the school telling my friends, I'm selling little bags of pot to the kids.

When the school administration caught on, Keith was fired abruptly. Jeffrey, now seventeen, got his GED in West Philly and left the group home, moving in with Keith and his mother and helping run her in-home daycare in exchange for free rent.

One afternoon, they heard that Keith's niece was being threatened by her boyfriend who had a gun. Keith took Jeffrey to her house to take care of the situation, not counting on the police to ensure their family's safety.[8] Jeffrey recalls, "Keith got a gun on him but New Year's everybody shooting their guns so he got his gun but it's empty. So now he goes into this drama with an empty gun, then I got a gun too and I got bullets in my gun." When they arrived at the house, it was only the niece and a few of her friends. Little did they know that the boyfriend and his friends were hiding around the corner. Keith relaxed, suggesting that Jeffrey "roll up a blunt." Just as Jeffrey briefly turned away from the wind to light up, he heard a "pow pow pow" and "I see sparks and I see him like falling between the cars. When I turn around I see the one guy running so I take my gun out and I'm shooting, boom boom boom."

Jeffrey vividly remembers:

> They say the fatal shot, when they shot my friend, they shot him right there, the bullet went in and it bounced. Like it hit, it bounced in here,

came out here, went through his elbow and his finger. It was a fatal shot, it hit a major artery. But I'm sitting there, I see the hole, I try to plug his hole up with my jacket. I take his gun off of him, like get him out of here. I'm trying to plug his hole up, somebody call an ambulance, ambulance never came. It took like ten or fifteen minutes to come. Now my friend he's still bleeding, and you can see the blood. I try to hold his head up and as soon as hold his head up, blood come out of his mouth. His heart, I still felt like his heart.

Jeffrey pauses to catch his breath.

I'm like, "Where's the ambulance?" Then a cop come, female cop, she's flashing the lights, she called backup. Another cop car come, two guys. They roll my friend over on his back, whole jacket is filled with blood. Took my friend up by his legs and arms and put him in the back of the cop car. When they threw him in the back of the cop car, they leave then the ambulance comes. I'm like, "Yo he's in the back of the cop car." So the ambulance goes behind the cop car, we get in the regular car and go behind the ambulance. So we get there, we're driving. As soon as I get to the hospital, they like he ain't making it. I'm just saying to myself they lying, I'm going to wake up tomorrow, he's going to be in the hospital, they just lying, I'm just tripping. He too big, like ain't no way in the world one bullet [could kill him], no he ain't gone.

Once Keith died, Jeffrey "wanted to put the gun in my head, he was gone. What am I going to do now? He was like my dad. I ain't know nobody, I ain't have nobody. I was pretty much lost, on my own." He found himself going "crazy": "I promised I would never let nobody else die. It was like I took all my friends, I said I'm going to be on the front line for y'all. I ain't letting nobody else pass. And I had that attitude so that's why. If I got my gun, I'm shooting. I wound up selling drugs, I wound up getting drugs cases, gun cases, stuff like that."

In the early 2000s, he says, "there was so much going on. I had another group of friends that was really big into like selling drugs. That's how I wound up getting the charge cuz they was actually coming out here [to the coal region]. I was right near your college!" he points out excitedly, to me. "What were you selling?" I ask him. "Crack," he replies. "I don't know why I did this dumb shit, I had a job and everything. I ain't had to do this, I just kinda wanted to fit in to help my friend out. Well, I ended up getting pulled over, police ran my name, I had a warrant so then I got locked up, then I'm in jail." Although Jeffrey did not have drugs on him, he argues, his friends "flipped" on him: "I'm like, are you fucking kidding me? My own friends." Jeffrey recounts how his lawyer, who charged him $5,000, advised him to plead "guilty to possession with intent of delivery," assuring him that he could do "one year upstate compared to seven years in the federal penitentiary if I take it to trial. So I'm like, alright, I probably got nine months in the county already so I'll take the one year. So I waive everything. I say, 'I'm going to work on myself mentally, physically to better my life.' I said I apologize for whatever harm I've done."

Then, to his horror, "she sentenced me, she hit the thing, I wound up getting two to ten years. For nothing. They didn't catch me with no drugs, they didn't catch me with nothing, they went by somebody else's word." After serving three and a half years in state prison, he was paroled. He reflects: "Once I heard about parole, you can do the slightest thing and parole can lock you up at the slightest anything. And it was like seven years of that, I couldn't do that in the city." Jeffrey left the city and moved into a halfway house near Harrisburg, Pennsylvania. He "didn't look back"—"I say to myself I'm going to start meeting important people. If I can't benefit from you, if you can't steer me in the right direction, I don't want you around me." He reasons: "It was either I had to change my life, or somebody would kill me or I would be in jail for the rest of my life. I got to say if I wouldn't have came out here, I think I wouldn't have made it. I know I wouldn't have made it cuz it's just the area that I'm from. If I would have gone back there, them dudes is just crazy. Really, really crazy. I can't deal with all that."

Jeffrey completed his parole with only one short return to jail: "my girlfriend's birthday party. She took pictures of me with bottles and posted them on Facebook. Parole seen them and locked me up." Once he was off parole, he moved to the coal region with his girlfriend, a white woman whose family has lived in the coal region for multiple generations. They are raising their five-year-old daughter together. Jeffrey's older brother, who stayed in Philadelphia, provides a tragic counterexample. He is serving life in prison for a murder he committed while high on PCP. As Jeffrey explains sadly, "the bad part about it is he got locked up in '95 and he got multiple sclerosis, and he's in a wheelchair right now. So he's going to die in jail with multiple sclerosis."

Since his move, Jeffrey has built a life that he is proud of. He emphasizes how he "can walk around Coal Brook and everybody say, 'Hey Mr. Wilder,' and I can feel so good." He repeats how he knows "important people" now, appreciating the newfound sense of social inclusion and self-worth that he never experienced in the city. It has not been a seamless transition: Jeffrey recently quit his job as a line cook at a popular local restaurant after getting in a fight with a server who called him the "n-bomb." "I kinda got upset so I was like, 'You fat B,' so I kinda fell into her trap. So they were like you need to talk it out, y'all are my best whatever. So she ain't really want to talk it out so I'm like listen, I'm done," he says regretfully. But he nonetheless tells an earnest, emotional story of racial progress and positive change in direct opposition to everything he has lived through:

My daughter, yeah she's cool, but she is so smart. She told me about
black history month, and Martin Luther King, she's only five. She was
telling me 'bout segregation and why blacks couldn't use certain water
fountains and why we couldn't like . . . and why Martin Luther King was
assassinated. Like she was telling me stuff, I teared up. She like, "What's
wrong?" I'm like, "Do you hear her?" That is so crazy, for her to be that
young and to understand she's mixed, and understand what your other
half, and now you see things are different. Like look at me and mom.
There's been a change.

Previous research has found that black men embody a "caring self" comprised
of altruism, generosity toward a larger kinship network, and a commitment to
working for social justice—a way of ascribing meaning to one's life that stands
in sharp contrast to the ethos of the self-made man.[9] The sociologist Michele
Lamont discusses how African Americans in the United States draw upon
narratives of past collective struggles against racial domination such as the civil
rights movement or the Black Panthers to make sense of, and imagine a way out
of, present barriers.[10] Jeffrey's story of the self weaves in elements of the "caring
self" as he emphasizes his connection to family, fatherhood, and community.
He articulates a hopeful vision of history that is moving toward justice—that
"things are different" and "there's been a change." He "tears up" as he thinks
about how opportunities will continue to improve for his daughter's generation.
But he also restricts the sphere of obligation to himself, his partner, and their
child, retreating into a smaller, more manageable sphere of action in which he
has some hope of creating a worthy, safe life.

Jeffrey voted for Donald Trump. "I'm always going to be voting, regardless of
whether the person is . . . you got to. I'm going to vote. If there's two bad people
and I got to vote, I'm going to vote for the one that's less bad," he explains. Jeffrey
was alarmed by Hillary Clinton's inability to win voter support during the campaign season—"it's just like, she's been trying to get there for a little while and
it's like she ain't, what's going on? On top of that you got Bill and you still can't
make it there, like what's really going on?" Trump, on the other hand, "he did
say if you're a family, like a husband or a wife and you got a family, he's going to
help the family. With the jobs and stuff like that. I'm kinda okay with him if he's
going to help." As the sociologist Corey Fields observes, while black Republicans
are often accused of voting against both their racial and economic interests, this
paradox disappears when they express their support for lower taxes and pro-
business policies in a context of racial uplift.[11] Furthermore, it is possible that the
networks that sustain his sense of social inclusion, especially among "important"
families in the coal region who are connected to his girlfriend and his former
boss, make voting for Trump the reasonable and obvious choice.

In the end, though, Jeffrey's belief in democracy is fraying at the edges. The topic of veterans, in particular, reveals his conviction that patriotism is built on a lie:

> I respect anybody that's . . . any veteran that put their time in the serv-
> ice. Me personally, I can't do it cuz I don't even know what the hell we
> fighting for. So I'm not going to go to be able to kill people that I have
> no problem with. I don't have no problem for these guys. But I feel like
> they brainwashed them to believe that they are the bad guys. They be
> brainwashing people. But everybody got their different opinion about
> it. Some people feel like you're more American if you go become a
> veteran or you give up your time or you participate in those kinds of
> things. I don't feel like you're a better American than anybody else that
> don't do it.

According to his logic, veterans are not a symbol of masculine pride, a broken social contract, or a forgotten hero, as these things were to the white women and men in previous chapters. In stark contrast, the ideals they are fighting for never existed in the first place. Reconceiving patriotic sacrifice as "brainwashing," he chips away at the belief in something bigger and more honorable.

Even as Jeffrey Wilder votes for Trump, he agrees with the other men in this chapter who "don't even know what the hell we fighting for" and believes that the United States is "ran and controlled" by "bullies." Jeffrey's suspicions bleed into conspiracy theories. "I can't even talk about politics cuz I start talking about the Illuminati cuz I believe in the Illuminati," he raves. "Listen, you have to be-lieve things are being ran and controlled. Like TV, look at the Simpsons. The Simpsons was talking about this shit when he would become president. Donald Trump. They had a statue. He's butt naked and he got a Illuminati ring on his finger. I'd seen [it] on YouTube."

"I'm Here Now"

Coal Brook, finally, is a place for these men to reclaim their humanity—to find personal redemption and protect their children's futures, even if they do not believe in a better future for themselves. Rafael de Sousa, a thirty-six-year-old man from Harrisburg, Pennsylvania, proudly flies a Puerto Rican flag off his cluttered porch, adding a splash of brightness to its rotted-out steps and chip-ping paint. Just two doors down, an attached ramshackle row home boasts a sign declaring "The Silent Majority Stands with Trump." Rafael keeps his shades drawn and his lights off all day. He tells me candidly that if I had come to his door unannounced, he would have slammed the door in my face. Fortunately, another research participant on the same block vouched for me, assuring him that I was not, in fact, a cop.

Once he lets me in, Rafael talks for almost four hours, with a brief interlude to make egg and baloney sandwiches, fried in butter, for each of his five kids. He shares his life story with urgent intensity: "I said, 'Man, she writing a book?' I said, 'Man, I don't need to get paid. I want them to know about this. I don't need to get paid. I'll sit down and conversate with her for free.'"

Rafael begins his life story by pointing to his flag: "I put that flag on my porch for a reason, you know what I mean? To make that statement. Wherever you go man, I don't care what you are, what you do, as long as you're a human and you treat me kind and you treat me with respect, I will do the same thing for you. They label you because of where you're from and how you grew up," he says critically. "I heard that the people here assume everyone who moves here is selling drugs, went to prison," I reply. "Yeah, I did a lot of that," he admits. "But not now. I'm here now. That's why I am here. I don't want that for my kids."

Rafael's father migrated to Harrisburg from Puerto Rico in the 1960s at age nineteen. He had "nothing but a eighth-grade education" and was "drafted straight to Vietnam." Rafael explains how his father came in search of "more liberty, more freedom, more opportunities that they didn't have in Puerto Rico." After being honorably discharged from the military, his father brought Rafael's mother to Harrisburg and they got married. Rafael's father worked as a truck driver, and his mother worked as a maid, "cleaning houses in nice areas." In his neighborhood, where there was frequent violence and the sound of gunshots was commonplace, Rafael recalls, "you had to grow up to be a man too fast." He describes: "My parents taught me right. I chose wrong, and I chose that because if you didn't live like that, you were getting eaten. You know what I mean? If you didn't have that savage life, you know what I mean? Yeah, I still feel like a savage when I go down there."

In the city, he regrets, "that side of me, that part of me gets me in a lot of trouble" but understands it as a requirement for survival. Rafael does not like that side of himself—the hypervigilance, the need to constantly project fearlessness and aggression: "In Harrisburg at night, you gotta be looking over your shoulder, you know what I mean? You don't gotta do that here. I want my kids to have a peace of mind." He shakily recounts the series of events that inspired his move to the coal region:

> The dude got outta the car, people on the porch, he just started shooting all over the place and running. And the other car started driving, look my hairs are standing up [he points to his arm as he speaks]. I'm telling

you. Three days before we got here. And we couldn't find my daughter. I was screaming and crying and all types of shit. And I was running out back when she was sitting out in the backyard. Because when we was looking out front, we had all the kids but except my daughter. So we started, you know, I was freaking out. But the whole time she was in the backyard, thank God.

Rafael expresses relief at no longer having to be constantly watching, ready to fight, ready to protect himself and his children, terrified that they might die under his watch.

When visiting his sister, who moved to Coal Brook in 2008 and bought a house for under $30,000, he met a man who had bought up dozens of blighted properties postrecession. "He told me, oh you help me fix the house and you won't have to give me a security deposit. So we helped him fix the house up and things like that. We didn't have no walls, no ceilings, no anything. We rushed to move in. It's cheap, we were paying $600 bucks for a two-bedroom apartment and we got all these kids. And that was before the extra two came. Now we pay $400 a month." Rafael foreshadows his story of suffering, resilience, and refusal to succumb to despair: "I been through it all. I been through it all and there is nothing that's gonna take my humanity. Because I was in a lowest point in my life plenty of times. I was homeless, I was on drugs. I was in jail, you know what I mean? I've endured life for real," he says forcefully, emphasizing his words by repeatedly hitting the table with his fist.

Rafael was first locked up when he was twelve. He has been "upstate" twice on felony charges and spent years in prison. As he moved in and out of jail, he and his girlfriend started having children. He now has six children with her and two who live with a former girlfriend still in Harrisburg. He tells a story of finding redemption through fatherhood, of how he "started thinking about them instead of thinking about the way I had to live. Then I said, 'Wait a minute, I don't want them to live what I lived.'" Even when he got his "second number and went upstate" to serve time in prison, he diligently pursued numerous certificates and his GED. Rafael leaves the room and comes back with a stack of papers. "Look," he points to his forearms, his voice trembling, "my hair stands up when I talk about this. Because when, when I went through that stage and I tried to make it right, I came with all these papers and diplomas. I came home with all this." He sorts through them, displaying each one proudly: there is one for anger management, one from pharmacology, another for parenting skills.

These "papers" are deeply meaningful to him, a thin stack of hope and redemption in defiance of a world that "don't care." He asserts willfully that he is still here, claiming recognition for his efforts, and mourning what he "coulda did" had he been given the chance:

> I'm not stupid. I'm very educated. And I feel very proud to be still here, at this table and having a conversation with somebody. I got two felonies, alright, but I'm a human, and I've tried. Nobody knows that, you know what I mean? Nobody knows that but me. It hurts. It really does. Because I coulda did so much. I coulda did a lot. But the society I grew up didn't let me. Cuz every time I tried, it was like no. For every-thing. For everything, ever since I was a kid. I was taught like the world don't care.

And despite all of these certifications from prison, Rafael found that "when I came home and tried to better myself, right, they shut me down."[12] Dismayed and defeated, he learned that:

> I couldn't get a good job. I tried to get a good job. even with all this paper, you see all this? I did all this. And I tried to reintegrate myself, as they said, we're gonna get you ready for reintegrate back into society, is what they told me. That's what they said they did. Then they put me back in there and society like they said, right. And I had, did all this, for almost two years. It's what I did for them two years I was there, you know. And for what? I cried like a baby to my mother and my father.

Rafael collects Social Security Insurance for numerous kinds of pain. "I don't know what happened. I did something to either in my back or something in my nerve or something. I had hurt myself pretty bad, and I've been diagnosed with generalized anxiety. I take pills every day." The family relies on food stamps—"if we didn't have that, we wouldn't be able to eat." Before his injury, he also did odd jobs for his landlord, dry-walling, carpeting, and painting. He cooks every day, often liver and rice. "I grew up in the slums. I did," he repeats. "But guess what? I'm a good person."

At first, when Rafael and his family arrived in Coal Brook, the stares of the white residents unnerved him. "They're trying to say, 'Oh before y'all came up here, this town was peaceful.' So before we came up here, all them overdoses ain't been happening before we got here?" he scoffs. "It's about to be 2017, and they're still stuck in 1935. And if you honestly look at it, it's like my dad said, there is no pure race. We're not even one race, us Puerto Rican people, we're like three dif-ferent things, you know what I mean?" He suspects that white people "already have Klan meetings, pass out fliers, they run around here with their weapons and flags. I never knew what a sand[n-word] was till I got to fuckin' Coal Brook, excuse my language, oh my god." Tensions culminated one night in a brawl out-side his home: "I couldn't take it no more. I said what I said, people said what they said, and then around twelve o'clock, one o'clock, midnight, somebody came here out front and we just defended our home. And I went to jail. For thirty-eight days, got a year probation, and a $700 fine. Whereas in Harrisburg, if I'd have had a fight, that'd have been a fine only." The violence and surveillance of the city continue to haunt him in his place of refuge.

Rafael calms down when he thinks about his children, who are thriving in Coal Brook: "My oldest daughter that lives here with me, she has straight As. She goes to basketball. Like it's opportunity and things that I can do here with my kids that I can't do in Harrisburg. I freely let my kids run around here, whereas in Harrisburg, they couldn't even hit the corner." In just his mid-thirties, he has suffered from kidney stones, and has delayed having a recommended colonos-copy for over six months. He explains: "I was huge. My cholesterol was up, my triglycerides was up." But he hasn't been back to the doctor out of his conviction that his life is already over: "I'm scared they gonna go and find something else. Cancer runs in my family. I'm scared. Diabetes, heart, blood pressure, all that, that stuff run in my family. And I have bad habits. I eat a lot of red meat. You're not supposed to. They told me you can't eat a lot of red meat." Watching the smoke swirl off his cigarette, he says with quiet conviction: "*This is all for the future of my kids.* I don't want my kids to go through the same struggles I did. I know we don't have it all. But we have a roof over our heads and a peace of mind because I can let my children run around here. And I just want them to know that there is bigger things and better things than bigotry, racism, poverty. You have choices. Instead of getting a job, get a career. You know what I mean? I talk to my children all the time. Drugs, sex, everything."

The achievement of well-being—forging a sense of self-determination, redemption, and dignity even when recognizing that the system is against him—is an extremely painful process. Rafael renounces his former self—the law-breaking, violent, fighting self. He remains crippled by the wear and tear of his former life, in constant pain, smoking to quell his racing thoughts, and viewing the world through the fog of anxiety. He tries to live a life of resiliency, but he can never forget the limitations that his society imposes on him. As he states, he expects nothing from his own life; it is all for his children at this point.

Rafael turns an unapologetically critical eye on the history of the United States and the myth of a golden past full of opportunity and justice: "I have never seen an American Dream. I don't know how you grew up, but there is no such thing as 'make America great again' cuz it was never great. It was never great. They came here, they took the Indians off they land, took the natural resources. Same thing they doing with other places for their rice, for their coffee, for the oil, for the gas. They just bullies." He expresses a complete lack of faith in the United

States as anything other than a greedy entity looking to plunder other country's resources: "You know why terrorism happens? Because they're being bullies to all these places cuz they want what their natural resource is. They just wanna take it. And they wanna use everything like religion and all this other stuff to cover up the war." He ties this sense of betrayal into his own biography: "I mean, my dad came down here with no education, no nothing. Didn't even know English. And they just drafted him straight to Vietnam. And that's why I don't vote."

Rafael, on his own, maintains a sliver of hope. He moved away from the city and abandoned the person it made him into, to build a new life, facing down racism along the way. Rafael believes in a better future for his children, but his story is hardly one of rosy optimism about life getting better and better. It is a story of grim determination. He muses: "I'm thirty-six and I feel, I feel like lost sometimes. And it's, it's just, I just worry about their future and what it holds for them because I'm done, I'm good. I'm just waiting now. Hit seventy or whatever, watch my grandchildren grow up. I'm just waiting now. I'm done. You know it's sad to say that at thirty-six years old, but you know what? I'm good where I'm at. I love the world, but it doesn't love me back."

We now turn to explore the lives of the "newcomer" women in the coal region.

Something We Never Had

The black and Latina "newcomer" women who migrate to the coal region leave behind traumatic histories—stories of early childhood abuse and neglect, poverty, extreme neighborhood violence, and drug abuse. Some of the women I spoke with were brought to the coal region by relatives fleeing controlling men and life-threatening crime. They stay out of obligation to their families, trying to build a life in an unwelcoming place. Hardened by their own early experiences with drugs and violence, other women view the coal region as a place where their children will not have to grow up the way they did. Starting over often means starting over alone.

Upon arrival, the newcomer women face painful accusations that they are unfit mothers, have poor work ethics, and are undeserving of government aid.[1] They nonetheless fight fiercely and relentlessly to get a fleeting shot at opportunities for their children that they themselves never had. These women encounter multiple predatory institutions waiting to take advantage of their optimism—whether for-profit colleges that leave them in debt and unprepared for jobs, or landlords who know that blighted housing is all they can afford. They inure themselves against despair by framing the American Dream as a long, steep, difficult ascent. Through small, everyday acts of civic engagement, they hold the police, their neighbors, local businesses, and the schools accountable for their loved ones' futures. Living a life of emotional turmoil, relationship flux, racial hostility, and poverty leaves these women emotionally raw, deeply distrustful, and physically depleted. They can devote themselves only to their immediate kinship circles, determined to heal themselves on their own.

They're Supposed to Fix the Problems, Except
That They're Causing Them

The sociologist Shirley Hill writes that women of color are often assumed to be strong mothers, self-sacrificing caretakers, and fierce activists, able to endure no matter how difficult life gets.[2] Previous studies have documented the significant emotional and physical costs borne by women of color during their struggles to provide adequate care when poverty and racism limits the control they have over their own bodies, their health, and their ability to ensure basic economic security for their children.[3] Stephanie Rivera, a twenty-three-year-old woman who identifies as black and Puerto Rican, spent the early years of her life in a public housing project in Brooklyn, New York. She lived with her mother, two siblings, and her grandmother. Stephanie describes the neighborhood she grew up in as "not all that great. Like you can't go outside by yourself. It was like you can't go to the park cuz you never know what they're doing, like either selling drugs, having sex." To this day, she does not understand why people think of New York City as "this nice place you can go hang out in—it's not."

When Stephanie was ten years old, her mother decided to move west to Lebanon, Pennsylvania—"that's where everyone at the time was going, like everyone that wanted to get out of the city was going, and for her it was like, complete life-changing." Her mother, Clara, who was pregnant at the time; her mother's boyfriend, Charles; and the three children moved into an apartment in Lebanon. "My mom was the good one," she explains. "She worked at housekeeping in hotels for years. The only problem was she was never really around." Stephanie foreshadows a long history of disappointment and distrust in men: "Everything was her responsibility. I can't remember my stepdad working ever."

Stephanie never knew her biological father and despised all of the men her mother dated. As a young child, she lived in perpetual fear because one of her mother's boyfriends "used to lock my mom in the house, like he would lock her inside from outside and he'd like strap her down and shit, like she was not allowed to leave." When asked about Charles, her mother's longest-running boyfriend, she says with disgust: "He's fat as hell, he's a big lazy man, sitting there and we would do everything for him kinda thing. The type of laziness he was, he would go into the kitchen, pull out the ramen noodles, then go to one of the kids and say, go make that for me. And my mom would come home late and always tired." Isolation and fear defined her early childhood years: "Like we never saw her. He would do the disciplining, we got hit, until my mom would be like, okay that's enough."

When Stephanie was in high school, her mother was almost killed in a serious car accident driving home from her job as a hotel maid in Harrisburg. "She almost died from what they say in the police report, cuz she doesn't remember anything and we wasn't there so we don't know," Stephanie explains. "I think the guy was eighty-nine and I guess he tried to commit suicide or whatever, he was driving on the opposite side of the road. And he bashed right into her car. She lost her memory for about a week and that was hard for me cuz I thought my mom was going to die, she was like paralyzed for a few days then she finally got her mobility back." Since the car accident, Clara has not been physically able to clean hotel rooms and has collected a monthly disability payment.

The intense emotions brought on by the near-fatal car accident—trauma, anxiety, gratitude—spurred Clara and Charles to get married. Clara initiated divorce proceedings after just three months. This breakup led the rest of the family to the tiny town of Coal Brook, a hidden refuge from Charles's relentless control. "The only reason why we came here is because my mom and my stepdad were splitting up and he was like the type of person, he didn't know how to let things go," Stephanie explains. "This was my senior year in high school, so five years ago. She felt if she left and he didn't know where she was, it would finally be like peaceful." After watching her mother's experiences with men, Stephanie swears she will never, ever get married: "I've seen so many marriages fail, I can't. I will never, ever, no matter what. I could be madly in love with someone, I would never. And I feel like it's all about money, too. You pay so much money to get married, then you fight."

Despite her mother's longing for peace and safety, their first apartment was "horrible"—"the landlord was this drug lord." She remembers: "A pipe busted and I don't remember if it was in the kitchen or the basement and we kept saying like our water bill was getting higher and higher and higher, and finally it burst, to a point where you stepped foot in the living room, your foot would go in the rug cuz there was so much water. We couldn't live there." With no money left to put a security deposit down on a new place, they turned to public housing assistance: "So we went to the housing office. My mom didn't know what else to do, she went to the housing office and they placed us within a week. But that was even worse then cuz the housing there, they are so nosey. You can't have company. If a car comes by your house, they'll question you. Whose car was that, why were they here?"

Desperate to escape, Stephanie completed her high school requirements but did not even stay in town long enough to walk across the stage at graduation: "The day they said okay you're done, I was outta this town." She moved back to Lebanon and lived with her cousin, finding a job at a Rent-A-Center. In Lebanon, she also met her daughter's father, who was working construction. But Stephanie worried constantly about her mother, Clara, whose mental and physical health had never fully recovered from the car accident. Clara was living alone after sending her fifteen-year-old son to live with his father in Florida because she feared his escalating encounters with the local police. "When the cop was picking on my brother, when he brought him in, it was so long ago I don't remember why he brought him into the station to begin with, but they tried to get him to admit to something he didn't do," Stephanie explains. "Like vandalism or something, he absolutely didn't do. He wasn't even there. So afterward, he [the police officer] kept picking on him." Worried about Clara's deteriorating health,

Stephanie and her boyfriend moved back to Coal Brook, renting one side of a half-double home. She got a job at a discount smoke shop that she could walk to, while her boyfriend got a job working in the shipping and receiving department at Walmart.

The neighbors, however, "were like doing drugs there, and they caught a sofa on fire and it came into our house. It was horrible. And then we were home-less for three weeks cuz we lost everything. I was three months pregnant. When I say we lost everything, the only thing we had was the clothes on our back, the phones cuz we all sleep with our phones." Homeless, she returned once again to the housing office. She points down the street:

> If you go down and make a right, there's a red door. I lived there and it was the crappiest place I ever lived in my whole life but I had nowhere else to go. Like, the Red Cross paid for I think security, and we had just paid rent. My job was in the next town over, I worked at the smoke shop at the time, I had no way to get to work, I didn't have a job anymore, I didn't have anything.

Stephanie sums up her attitude toward the world: "That's the people you're sup-posed to, if something goes wrong, they're supposed to fix the problem, except that they're causing them. And that's the main problem I have."

Stephanie offers plenty of additional evidence for this worldview. When she got pregnant, she explains, she went to the local doctor and insisted something was wrong. At twenty-nine weeks "I kept saying I thought my water broke cuz I had like fluid leakage. They said nope, it's not water, it's normal discharge. It was amniotic fluid coming out." It turned out she had preeclampsia, a serious and sometimes fatal complication. Stephanie finally went to a large hospital about twenty miles away with a more advanced maternity unit. She learned: "My pre-eclampsia was so severe. They explained to me what it was, high blood pressure during pregnancy. So I was high risk since I was twenty-nine weeks all the way to thirty-eight weeks and no one told me. And nobody said anything. I was working all the time. Always on my feet."

To make matters worse, she adds, the doctors "thought I was on drugs be-cause of how small she [her daughter] was, but it was because they neglected my pregnancy. She wasn't getting the nutrients because of the preeclampsia. She was born five pounds. Itty bitty little thing." Stephanie, who does not smoke or drink alcohol, continues with outrage: "They tested her without my permission for alcoholism and marijuana and all of that. So they came out, 'Oh yeah by the way she doesn't have alcoholism' and I was like wait, what? They said, 'Oh yeah, we tested her.' " Stephanie suspects that the hospital workers automatically assumed that she was a drug addict because she was poor and not white.

Throughout this turmoil, Stephanie and her boyfriend were arguing constantly, and they finally called it quits. Their shared desire to give a child a better life could not sustain them through the trials of raising an infant in the throes of poverty, housing insecurity, and family turmoil. She remains frustrated that "he doesn't really talk. That's one of our main problems in our relationship." Nonetheless, they still live together, splitting their $425 a month rent and raising their daughter together. "And he feels like, oh if we moved to a different place, got to a place where we never argued before, where people don't know us, we'd get back together," she says wistfully. "We don't hate each other or anything. My daughter loves her father," Stephanie insists, "I would never like, ever, ever take a man away from his child, especially being a black man that wants to be a part of his child's life. I would never stop that."

Stephanie has shifted her focus toward self-improvement since her daughter's birth: "I don't want to go from job to job when I get older. I want a career for my kid." She found a nearby for-profit college that, she now realizes, "does anything to get you to go to that school. I literally went to school and they wanted me to sign up for the class that started three days later." Skeptical of how eager the college was to sign her up, she adds, "That's how bad they were. I'm like, if you ask me what I wanted to do, like job-wise, where do you want to work? I don't know." Bewildered, Stephanie chose to pursue a two-year "medical assisting" degree. Despite being told that there were grants available—"they always say, oh you have grants and everything available to you and scholarships"—she soon realized that "they don't even cover half my, it didn't even cover a quarter of my education quite honestly. I had the Pell. I think that was $5,000 a year, $10,000 all together but my tuition was $50,000 for two years. It didn't cover anything."

After completing her online classes, she found out that she was required to complete an unpaid externship in a doctor's office. She quit her job and took out more loans to live on. She fumes: "What they taught me in school and what I'm learning in my externship was two completely different things. Like they don't explain to you, I have a bad problem with like body odor, bad body odor, the smell of urine, the smell of poo, the smell of saliva . . . if they would have embedded that in my head before, I would have been prepared for it." She already suspects that her educational gamble will not pay off:

> So if I am just a medical assistant, my average pay would be $13.00 an
> hour which that's another thing I was mad about, cuz some people at
> Walmart make that money and I went to school for two years and they
> made it seem like it was way more than that. They told me I'd average
> $17 an hour, at the time when I looked it up, like the sheet they gave
> me it was that. I don't know if it changed, I don't know why it would go
> down. But then I found out I could have just gotten my LPN, been in

school for one year and pay only $15,000 instead of $40,000. It's like,
and LPN pays twice as much. Their average pay is $25 an hour, and you
go up with experience and raises and everything. They [the for-profit
college] just do so much to get you in there.

Stephanie sighs, shifting from anger at the institution to anger at herself. She says
with resignation, "And I mean it was my fault I didn't do my research, I had no
idea that I was going to be an M.A. [medical assistant]."[4]

Aside from her externship, Stephanie mostly stays in the house and takes
care of her daughter. "I don't really go out besides work. Would I walk around at
night? No. No," she says firmly. "There's a lot of drunk people around here, just
stupid things. One time when I was trying to drive away, is when they was doing
the fireworks [during the Fourth of July], I had a crowd of people around my car
yelling the n-word and all this at me. My daughter's crying in the backseat, cuz
she didn't understand what's going on. It was horrible. It was the worst. I cried,
I never cried so hard in my entire life." When I ask her if she ever attends the
festivals and parades in town, she shrugs: "I never know about them. Um, even
when they have like parades, I never know about it until it's happening." Her
isolation from the community dovetails with complete and utter disengagement
from conventional politics. She says dismissively: "Not to say I'm stupid, but
I don't understand it. It's all like, what is this? I think it's cuz I don't care for it.
I don't understand it. I don't understand the point of it, all of it." She has never
registered to vote.

Stephanie names one act of civic engagement that she is fiercely proud of: she
filed a complaint with customer service at Walmart, where her daughter's father
works, asking that their workers not be allowed to smoke cigarettes by the store
entrance. She states passionately: "I made it my business for me and everyone
else who didn't have a voice to stop the smoking in front of the store. For a whole
week, every time I went to Walmart purposely three times a day, I took a picture
and I came here with twenty-seven pictures. And I sent that over to the corporate
office and they stopped the smoking in front of the store." Stephanie justifies her
activism in terms of a need to protect her daughter's well-being: "Cuz I shouldn't
have to walk out of the store with my child to walk into a cloud of smoke!"

Stephanie and her boyfriend rely on food stamps. "Like I used to go to self-
checkout all the time just so no one sees me using it," she admits shamefully.
"Then you realize everyone around you is on it. Everyone." At the end of our
conversation, I asked her if the American Dream is working for her family. She
replies succinctly: "No." She continues:

I mean if I had a choice of what country I wanted to be born, of course
I would say America. But American Dream? No. Cuz everyone thinks,

okay I'm going to move to America and everything's going to get so much better. It doesn't. You have to work, you have to build yourself up from no matter where you are. It's just easier here than in other places. That's the only difference. It's just easier, it's not, "Oh let me move to America and then I'm going to be rich and have my own restaurant." It doesn't work that way. You're going to move to America and you're going to be homeless for a few months until you get to where you have to go.

Stephanie does not believe in any kind of "dream," but accepts the harsh reality of her life, with her eyes wide open.

Fighting for a Better Future

Daniela is thirty-one-years-old and identifies proudly as Puerto Rican. Daniela tells a personal story of redemption and upward mobility, of leaving a life of pathology and pain behind and achieving a piece of the American Dream. Daniela takes it upon herself to improve her family's life chances, not through conventional means like marriage or joining civic-minded groups, but through minute interactions in her everyday life in which she sees her children's futures hanging in the balance.

Daniela and her boyfriend, Andres (who appears in chapter 4), have lived in the coal region for ten years and are among some of the earliest newcomers in the area. Daniela never met her own father. She says flatly: "My mom didn't work, my whole family didn't work. We was on the streets. So that's how we got our money, from the streets. That's the only thing we grew up on." Raised in North Philly, Daniela reports that she was accustomed to seeing "people that do drugs laid out in the streets" and "violence everywhere." She learned to distrust people in authority early on: "When I was younger, life was different growing up. You had cops coming up to you, cursing you out, spitting on you, and saying things to you, then they come out and they take their badges off and they want to sit there and try and fight a minor."

Daniela went to multiple high schools—Edison, Kensington, then finally a "CEP school"—referring to the schools that provide alternative education and free nutrition to underprivileged and poor youth. To this day, she says, "I don't know why they put me there, I try to figure it out myself sometimes." Daniela and her boyfriend met at CEP and both dropped out at age eighteen—"there was too much money to be made in the streets," she shrugs. When Andres's sister's husband moved to the coal region, Andres and Daniela decided to go there too. "I moved out here to change my life, just change myself and where I was growing up from. I just needed a way out," Daniela says quietly. Daniela has received SSI for a mental illness since she was in Philadelphia. She explains, "I get drugs, I get transportation, I get everything. If I have appointments and stuff I get transportation. You got to be at certain hours but it's okay. You have some people who get coverage for medical insurance and they have to pay for the medication, I don't have to do that."

Daniela sticks to herself, going mainly to the grocery store, her children's school, doctor's appointments, and home. She feels like she lives under constant threat, yet she remains determined to stay in order to build a better life for her children:

> We have to protect ourselves. Because not too long ago somebody broke into our car. So therefore we got to sleep with one eye open, one eye closed. They were testing us. We don't mess with nobody and we told a lot of people, we told them we stick to ourselves. We live to live our lives. To make a better life for ourselves and a better life for our children. A home that my kids can grow up in and stuff like that so I don't bother with nobody. Something we never had as a kid.

Although she is devoted to building a stable home, she refuses to marry Andres—she confides, "He asked me to get married and I told him right now, we go through our ups and downs and stuff but we manage to still stick with each other. But if you want to get married and like, just because we're married things will change differently." She does not regret the decline of nuclear family structures, lasting marriages, and children raised by married parents.[5] On the contrary, Daniela fears that there is something about being married that "would change everything, worse rather than better"—for example, "I've seen people get married and stuff didn't work out. Like my mom and my stepfather, they got married. They got married on a Friday, the weekend hadn't even passed, the night wasn't even over, and they both threw their rings at each other and they wanted a divorce Monday morning."

Resisting a formal commitment, she elaborates: "I'm waiting for when I'm ready. I'm waiting till I'm ready for it 'cause right now I'm not ready to have someone else's last name. I mean, I love him to death. The way I see it, it's like why do that? Waste money on buying dresses and buying all this stuff if it's not going to work out." To get married is almost to jinx their ten-year stability, to threaten the already tumultuous "ups and downs." Daniela is reluctant to tie her last name to someone else's, even someone she loves deeply, to protect her independence. Marriage does not hold the same appeal that it does for the young white women in chapter 3, such as Danielle or Lucy, for whom being and staying married signals self-worth and warrants social honor regardless of the quality of the relationship.[6]

Unable to work, Daniela receives food stamps and health insurance for herself and the children. When I ask her if she thinks that people deserve this kind of help, she reflects:

> I mean, yeah, for people that need it. I mean not everybody need it but the ones that do, yeah we need benefits. Yeah we need stuff like that, our insurance and stuff like that. Not everybody got that privilege, not a lot of people can have medical, and not a lot of people go to the doctors to get checked because they don't have medical insurance. Like the majority, you know people got 401 plans, people with raises, their parents are doctors, you know they have something for them. As soon as they're born, bang they're born.

Her own narrative of coming to the coal region is one of diffident pride—she understands that the lottery of birth allows some people to get ahead in life while others need additional help. "Basically where I'm at today, because some people when I go down to Philly be like, 'Oh you living that rich life.' I'm like, 'I still struggle like you,'" she says modestly. But she believes that "the school system is way better up here than it is there [in Philadelphia]" and is pleased that her children "won't see all the stuff that's down there. We don't want them to witness what we witnessed."

Daniela is generally content with the quality of the school system: "My daughter's school, has this zero tolerance for bullying. I never seen something like that in Philadelphia. I also love the fact that they have armed guards in the school" and that "if I send my mother-in-law, father-in-law, sister-in-law, to go pick up my kid, they have to show ID." Security and protection are her main concerns. But she also reports numerous incidents when she has had to go to battle for her children—fighting for their safety and making sure they get the opportunity they deserve. When her daughter was in third grade, for example, "a kid threatened to kill her. So the next day I went down to the bus stop and I told their parent. They been going to Head Start together, third grade, second grade, whatever. So my daughter hit third grade and they were in the same bus together and the girl kept messing with her, calling her the b-word." Daniela put an immediate stop to this harassment: "I'm coming to you now and I'm going to tell you your daughter is disrespecting my daughter, calling my daughter names. So I told her, if it continues we're going to have problems, and she was like all right."

Another time, when checking her other daughter's homework folder, she suspected that the teacher had made a mistake: "I'm reading the math and stuff and I'm like, this is right, why did she mark this wrong?" When she and Andres went to their parent-teacher conference, "we bring that up to her, we were like, look, this answer right here is right. She was like oh yeah, she messed up and she had to mark it right. That's why, I said, you're a teacher, you're supposed to be on top of that, you're supposed to pay attention." Daniela is still angry, feeling that she has to be constantly on her guard to make sure her child gets the opportunity she is entitled to: "That's putting my child's grade down. Like they'll put that as a fail for her or something. Every homework paper counts." Daniela carefully monitors her children's teachers, watchful of any unfair treatment, and ready to fiercely defend and protect their every opportunity, no matter how slight.

Daniela is careful to limit the scope of whom she cares about to her own children, saving her energy for what truly matters: safety and a fair shot at a good life for her children. She states deliberately: "I believe in God. But I also believe we're on our own." She uses this same logic to explain why she does not vote, follow the news closely, or get involved in any kind of activities or groups outside of caring for her own children. "I don't care what's going on in the world," she says defiantly. "I'm living for the day. I'm living for my children. I'm not worried about them [*gestures toward outside*]. If the world's going to end, it's going to end. We can't do nothing about it. If this world's going to end, if there's a war and people's out there, we can't do nothing but stay to our self." As long as "nobody's messing with us, and nobody comes to my door and nobody's threatening me, putting a gun to my face, I don't have to worry about nothing," she insists. Narrowing her focus, she worries solely about building opportunity for her children in her daily interactions, one hard-won homework problem at a time.

Confronting Discrimination

The "newcomer" women express a sharp awareness of inequality, especially when it comes to protecting their children and intimate partners. They are openly watchful, speaking out against the lack of good jobs, the surveillance of men of color, and the racism of the criminal justice system. Mikayla Gabriel, a thirty-four-year-old black woman, grew up in Queensbridge, the "projects" in Queens, New York. She lived with her "grandmother, her boyfriend, my mom, my uncle, me, and my brother. So it was six of us in a two-bedroom apartment. It sucked." Her mother was a corrections officer on Rikers Island and worked as many shifts as she could get. Her mother always wanted to move them to a safer apartment, but the rents were too high. When Mikayla was seventeen, her mother decided to relocate the family to Decatur, Georgia—"so the amount that she was paying for an apartment in New York, she could get a house in Georgia. Then she met my stepdad. They got married, and he's a cop out there." Mikayla describes Decatur as another "bad place to live," but her mother and stepfather have since "moved to a more chichi neighborhood."

Mikayla describes her mother's epic transformation, which she views as the result of her new Polish/Puerto Rican husband: "He's like ex-military and things like that so now that she's seen the other world, of where she grew up and everything. Now she's political, now she goes to church, and now she does things she never did when I was little." Since the election has just passed, I ask her if she knows whom her mother voted for. She laughs drily: "Trump. I just think it's so weird. Me and her were going back and forth the other day. I said, you know, voting for a Democrat was fine when you were getting all those free benefits but now that you're married and you're not eligible for that anymore, it's no longer fine. We got food stamps. We had assisted living." Mikayla, who works for an insurance company and has been able to afford health insurance only since the expansion of the Affordable Care Act, voted for Obama in 2012 alongside her mother. She says bitterly: "Now that you [her mother] don't qualify for benefits, you turned your back on it."

Mikayla frames herself as a self-determined person with the drive and motivation to transform her life. She now has four children. She credits her oldest daughter's father for "showing me the other side of the world," that "I didn't have to live the way I grew up and basically he just pushed me." When this man, who was her boyfriend since her junior year of high school, asked her to move to the coal region with him a decade ago to work for his friend's father's plastic company, she agreed, quitting her job as a bank teller. At first, she regretted the move. She remembers: "When I first came out here I moved out here without even visiting. So I was like what the hell did I do to myself? Why did I come over here?" Mikayla soon discovered she was pregnant, and they "wound up staying," buying a house together. They never got married— "I was like what's the difference, we were together, we bought a house together, we skipped all the steps, we had a baby. But then thankfully we didn't. I can't see spending money to get married like that." Like the other women in this chapter, she points to the needless expense of an elaborate wedding for a reality that will not live up to romantic ideals. They are no longer together but are committed to raising their daughter on civil terms: "I can make it easy to just be like obviously we cared about each other at one point so why hate each other now just cuz it didn't work out. Luckily he's the same way, and we can keep it cordial."

As the primary breadwinner for her children, Mikayla has worked as a telemarketer, a home health aide, and an insurance representative. Over the years, she has had a series of relationships that have not worked out. The father of her youngest, a toddler, is currently living with her. "My life is crazy. Currently, my youngest one [child] is with someone, we're not together, but he does live here.

He's on house arrest. So um, just until his house arrest is over. Then he can move. He needed a home plan. But me and him, we're okay."

Taking a political stance, she describes how he was "definitely targeted" unfairly by the police, that their search was illegal, and that his case was "all bullshit":

> I contacted the NAACP for everything. It was illegal what they did. They were looking for someone else that had a warrant. The person was right there, they had them cuffed and everything, and because of who he was [her boyfriend], the guy was outside and they said, "Who's in there?" And once they mentioned his name, he was like, "Oh search them all." When you do that, you're only allowed to pat, and if you feel something that feels like a weapon or drugs then you can actually go into someone's pockets. And they didn't do that, they just went into his pockets and they found half a gram of coke. You can't feel that when you're patting. So they arrested him for that.

While those possession charges were dismissed, this man is currently on house arrest for earlier convictions. Mikayla does not dispute the rumor that some of the men of color who have moved to the coal region do indeed sell drugs. "It is a shame," she shakes her head. "But the way that things are set up around here, people don't have another choice. It's sad to say but they really don't." She elaborates: "They see how cheap it is to live here and they move. It has nothing to do with, 'Oh I'm going to come right over and sell drugs and that's how I'm going to make a living.'" She points to the lack of transportation and the reluctance of local employers to hire these men: "I didn't know that it was so hard to get a job out here. Or how racist they are, and you have to have a car, and that there is no public transportation. I didn't know any of that. So these people move out here, they see opportunity. Maybe they're naïve, maybe they should have looked into it. Because there really isn't much." She is staunchly against collecting child support payments from any of her children's fathers: "No, none of them. I feel like if a father has to give 60 percent of his paycheck to take care of his kid, then that mother shouldn't have their child. They might as well be with the dad. And how are they supposed to live? How are they supposed to pay their bills? What do they do? They sell drugs." Mikayla believes that her worldview frees men from the mandated provider role because it could induce them to commit crime and become a victim of the criminal justice system.

"So I don't look down on anyone, on people who come out here and they do sell drugs to support their family," she says defiantly. "Then people complain about the fact that there's drug dealers here. If the parents here raised their kids better, they wouldn't have to worry about, drugs dealers wouldn't be here if they weren't addicts," she insists angrily. "They wouldn't be here if there weren't people enabling these addicts to have the money to spend on these drugs, to support these drug dealers. For anyone to say anything about a drug dealer, you need to look at the core problem first, you can't just look at the people who are selling the drugs." Mikayla believes that the true criminals are the white doctors in town who prescribe opiates indiscriminately: "I think [name of the local doctor] actually started this whole heroin epidemic out here cuz he was prescribing Percocets and then cuts everybody off, just dry like that. Now they're withdrawing. Heroin is cheaper than Percocets."

Mikalya is losing faith in all of the institutions around her. Constant bullying and racist slurs from a white child led her daughter to switch to homeschooling. "I actually told my daughter if she confronts her or says something to her again to hit her. Then it's really going to be a problem. So I'd just rather take her out of school," she sighs. Two months ago, Mikayla joined a Pentecostal church so that her daughter could partake in the youth-group services to replace social interactions she was missing in her online, self-directed classes. Unfortunately, the political message from the pulpit the Sunday after the November 2016 election made Mikayla feel unwelcome and unsafe, and she has not returned since. "Like they would try to make it seem like Trump was the Savior. They said God decided to give us another chance so that's why they gave us Trump. And basically that if you feared anything that he was going to do that we needed counseling. That was it for that place."

Mikayla's favorite presidential candidate was Bernie Sanders—he is "my guy," with a "good heart" and "he wanted what was best for us." But Mikayla, a registered Democrat, despised Hillary Clinton so much that she did not vote. She ties her assessment of Clinton to her own contradictory feelings about what it means to be a woman:

MIKAYLA: She's deceitful and I don't trust women. I just don't trust women. I feel like we lie with such ease, and we do some very deceitful evil things. And with her track record I just didn't feel like she was a good fit.

JS: So do you trust men more than women?

MIKALYA: Oh yeah, definitely men more than women. I just feel like women tend to go more off of emotion, we don't really think first before we react. So, and just knowing what she's been doing, I just didn't think. . . . There was no trust for her. I think a woman would do excellent as a president, I mean we bear children, we financially take care of them, we're more mature. But she just wasn't the one.

Mikayla ties women's potential to lead to their ability to care for children, to step up and take care of them on their own. But she still believes, like many of the people in this book, that women are untrustworthy, manipulative, and emotional.

She asserts: "We killed the American Dream ourselves, cuz we don't have any pride anymore. Our people don't stand for anything anymore. There's nothing that we do. Like the US is just known as a taker. We do things because we want it and that's it. There's no more values." She wants the United States to "stand for" something that is bigger than our individual greed. Even as she believes that racism used to be worse, she pines: "I just wish my kids were growing up in the '50s and '60s.There's nothing here for them. There's bars, churches, and addiction help centers. That's it. That's all that there is. Like what ever happened to like Big Brother programs? We don't even see that out here, why not? It's nothing. It's sad." Mikayla decides that success stems only from her own personal ability to resist being pulled back into the lifestyle she was raised in: "I think you have two ways of looking at life. Either you fall into the same system that you were raised in or you fall into the system where you never want to go back to how you were raised. So depending on how you look at things and the people that you surround yourself with, is the outcome."

Hell on Earth

For Eva Torez, well-being also entails cutting other people off and making it on her own. Eva was a child when her grandmother moved her to the coal region from Red Hook, New York, fleeing violence and trauma within the family. The past is not so easily shaken off, and Eva—who, at only twenty-one, has battled heroin addiction, abusive relationships, and severe depression—describes her life as hell on earth. She is in the process of removing negative people from her life, refusing to live under the thumb of controlling men, and becoming a person who relies only on herself. Cutting herself off from other people entails embracing utter political disengagement: "It's not happening around me, I don't really care," she says brazenly.

Eva describes her early childhood as "pretty bad." Her mother was a "drug addict," hooked on crack cocaine and heroin, and her father was in prison. When I ask her why her father was incarcerated, she tells me the following story: "When I was a baby, my mom cheated on my dad," she explains. "And then my mom came back to my dad. And he took her back, he loved her. But the guy she cheated on him with was upset. And he shot, like me and my grandmother were in an apartment, and he shot the whole place up." Eva adds nonchalantly: "You know, we didn't get hit or anything. But my dad found out. And he went to the guy and he flipped. He didn't kill him, but he hurt him pretty bad." By the time her father was released, Eva was four years old and living with her grandmother and great-grandmother. Her great-grandmother, "had a few mental problems. And she'd lock me in closets. She was delusional, schizophrenic, and a few other things."

Although her father was in prison when she was younger, Eva is now close with him and speaks warmly about his devotion for fatherhood: "He got his GED when he was in jail. My dad had me when he was young, seventeen. And he dropped out of school. And when he went to jail he got his GED. Cuz I know he always wanted better for me and so he did all that." But Eva's grandmother was worried when Eva's father got out of prison, when Eva was in elementary school, because "the kind of stuff my dad was into, it was like dangerous for me and them."

In the coal region, her grandmother found work as a school janitor, and her grandfather supported the household with his army pension. Although her new neighborhood was quieter and safer, Eva struggled with "severe anxiety and major depression" throughout her adolescence. She found herself "dabbling with drugs and getting myself in trouble, getting in fights, having like behavioral problems" by middle school.[7] By then, her father had settled down and gotten married to a woman whose family lived in Coal Brook and they "were trying not to get in trouble anymore." Eva moved to Coal Brook with her dad and stepmother when she was in ninth grade because "it was getting too hard to watch him go" when he visited. Her stepmother works as a cashier at a gas station, and her father collects SSI from a car accident injury. Eva notes that as a "convicted felon," even though it was twenty years ago, he struggled to find a job.

Eva dropped out of high school and moved into an apartment with her boyfriend, paid for by his father, a longtime resident of the coal region. For over two years, they were both addicted to heroin, living only for their next fix. When he was sober, Eva recalls, this boyfriend was often cruel—"It was never like physical abuse, nothing like that. But things he would say to me, it like really took a toll on me. It was pretty bad. It's like at that time you wish you, he would just hit you instead of saying like what he's saying. That's how I felt." To pay for the continuous supply of drugs, Eva's boyfriend found her a job as an exotic dancer in a town about forty minutes away so that she would not run into too many people from the area—"cuz he didn't want to do anything. I didn't make that much. But it made enough money for us to go get our next fix." She shrugs off my concerns: "It wasn't bad. I was high every time we danced. So it was like, it really wasn't a bother. I mean now I don't see myself doing it. And it was, it was messed up."

Eva has been sober for six months. Her sobriety was abruptly forced upon her when she overdosed on heroin last November and her boyfriend called 911. She explains:

They shot me with Narcan [a medication used to block the effects of opiates]. At first it wasn't bringing me back. But the second time they shot me with Narcan. The police shot me the first time with it and it didn't bring me back, and I was still in the house. By the time the ambulance came, they were like losing me. And they put me into the ambulance and shot me with Narcan again. They said they didn't think it was gonna work at first cuz it was taking a long time for me to wake up. But I woke up. I think it was scary waking up. Like I knew what I was going into, but like waking up with all the, everybody being around you. Like three people in your face, sirens. It was pretty scary.

Eva spent two weeks in a mental institution and was then referred to a counselor, who oversees her Suboxone treatments to help her stay sober. To treat her depression and anxiety, she explains: "I'm supposed to be on medication too. But I noticed that like when I'm on my medication I feel like a zombie. Like I'm so slow, I don't wanna do anything. So I stopped taking my medication and I feel much better. I mean I still deal with the stuff I deal with. But I think it's better."

Eva has decided to take control of her own medication because she does not like the counselor she is required to see as part of the treatment program for Suboxone. Eva complains: "She's very judgmental. She'll call me names and she was saying that I make it seem as if I'm innocent and I'm naïve and I have to take more acceptance that I was an addict. Like you don't know my story! It just came out of nowhere. And it's like I'm not, how am I innocent? How am I naïve? Like I know what I'm doing." Eva reclaims her pride by insisting that she is responsible for her own life choices: "And I know that, I know when I'm not in the right situation. So I'm not trying to make myself seem innocent, not trying to put the blame on anyone. Cuz it's no one's fault. It's my own." She notes one ally—a local police officer who has pledged to "stand by me to show the judge that I'm not a problem in the community. He knows I'm not really a troublemaker. And you know he does notice that I am doing good. Like I'm doing a lot better for myself and he wants, he wants to support me."

The biggest lesson Eva has learned from growing up and watching her own family's trials has been that she needs to become financially independent and not rely on men. While her current boyfriend, also a recovering heroin addict, wants to move in with her, she "told him to just kinda wait it out, kinda get yourself better while you can. Stay at the halfway house and stuff like that. Like I wanna have my own place." For now, Eva lives with her father and stepmother and is trying to find a job. Describing the women in her family, she realizes how "they always have to rely on someone," which leaves them battered, trapped, and betrayed:

My cousin, she just got married to this guy. He beats her. She's actually pregnant with his kid, but she knows she can't, she thinks she can do it on her own. And my aunt, well my godmother, she's with this guy. She knows, she has a kid by him, she knows he's cheating. You know her young daughter would come to her and say, "Mommy I saw daddy flirting with this girl." And he cheats on her. She's like, she's like, "I'm not gonna leave him because I can't pay our rent by myself." Yeah, my other cousin, she has two kids by this one guy. He was just in a serious motorcycle accident. I mean he was in a coma for three days. But he's recovering. And he, he actually knocked her two front teeth out, like early in the relationship. So now she has like those fake teeth.

Recovery is not just about not using drugs. She has tried to learn from her experiences and always be able to take care of herself—"I don't want my sister to end up like me. I don't want anyone to ever end up doing what I was doing. I don't want anyone in my family dancing just to get by. I don't want that. I don't want them having to rely on any guy."

Recently, she "officially cut my godmother off like, I told her I want nothing to do with her anymore. And so I don't talk to her anymore. And I think that's for the best. She's supposed to be like a big influence in my life, but she always had dudes in and out of the house." Eva shakes her head in disgust, as if shaking off the people in her life who broke her trust, disappointed her, violated her moral code, and let her down: "Her daughter would always come wake me up because she left the room, her mom's room. She stayed in the room with her mom. And she always heard her mom having sex." She has decided to no longer tolerate people like this in her life. Although Eva says that she would like to "help some of the people" she knew when she was using, "I noticed I'm getting taken advantage of. Yeah, every now and then. Like everyone will just hit me up out of nowhere, like do you want this, do you need something, or can you get me this? And so I stopped with that." Instead, she has decided to face life alone: "I'm one of those people that if it's not happening around me, I don't really care. I mean it's horrible what other people are going through. But if it's not affecting me . . . I think out of all the kids, my parents will tell you I'm the most independent. Like I don't need anybody to rely on."

Eva has not had any experience of being politically engaged or connected to others, and she reports that she has no knowledge of her parents or grandparents ever voting. We have the following terse conversation about voting:

JS: And how about politics? Do you follow politics at all? Do you vote?
E: No. I'm not into that.
JS: Do you think you will vote in November? [It is July 2016.]

E: No.

JS: How about your mom and dad? Do you remember them ever voting?

E: No.

JS: They are not political people?

E: No.

Eva does not believe in the integrity of the political system enough to spend her time engaging in it. For example, she is critical of the United States and of the blind patriotism that she believes characterizes the coal region. "Everyone says, oh you know, if you ask someone why they like America, they always say because it's free," she observes. "But like Canada is free. Europe is free. We're actually the lowest in everything. And you know, I think we're in twenty-fourth place for having the highest math scores. And it's just, America sucks. And I wanna be Canadian. I wanna live in Canada." She quickly backtracks: "Like I'm a proud American. But I would be a lot more proud if America really stood for something." She echoes the common theme of wanting to restore meaning to the word *America*—of wanting to believe that being American actually means being part of something bigger and more noble than herself.

Eva's distrust in the media, the government, men, and other people more generally, curtails all traditional forms of collective civic engagement. "You never know what you're being shown, so you can't judge. And there's always three sides to every story. There's one person's side, the other person's side, and then the truth. So it's, you don't know what's going on." She says dismissively, "I know a lot, but it doesn't affect me." Eva sees her own effort as the only force that matters in her success: "On the path that I'm taking, I think my future's gonna be pretty bright. I realize I'm one of those people that actually has to work for my future. I won't have it easy. So I need to do what I have to do to make my future the best."

Finding Common Ground

Over the last four chapters, we have examined how the different groups of people in this book—white working-class men, white working-class women, black and Latino men, and black and Latina women—create bridges between their life histories, experiences of suffering and renewal, and political worldviews. Each group puts forward markedly different interpretations of the past, assessments of the present, and predictions for the future, resulting in diverging expectations of what makes a worthy life. In chapter 6, I turn to examine what unites the different groups across race, birthplace, and gender: their disenchantment with mainstream social and political institutions, and their decisions to disable themselves as a larger political group. I explore the everyday practices and rituals that take the place of political engagement, diving into the self-help mantras and conspiracy theories that promote individual over collective efficacy. This willful isolation raises serious questions about the shared identities, alliances, and values upon which any kind of political mobilization might rest.

Democracy Denied

At just twenty-one years old, Austin Adinolfi, a pizza deliveryman, already takes a dim view of his own future. Austin is currently in his third year of a two-year associate's degree program and will graduate in a few months with about $45,000 in debt. "I'm doing a two-year program, but I'm going to be there for three because I switched for a semester and went to art, then switched back to what I was originally in. I'm in electrical," he sighs. "I feel like I could have done this without going to college," he adds with frustration. "I kinda regret it now just because it's a lot of money. I have friends that didn't go to college, they just went straight into the work force and they are just out there making money. They don't have anything to pay back. So I feel like I'm already starting behind rather than just with a clean slate." Austin condenses his philosophy toward life into the following reflection: "When you're a kid, you mostly get told the good things, you don't get told the bad things. You paint a picture that the world's a good place and then you grow up and realize it's not."

Austin's family story chronicles a long, multigenerational disengagement from social institutions and an accompanying loss of faith in American democracy. While his grandfather was a war hero, his own father, a nurse, received a dishonorable discharge from the air force because "when my pap [grandfather] was getting sick, they weren't letting him go see my pap so he got a dishonorable discharge because he just kinda left. He wanted to be with his dad until his last days." The family has not attended Catholic Mass, aside from weddings and funerals, since his grandmother passed away. His mother's business degree from a for-profit college did not lead to the kinds of opportunities she imagined. As Austin puts it, "They are in their forties and they are just now getting their loans paid off. My mom can't even get a job for what her degree is in, but she's still paying loans. That was why my mom was like, with art, are you going to be able to get a job and start paying back the loans?"

Austin grew up hearing about how his ancestors were "really poor. My grandpa used to always tell me how he would buy a pair of shoes that would last him three years." He believes that everyone deserves to have a stable life, no matter what kind of job they perform or what rung of the class ladder they occupy. He asserts that "college should be free," because "if you do go to school you're bettering yourself, you're doing something that's going to help provide for your community, help provide for where we live and everything." He supports raising the minimum wage: "As long as people are all trying, we need people working at McDonalds and fast-food places, so they need to be paid equal amounts so they can live. So they can afford a house or an apartment and a car to get to work and everything." Although Austin emphasizes that people not be allowed to take advantage of the system, he supports help for the "deserving." For instance, "if you are a single mom, you can't work because you have to take care of this kid. You should get help." Austin endorses decriminalizing marijuana and points to the devastating effects of drug convictions on youth—"Like how marijuana is classified as a Schedule 1 drug but there's no reported deaths from it. You take a kid in front of a judge who had a little weed and they say you either go to rehab or we put you in jail for a couple of months. So it's rehab or jail, both of them are negative."

In 2015, Austin is most drawn to Bernie Sanders, the Democratic primary candidate who identified as a Democratic Socialist, yet dismisses his chances as "unrealistic." Austin, who gets most of his political information from Twitter, plans to vote for "no one." I push him, asking, "If the election were tomorrow, who would you choose?" He resists: "I would probably write in a candidate. I don't trust anyone." This is because Austin expresses sheer disbelief that any political candidate would ever support his interests. With chilling cynicism, he proclaims: "Big money runs this country. They just serve whoever is in their pocket. We have a bunch of rich old people who do nothing half the year making decisions for everyone. If you think they'll take less so you can have more, you're ignorant. They keep us bickering amongst ourselves while they live above the law." He insists that "the government and the media put out news to get people going, to get them mad at another group of people because they get more ratings. Most of it is fueled towards money. Like the fake ads that come up with some fake news story to get you to click on it, a lot of people read those news stories now thinking it's the truth but it's not. It's something to get you to click on ads." He ultimately does not see any point in choosing a political party: "I just, we've had Democrat presidents, we've had Republican presidents, they've both done pretty much the same thing."[1]

Austin consciously separates himself from his father, a lifelong, blue-collar Democrat: "He's against conspiracy theories and all that, but I'm on the opposite side of the fence. Some of it doesn't add up so I feel like there is some kind of conspiracy behind it." Austin becomes especially heated when he discusses the attacks on September 11 that occurred when he was in elementary school. He muses: "If you watch some of the things, it doesn't add up. Like how the World

Trade Center just collapsed and they said it was due to like office fires but there weren't any planes near it. And it wasn't really reported in the news really, they might've mentioned it but it was all towards the Twin Towers that fell." He adds acerbically: "I feel a lot of people did make money after the start of the war in Iraq over oil and everything. It just so happens that they have all this oil, and now we're making money off of it?"

We end our conversation on the following grim note:

JS: What would you respond to someone who said the American Dream is dead?
AUSTIN: I'd probably agree.
JS: Who do you think killed it?
AUSTIN: Money. Money killed it.

From Allegiance to Alienation

In the 1950s, the political scientist Robert Lane set out to understand the political beliefs of working- and lower-middle-class men in Eastport, a small city on the Eastern seaboard of the United States. Most of the men Lane interviewed expressed allegiance: they believed that the American government operated on their behalf and that the rules of the game were both fair and effective. Lane chronicled a vibrant, robust sense of "we the people" among these men— although they might be powerless on an individual level, knowing that there were "millions like me" served to transmute them into "someone worth caring about" as a collective whole. These men believed that their social institutions were "positive, supportive, [and] nurturing."[2] Lane contended that allegiance serves an essential social function—that feeling like one mattered returned to men some of the pride and self-worth that industrial society "steals from him in other ways." Only a few men in his study were described as "alienated," defined as believing that the US government was not *their* government, seeing no possibility of changing the system through their own efforts, and viewing the rules of the game as unfair, rigged, and illegitimate.[3]

Throughout this book, working-class people who would fit Lane's criteria for allegiance are virtually nonexistent. In this chapter, I examine how working-class men and women in the coal region justify their political alienation. Freely letting go of patriotism, they negotiate and even break with the political traditions they grew up with. They scoff at the idea of their own efficacy in changing the system and also fundamentally believe that politicians have been bought off by powerful corporations. Unlike the men in Lane's study, many of the people in this book, especially the younger ones, feel a sense of security and pride when they are adamantly resisting any attempt to force them to believe that they live in a free, fair, and transparent democracy. Their ideal politicians end up being defined, as a last resort, simply as people who are not politicians.

Some scholars have suggested that the economic downturn of the Great Recession, and the issues of debt, immigration, and government regulation that it brought to the fore, might disrupt older political allegiances and spark the creation of new identities, solidarities, and divisions.[4] But "the people" can make democracy effective only to the extent that they can form associations based on a larger sense of "we."[5] Organizations channel existing identities by claiming to represent the interests of a larger group—such as when the United Mine Workers of America mobilized on behalf of "coal miners" across ethnic and religious divides—connecting their individual and personal struggles to broader, collective political identities and practices. For Austin and the other working-class people in this book, it is their deep condemnation of "the system" that unites them across their diverse experiences and backgrounds. Their disenchantment with mainstream political institutions—and the solitary re-enchantment that self-help and conspiracy theories offer—serves to fortify the echo chambers they build around themselves.[6]

Breaking with Tradition

Rachel Askey, a thirty-five-year-old white woman, remembers a mock presidential election in elementary school as her earliest experience of politics. "I went home to my grandmother, and I said, 'What am I? Am I a donkey or an elephant?'" she laughs. "And my Gran said, 'You're a goddamned donkey... and your goddamned grandfather will roll over in his grave if you're anything other than the donkey!'" Rachel's life history reveals a slow detachment from the civic and political institutions she grew up with. Learning to be distrustful, she displays a go-it-alone skepticism and rejection of "we the people," beginning in the most intimate relationships within the family and extending to a wide range of social institutions.[7] She provides an example of how the links between family, community, and political party have been severed across generations.

Rebecca works part-time as a certified recovery specialist at a drug and alcohol rehabilitation center. Gesturing toward her son, who is running around in the park, she says wryly: "If I wanted to leave his father, I couldn't, because I couldn't afford it." The only better-paying jobs that Rachel has found have lifting requirements above one hundred pounds. Although she put her resume on "Monster, Indeed.com," and applies "right from her phone," her life remains stagnant. She says flatly, "I always said I didn't want to live in a trailer, but then you just kind of have to suck it up."

Her mother, a secretary, and her father, a football coach, split up in a violent confrontation when Rachel was four: "He strangled our dog and killed our dog, and then called my mom at work and said, 'Come home, your dog's dead in the yard, come get your fucking dog out of the yard,' or whatever." For a while, the children saw their father every other weekend, but these visits ended after he punched her brother in the face. Rachel muses: "Crazy things happened, and the police were never called. I don't quite understand it. I don't know if that's just how . . . things are different now, but I think especially in the '80s, nobody wanted the neighborhood talking about them, so they wouldn't call the police. They were trying to avoid that at all costs."

Rachel, her mother, and her brother shared a one-bedroom apartment where Rachel was forced to sleep in the hallway. She describes her mother as "not a good mother":

> She has a gambling addiction. She had a shopping addiction. I re-member not eating. I remember her coming home from work, and I could see the McDonald's garbage in the car and smell it and being starving, and her being like, "Tough shit." Actually, I remember when I was little—it's one of my main memories of being hungry—I couldn't reach the spigot to get water, so I found a bottle of Dimetapp [cold medicine], and I drank the Dimetapp, because I was thirsty. I don't re-member what happened after.

Both Rachel and her brother experimented with alcohol and illegal drugs in high school. "Definitely pills were my favorite, because it was just easy. You just pop a pill and you feel better," she remembers longingly. She also references the infamous local doctor who would prescribe opiate painkillers and diet pills to her friends. "I used to think, in my opinion, the doctor is a very nice man, and I thought he's easily manipulated, and I thought that maybe he didn't realize the monsters he was creating," she ponders. "But now I think he knows and it's a money thing."

Rachel's father committed suicide when she was nineteen. Although she was "already using, when my dad committed suicide, that's when it was full-blown addiction." For the next twelve years, even while she held down a job at a dis-count tobacco store, she was either "so high you don't want to move, or you're so sick you don't want to move." Her addiction led her to occasionally use heroin: "Then what happened is, pills got really expensive and were harder to find, and heroin was around and cheaper and easier, accessible, so I did it here and there, but it was never my drug of choice." Rachel attributes her decade-long addiction to unresolved family trauma:

> I know myself, and a lot of other addicts I know, if you have any trauma in your past or in your life, once you take an opiate, it's like for the first time in your life you're numb from that, and you don't have to think about it, and it's in some ways an escape, but after you take them for a little while, you become physically addicted to it where you're ill if you don't have it. You can't function if you don't have it.

Four years ago, she heard people talking about "this medication called Suboxone," and hoped she might finally free herself of her addiction: "I tried to call and get on Suboxone, and that didn't work out. At the time, there was a two-year waiting list to get in, and a lot of the doctors were taking cash, cash only." Complaining that it was "even more expensive to get the medication than your habit between the costs of doctor's visits and the prescription," Rachel dismisses this treatment as "basically a money-making racket."

Rachel acquired Medical Assistance for Workers with Disabilities (MAWD) and enrolled in a methadone maintenance clinic, where she went for help every day for several months. She speaks with awe and gratitude about her experience: "You have to build trust. It's responsibility. I know when I started, I had to do an hour of therapy a week, and then an hour-and-a-half of group therapy a week, and it changed my life. It's like you have the tools you need to survive." Although Rachel feels "like shit, just tired and worn down," she is proud to have been sober for four years. Cigarettes remain the "only monkey on my back. I wish I could quit and it is so expensive. Smoking just does awful things to our bodies, and so, no, I don't feel healthy."

Rachel and her son's father, a mechanic, "don't have the greatest relationship," and marriage is out of the question for her. "Even his sister and brother-in-law, they were together for twenty-five years, and then they got married, and I want to say within a couple of months he was cheating on her with women on Facebook," she shudders. "And he was this loyal, devoted husband, and then once you put that label of marriage on it . . . marriage kind of scares me!" Rachel finds her boyfriend to be a perpetual disappointment, as he spends most of his time with his son watching television in the other room—"He's not the kind of dad that plays catch with their son and does stuff with him." She sighs. "When I was pregnant, he was like, I'm going to be the greatest dad ever, and I'm going to do this and that, and none of that happened. He blames his childhood. There's lots of stuff that happened to him when he was little, or the way he was treated when he was little, because he has a messed-up situation himself." She adds dismissively: "He talked a good game."

Her methadone maintenance group is the only voluntary source of social interaction with others that she trusts and feels grateful for. But her doctors, her partner, her parents, the police—all of these formal sources of care have failed to live up to their duties. She summarizes: "Trust has to be earned, but it's tough. I think that's just because of my life and the things that I've seen and been through. It's hard to trust people. I've been fucked over a lot." Rachel adds organized religion to the list—although she received all the Catholic sacraments from baptism to confirmation, she stopped attending Mass and believes "I can speak to the higher power myself or confess my sins to myself." She separates herself from earlier generations, who believed wholeheartedly in the goodness of the clergy: "Even my grandmother and stuff, they would treat a priest like he was a king. You have to tell him your deepest, darkest secrets and sins, and I could see how they can use that to take advantage of children. It kind of poisoned it."

Rachel possesses a rich knowledge of her family past. She recites: "My great-great-grandfather, when he moved here, was a coal miner, and then my grandfather and his brothers were coal miners, and my grandmother's first husband, my mother's father, and my grandmother's dad was a coal miner." Her historical analysis of her family's mining history is infused with the politics she was raised on. She recounts: "I know that my grandfather had black lung and died from that. I know he died pretty young, I want to say maybe in his early thirties. I mean, it was nothing heroic, no one being trapped or anything like that, but I do know that it was very difficult. I know they had to buy their stuff from the company store, so they were kind of a slave to the coal company." She continues: "And I know a lot of people were conned out of their land by the coal companies. The companies were greedy."

Rachel is a registered Democrat and attests to having voted for Barack Obama for president twice. In late July 2016, she is gravely disappointed with Hillary Clinton's victory over Bernie Sanders as the Democratic nominee for president.

> I love Bernie Sanders. He's such a good guy, and he's the only candidate that I really felt was sticking up for people like myself, and I used to love Hillary Clinton. I used to love her, and one of my big things was universal health care. We're one of the only countries in the world that make our citizens pay for health care, and it should be our human right. It should be put in with our taxes, and when she was married to Bill when he was president, she would go speak out for universal health care, and then once he got a huge donation from Humana, the one health care company, she changed her tune, and all of a sudden, it was back to this free market of health care, and it really upset me. When I found out more about the money she was getting from Goldman Sachs and other banks and stuff like that, and I learned that stuff from Michael Moore movies, not even from Bernie or anything like that . . . I've known this stuff for years, but it makes me feel like she can be bought and she can

be swayed with money, and I don't like that, where I felt like Bernie had people from here's best interests at heart.

Rachel believes health care coverage should be universal and paid for "with our taxes"—a starkly different vision from the "money-making racket" that she confronted when she desperately needed treatment. Rachel links Hillary Clinton to her husband, Bill Clinton, suggesting that "when she was married to Bill when he was president," she was more effective and sincere. Since then, Rachel frames Hillary Clinton as increasingly corrupt, "changing her tune" and endorsing a "free market of health care" as she was "bought" and "swayed by money."

Rachel remains critical of economic inequality and does not cast blame on people who depend on food stamps or Medicaid. She asserts: "My boyfriend was making $7 an hour, and this was in 2006, and our gross was $25 above the poverty line, and we got denied. It's tough. I don't fault people for needing food stamps. I need them, and I can't get them." She decides, "You're always going to have people that take advantage of whatever system, so I don't care." She understands her own life circumstances as fundamentally shaped by inequalities of resources like money and knowledge: "There's all these things that if I would have known, my life would have been so much different. People that I see from this area that have gotten out and done well were people that came from well-to-do families, and they had their college paid for, and they didn't have to worry about working when they were in college." She sounds more mournful than bitter when she reflects on the American Dream: "I think if people are in the right place at the right time, coming from a poverty-stricken area, they can follow their dreams. But I know even for myself, I didn't have anyone to show me how to fill out college applications. I didn't have anybody to show me how to fill out loan paperwork. No one ever taught me that credit was important." She hopes her own son will graduate from college so that he might be able do better than his own parents: "I don't think I'll ever be able to have a college fund or be able to save money for him, but I help him with his homework and help him do good in school."

With this tepid endorsement of the future, Rachel leaned toward not voting in November 2016, and was not sure if she even believes in democracy at all anymore. She sighed: "I just think people around here just aren't very smart." To express her frustration, she summoned an example from popular culture:

> I think we live in a very idiotic society. I don't know if you've ever seen the movie, *Idiocracy*. It's a movie from the early 2000s. Luke Wilson's in it. It's a comedy. At the time, it seemed very dumb. It's about the future, and in the future this society is so dumb that this average guy, Luke Wilson from the past, is the smartest guy in the world, and they're

watering plants with Gatorade. They have a professional wrestler as their president, and it's almost like we're becoming . . . it's like this movie predicted the future, like we're just getting dumber and dumber. I even notice with music, it just gets dumber and dumber.

When Rachel engages with politics, she is completely removed from real people—that is, she has no one to talk to or debate with around her, and no vehicle for collective action, despite her sharp critiques of the world around her. Hollywood's rendering of the problem of idiotic citizens confirms the disappointing, senseless world she sees around her.[8] Absorbing fictional accounts, yet detached from other people in the same precarious situation, she becomes a critical yet passive observer of politics.

The Lure of Conspiracy

In contrast to Rachel's weary resignation, the only time I heard passion and excitement in discussions of politics was on the topic of government conspiracies. Belief in conspiracies, as Jesse Walker writes in *The United States of Paranoia*, may "sa[y] something true about the anxieties and experiences of the people who believe and repeat it, even if it says nothing about the objects of the theory itself."[9] Betrayed by institutions, detached from political and religious organizations, and distrustful of government, young working-class adults briefly lit up, their faces flushed, words flowing quickly, when they proved to me that they could not be fooled by the illusion of democracy.

Scholars in the mid-twentieth century tended to characterize people who believe in conspiracy theories as psychologically abnormal or even delusional.[10] But the political scientist Michael Barkun argues that "fringe ideas" have spread rapidly to the American mainstream in the late twentieth and early twenty-first century.[11] New forms of social media have allowed conspiracy theories to break out of isolated subcultures, transforming previously stigmatized knowledge (e.g., "the government created AIDS") into widely available and accessible ideas. There is widespread favorable reception of conspiracy theories in the United States today. For instance, 54.3 percent of Americans in a 2016 Chapman University survey agreed or strongly agreed with the statement that the government is concealing information about the attacks on 9/11. One-third of people surveyed believe, as many of the men in earlier chapters do, in conspiracies surrounding Obama's birth certificate and the origin of the AIDS virus.[12] Conspiracy theories flourish when people feel as if they are under threat.[13] In this mode of thinking, nothing happens by accident, nothing is as it seems, and everything is interconnected.[14]

When I arrived at Graham Hendry's mother's white frame house on the morning of election day, Graham is sitting in a rocking chair on the porch, chain-smoking Newport Menthols. Graham is twenty-five-years-old, white, and has been smoking since he was nine. He is bleary-eyed from pulling the night shift at the "short-staffed" nursing home where he "takes care of like thirty people" by himself. He calls his job "very rewarding" but "doesn't pay well right now." He is currently in community college "for the RN though so I'll be doing well. In about a year I'll graduate."

When I pull up to his house, I am wearing my "I Voted" sticker, having just cast my ballot at the local library before driving to the coal region. Our conversation does not begin auspiciously. His eyes flicker disdainfully over my sticker.

GRAHAM HENDRY: This election doesn't matter, it's not the people's choice, it's *their* choice, you know what I mean?

JS (LAUGHS): Maybe I'll take my sticker off after this conversation.

GH (NOT AMUSED): I'd advise it. I wouldn't be proud of it, no offense.

JS: What makes you think that?

GH: You don't see that yourself? Are you paying attention to what's going on around you?

Graham tells me about his childhood, when his grandfather, a coal miner, "would go to pick me and my sister up, just like that, he used to throw eight-gallon buckets of coal over a twenty-foot wall, strong guy." Although Graham is young, he still harkens back to a more vibrant past: "Yeah, it's crazy how it changes like that. Economy was better, like we had three movie theaters. I think it was, yeah, three movie theaters in town, we had all those big stores, JC Penny's and stuff like that."

After his father, a truck-driver, died of a heart attack when he was nine, Graham began smoking, getting in fights, and drinking. He spent time in juvie and believes he "got a shitty education" in the coal region. He lives with his mother, who has a two-year nursing degree, aside from an earlier brief stint living in an $800-a-month apartment with his ex-girlfriend. "Yeah, cuz minimum wage, you have to get government assistance to live off of minimum wage. Cuz right now I don't get paid that much, that's why I'm fortunate at my mom's house right now," he admits.

Graham believes that people with power are focused on making money instead of on doing what is right. Taking the example of police officers, he fumes: "I don't trust cops, I hate cops. Like, 'I have this badge so I can do what I want in this situation' kinda." He says indignantly: "Back in the day, they weren't trying to make money. If you were drunk, they'd take you home and drop you off, let your parents deal with you, you know what I mean? Now they're all about their money and they're ruining kids' lives." His words drip with sarcasm: "They say, 'I'm here to help you.' Yeah, give me something on my record and a fine, that's really helping me guy, you know what I mean? We're doing the same shit you were doing when you were a kid and you were probably younger doing it. They take power in their own hands, you know what I mean? It's like a complex, a god complex," he says heatedly.

Graham has "lost three friends in four months, like brothers," from the heroin epidemic. "One was my best friend my whole life. I lost him. That killed me. He was seven days younger than me. We had our birthdays together every year. I went to his mother's daycare." He targets the drug manufacturers and their limitless greed: "These people don't care about people's lives. They're putting Fentanyl in the shit, it's killing them." Graham then laughs about how he almost got into a fight just this morning when a passerby suggested he turn down the music in his car: "I am just a bad kid. Someone's gonna start, I am gonna finish it, that's just how it was. I still am like that too. I almost got in a fist fight today, this morning." He distrusts everyone. "I don't want people to know what I'm doing," he explains. "That's why I don't even have a Facebook. I'm like the only person I know that doesn't have a Facebook." While he was raised Catholic, he no longer believes in organized religion—"I believe in, well, church is man-made. Like if I can pray to my god right here, you know what I mean, I don't need to go to the church."

Graham unabashedly denies that the United States is a democracy. He insists that voting is simply a shield for a totalitarian global regime:

> We're not, it's funny cuz we actually fund wars on countries that aren't a democracy. When we're the least democracy out of all of them. Like Iran is more of a democracy than us. And they're on the axis of evil. They're a direct democracy, every vote matters in Iran. Here? Who the hell would even pick these two people? Like what the hell's going on? It's just subversion. Propaganda. It's not, I don't know. Sorry if you trust your government . . . but I mean we're the biggest terrorists in the world. What you're hearing going on in Syria right now, that wouldn't be going on if it wasn't for us impeding on everyone's well-being. We have a base in every country in the world. You know that, right? I think that's fascist. We're more fascist than democracy, but yeah. Not to be pessimistic here.

Graham's tone shifts rapidly from condescending to impassioned to weary. He repeatedly stops to ask me if I know what he is talking about, if I am informed, using the phrase "You know that, right?" as if to assert his unique mastery over secret, obscure information. He frames his knowledge as a burden: "When I first started like getting real deep into this stuff like, I was like ignorance is bliss right now, like I wish I didn't know this stuff." He casts himself as a long-suffering truth-teller who refuses to be complacent. "It's not conspiracy theory, it's conspiracy factual," he insists.

Graham has never voted, nor has he registered to vote. "I don't wanna get personal taxes. You know, they tax you for that. For registering," he informs me. He continues contemptuously: "Would you really think any of these two people [Trump and Clinton] are a good choice? Why the hell are we picking sides like that. Hell no, I am not voting today." When I push him to choose a candidate, he remains adamant: "I wouldn't, I'd say shoot me. You're gonna make me do something I don't wanna do." Among the other young people whom I interviewed, common answers to this question included "I'm shooting myself," "I'm shooting them both," or "I would write in a candidate." Compromise is unthinkable.

Graham connects his political alienation to his distrust of a global financial elite. "The thing is though, you gotta remember, you ever hear of like J. P. Morgan, Rothschild, the elitists. One percentile?" he asks. I nod. "You ever hear of Cecil Rhodes? Look up Cecil Rhodes when you go home. Learn about him," he instructs. "You know what a Freemason is, right? He brought the round tables from England over to here. I mean we actually have a Masonic lodge in every town, you ever notice that? Isn't that a little weird to you? I don't know, it just doesn't add up to me." He declares passionately:

> *They* run this country. The president's just a figurehead, it's like the queen of England. It doesn't matter. What, all they have is veto power and declaration of war. That's all the president can do. And by the way, Hillary killed over half a million children just so you know. Back in Iraq. Did you know about that? I don't remember the exact way they did it, she did it. Her and Madeline Albright, our secretary of state. And she actually released the documents on the Contra scandal.

As he moves rapidly from topic to topic, I ask him why all of these conspiracies exist. "Money," he says simply. "You ever heard of the petrodollar? In the 1970s, we were funding that shitty war in Vietnam. All the countries wanted their gold back. So we had nothing to back our currency. So we took the other route, the petrodollar, oil," he asserts. As he explains it, the United States removed the dollar from the gold standard and struck a deal with Saudi Arabia to standardize oil prices in US dollars, thus securing the American dollar as the world's dominant currency. As global energy markets fluctuate, threatening the US global economic hegemony, Graham points out: "The best place to control it is Iraq, you know what I mean?" He pauses, waits a moment, and looks at me incredulously. "I mean you don't see like . . . you don't really believe in 9/11?"

After confirming he is not "on a time limit with this interview," he unleashes his analysis of the terrorist attacks on the United States on the morning of September 11. He was in fifth grade at the time. He asserts: "You look at 9/11, you'll see building 7 fall, and this lady's doing the report, on the news, you can look it up on YouTube. I'm surprised it's even on the internet. And you can see the building still standing. She's saying the building just fell, you'll hear building 7 was behind the Twin Towers, cuz that collapsed too. Demolition-style." He concludes: "No building that gets hit by an object is gonna fall like that. Momentum and physics would make it, you know, it doesn't make sense. I don't know. How do you feel about it?" I stammer: "I've never even thought of it this way before." He shrugs. "Really? It's probably a good thing you don't."

Graham wants Americans to "wake up" to the treachery practiced by their government: "Like you ever heard of the term *subversion*? They make us look left while they move to the middle." His suspicion leads him to speak out against discriminatory treatment based on race, religion, or ethnicity. For example, Graham's comprehensive vision of a scheming "they" extends to FEMA, the Federal Emergency Management Agency, which he suspects is constructing concentration camps for racial minorities. "There's 808 FEMA camps in the United States," he reports. "And they all have railroads going into them and stuff like that. And they have these big silos and I feel like eugenics is gonna happen. They're gonna get everyone outside of the Aryan race, try to cleanse the world again. Like a race war."

Graham glibly dismisses a series of national tragedies—the Sandy Hook Elementary School shootings in Connecticut, the Boston Marathon bombing—as "a bunch of bullshit. The Sandy Hook obituaries were made before the situation even happened. The Boston bombing, if terrorists were really gonna attack us, you'd think they'd kill more than two people." He suspects that President Obama manufactured these events to "take the heat off of him and try to pull this shit so he can take the extended clips away. You know what extended clip is, right? He's trying to take our arms away. Once Hillary gets in, say goodbye. I'm surprised they're [extended clips] still here."

Graham speaks repeatedly of an evil, malignant "they" that controls the government. He is particularly concerned with chemicals in the air and water supply that allow the government to control people's minds, providing the following examples offhand:

> You ever see, when you were a kid you watched a plane go by, didn't the cloud dissipate real quick? You'll see those freaking trails up there for hours now. That's not just fumes, that's chemicals up there.
>
> You use like toothpaste with fluoride in it, stuff like that. Don't let your kids use that. Fluoride actually calcifies your pineal gland. And

that's a big thing they're trying to do. Aluminum oxides in your deodorant, that's what's in the air too. It's mind control pretty much. Your pineal grand is pretty much your third eye, you ever heard of that one before?

After these last pronouncements, he scrutinizes my face for a reaction: "I'm not weird, I'm just educated. Knowledge is power, my friend." Veering wildly from the Left to the Right and back again, he denounces the "mainstream media"—"don't trust the media. All the news like every Fox, NBC, they're all bought out by major corporations. I go to libraries and stuff like that, yeah. You can't change a book. You can't change things that's already written in print, remember that. You can manipulate stuff online, you know what I mean?"

According to a 2016 Gallup poll, Americans' trust and confidence in the mass media "to report the news fully, accurately and fairly" had dropped to its lowest level in Gallup polling history, with merely 32 percent saying they have a great deal or fair amount of trust in the media. More than half of Americans today acquire information from personalized social media news feeds that are curated based on what someone "like you" tends to like. Jettisoning the checks and balances on information that are essential to a well-functioning democracy, these social media echo chambers exacerbate political polarization and self-insulation. Many of us live in our own newsfeeds, immune from diverse perspectives, cut off from common experiences with each other. In such instances, "place-based communities" are supplanted by "interest-based communities"—as evidenced when Graham relies on his phone to eagerly investigate conspiracy theories in online communities on his own.[15]

Graham contends that "this election doesn't matter, it's not the people's choice." He adds despondently: "The only way anything's gonna change is gonna be a bloodbath. They have us by the balls pretty much. We'd have to kill all the old heads in office." Noting the flag flying above his mother's porch, he clarifies: "We're for our people, though, we're not for our government."

You Can Heal Your Heart

Like Graham and Rebecca, Jordan Madera, twenty-six, retreats from the public sphere. She attempts to manage the instability of her life by creating self-healing strategies. She tells a story of self-transformation through suffering—forging a temporary sense of control over the chaos of her life through yoga, reading self-help books, or Pinterest. Jordan was born in Puerto Rico and grew up in western Massachusetts. Her father abandoned the family when she was two, and her mother has been married and divorced twice since. Jordan describes the neighborhood she grew up in as surrounded by "drugs and women who like sell themselves." Jordan's mother eventually was able to buy a duplex in western Massachusetts and began renting out half of it to other family members. They joined a Pentecostal community that she now looks back on as a cult—"you're sheltered; you can't go to the movies. You can't do a lot of stuff; they say that it's worldly. Basically you stick within the church. We weren't allowed to like, well girls aren't allowed to cut their hair, you can't get piercings, you can't wear pants." Evoking the sense of social unmooring, she shrugs: "Yeah, I've like broken it all. I had a child out of wedlock, I'm not married, I lost my virginity before getting married. Like you're not supposed to smoke, you're not supposed to drink, you're not supposed to party."

Despite her early love of reading and her track record of "doing good in school," Jordan's life came to a screeching halt when she was arrested at a party at a friend's house where some of the kids were using heroin (she says she was not). She was convicted of heroin possession and sentenced to the maximum one year in jail. She left high school to serve her time. "It was my first charge ever. They didn't care that I was like doing good in school or nothing," she reflects. "Being in the wrong place at the wrong time kinda thing."

When she was released, she earned a GED and met her current boyfriend, the father of their two-year old daughter. As his mother was moving to the coal region to start a catering business, they decided to follow. She explains:

> I came out here to get away. I came out here to start fresh. Everything. Life. And I wasn't even gonna stay out here long, it was more like, the cost of living out here is super cheap compared to the city where I'm from. So I figured, you know, if I come out here, get myself situated, I had a lot of shit that I was like I just need to get myself together. I thought Coal Brook would be a stepping stone, I'd stay out here for at least a year or two. Save money, save money, and then just leave. And then I got pregnant and we just stayed here. And we've been here since.

Jordan was turned down for several jobs in the area. When she applied to work at one grocery store, she was subjected to references to *The Help*, a film about African American women in the 1960s who work as maids in white households in Jackson, Mississippi: "We had asked the manager like what positions are available, and he just looked at me and was like, well if you just put *The* fuckin' *Help*, you might get a job." At a bar, Jordan reports, "They were like, straight up was like, 'It's not that I wouldn't hire you,' they were like, 'My manager's not gonna hire you, you're not white.'" She finally landed a job working at a customer service call center from Sunday through Thursday, 7 a.m. to 3:30 p.m., making

$10.50 an hour. She and her boyfriend rent a $425-a-month apartment, and he cares for the baby while she is at work and does "odd jobs" on the side. She was denied a housing voucher at the office in Coal Brook. "Even when I didn't have a job they wouldn't give it to me," she says angrily. "When I was pregnant they wouldn't give it to me. Because of the charge that I had. Even though it's a misdemeanor and it's been more than five years. I honestly believe like it has a lot to do with like race down there."[16]

Jordan states that "jail was a day in the park compared to a lot of the other things that I've been through. I mean I've been through enough shit that I just feel like I have no choice but to be all right with it, even with things that I can't accept or come to accept or deal with." Although she and her boyfriend are technically together, and share their household with their daughter, he recently got another woman pregnant. She lives about fifteen minutes away. Jordan is devastated. "I don't know what the fuck we're doing anymore. I just don't know how to deal with it. I wouldn't wanna marry somebody who's not gonna commit to me and only me." She asks desperately: "If you're gonna give yourself to someone else in a way that you only should give away yourself to your partner, what the fuck does it even matter?"

Nonetheless, Jordan attributes many of her relationship troubles to her own untreated psychological disorders—disorders that stem, in her eyes, from the unhealed traumas of her life. She explains: "I just, just don't deal with shit. How I deal with it, when I deal with it, I snap, we argue. I just won't deal with it to the point that I just shut it off and then that's it, it's just off. And that becomes . . . we do a lot of silent treatment. There's nothing worse than not saying what needs to be said and lingering in the abyss of silence."

> I used to go to a therapist when I lived in Massachusetts. I have a whole bunch of shit. I've been through a lotta shit and I don't know, they say I've experienced trauma, post-traumatic stress. But I had to stop going cuz I just felt like she pushed the hard limits. She had me doing like this therapy which unlocked a lot of shit that I just didn't wanna remember and I blocked out. So maybe like worse but better at the same time if that makes sense?

Jordan diagnoses herself as emotionally broken by her past: "I know that I need help now, bad. But they just don't have it out here."

She searches for activities that serve the same function as going to therapy—shopping, cooking, reading—and self-medicates with alcohol when those fail. She elaborates: "Like literature, it's just a good way to express yourself, just to clear your mind of the madness. One book is *You Can Heal Your Heart*. And *The Power of Now*. So good. It definitely keeps you focused." These best-selling books from the self-help genre promise readers to teach them how to live focused on the present moment, avoiding painful or worrisome thoughts of the past or future, and helping them to find inner peace and the courage to go on. They "clear [her] mind of the madness." The other book she names as a favorite is *Random Family*, an investigative journalist's poignant account of a poor urban community and their intimate struggles with drugs, violence, family conflict, relationships, and childrearing.[17] Praising *Random Family*, a book that echoes many of the traumas of her own life, she says wistfully: "I wanna write a book like that someday. I read it in a day. It's a really good book. I couldn't put it down, that's a really good book."

Jordan is struggling to build a family with a man she can't trust in a town that mocks and rejects her. Invoking the language of therapy, Jordan discusses her online shopping habit as a temporary cure for her troubled soul. "Cuz I retail, I do retail therapy," she explains. "I like to shop my feelings away. Online. Online shopping is, I went like when I first found out about everything, I think that was like the first month and a half, I would get shit shipped here like every day. I like bought so much shit. I spent a lot of money." She explains her strategy of coping this way:

> But that's how I've always dealt with shit. I just feel like when you feel shitty you buy shit and you make yourself feel pretty and that's it. And you get drunk and you just get over it. You just keep drinking till you are over it. But I can't be like that no more cuz I have my daughter. So I just buy lots of shit. I don't know, just, I don't know how to deal with something so hurtful and then still live with the person, it's so hard. I'm barely holding on, it's just . . . [*trails off*]

Her routine—"Cook, drink wine, Pinterest, and Tasty videos"—gets her through the day when survival feels unbearable and she "lingers in the abyss." The only time during our conversation that she becomes energized is when she shares her favorite recently discovered recipe: "Do you like mozzarella chicken? You take like chicken cutlets, like the big ones, you cut it like this. And you season it however you want. And when you cut it, like that you stick parmesan cheese in it. You close it, you dip it in flour, egg, flour. Then you put the crumbs on it. You fry it. *It's the closest thing to therapy.*"

Jordan pays little attention to politics. She first deflects my questions by laughing, "Oh, we shouldn't talk about politics." When I persist, she reluctantly shares her opinions about the candidates in just a few sentences by referring to the racism of the coal region: "Trump? He basically, I just feel like honestly if you're voting for Trump, it's like, Trump should just basically have like the KKK as his shit. Like I just feel like that shit's all over the place here." When I ask if she would vote for Clinton, the Democratic candidate, she continues contemptuously: "And then Hillary . . . I'm not really into Republican or Democrat. It's more just like what do you have to offer, like how are you gonna make us any better?" She says scornfully: "I'm not voting. I've never voted. I was so hyped to vote this year, but I'm just like, what the hell are we voting for? We're fucked." But she also admits that, truthfully, she has little mental energy left for thinking about politics: "I haven't been like following it lately. I just been wrapped up in my own life's bullshit lately."

The therapeutic self—inwardly directed, preoccupied with its own healing and transformation—would seem to stymie civic obligation and collective action. The emphasis on self-change renders structural barriers into individual obstacles that must be overcome through willpower rather than collective action, detaching the suffering of personal life from its social and political roots.[18] In Jordan's story, recipes for mozzarella chicken become a quick fix for despair, and the idea of collectively working to remove the causes of suffering in the first place does not even occur to her. Jordan herself is fully cognizant of using online shopping and wine as a stopgap, but sees no other viable strategy for wrenching herself back from the "abyss."

Disengagement as a Moral Choice

While Jordan devours self-help and Graham delights in conspiracy theories, other young adults frame their political disengagement as a statement of personal resilience. William Lewis, a twenty-four-year-old black man who builds concrete beams used for bridge construction, insists that he cannot be swayed by external forces, including politics, and views control over his own life circumstances as a necessary part of survival. William's grandfather migrated from Mississippi to the coal region in the 1950s and found a job working in construction. Throughout his childhood William's father worked round-the-clock shifts as a cook at a casual dining restaurant. He has not seen his mother since he was two. "When my dad first had me, they were into drugs," he recounts. "My dad gave up drugs to take care of me, my mom didn't want to, she took me into a crack house. My dad broke into the house and stole me from the house and took me to the hospital cuz I had pneumonia." Amid this family turmoil, William pinned his hopes on a career in professional sports and excelled in football, wrestling, and baseball in school. His father had also harbored dreams of a football career, but could not play college football because of a career-ending shoulder injury.

When he was sixteen, William and his father moved abruptly from one town in the coal region to another after William encountered "legal trouble": "There was a messed up situation, like I ended up getting a felony charge when I was in high school and then they told me I couldn't play sports for the rest of the year." He elaborates:

w: These kids broke in a house, I stood outside, I didn't want nothing to do with it, and then they ended up, they didn't get in trouble, they said that I was the lookout and everything. So kinda screwed me over. There was a kid at a party who stole diamond earrings off of a chick, the cops came, and he still got to play.

js: Was he white?

w: Yeah. So Dad eventually said, "Forget it, let's move." So I ended up missing football season that year and then I came and wrestled for Coal Brook. It was all right. I don't regret any of it.

"Actually," he reflects, "the only reason I wrestled was a racist situation. I played basketball up until seventh grade, I tried out for the seventh- and eighth-grade team and me and this other kid, a black kid, we were awesome at the tryouts, then the coach cut us. Then I was like, I can't not play sports. So then I went out for wrestling." William "couldn't go out with certain girls cuz their parents was racist, I couldn't hang out with certain kids cuz their parents was racist." When he was in ninth grade, he was arrested for selling marijuana but not convicted: "I ended up not getting in trouble for it cuz they couldn't prove nothing about it. They kind of just wanted to slander my name. That's what the cop pretty much said when he arrested me. But it was front page. Stand-out athlete caught in drug bust."

William takes responsibility for his downward spiral into heroin. "I ended up getting in trouble again here my senior year. That's the thing, there's like a quote, 'If nothing changes, nothing changes.' So if you don't change nothing about yourself, you're going to end up doing the same thing. So what I did was just find the same people, just different faces." He explains: "I became opiate-dependent, on opiates like Percocet, Vicodin, and stuff like that. I eventually ended up doing heroin, and I sold heroin after I graduated to support my habit and then I went, and then I got arrested. Heroin isn't a drug you can just do and stop and walk away from. There's not many people out there that have done it and walked away from it."

William describes the confidential informant system that led to his arrest as "so ass backwards" because it puts addicts in need of treatment "back on the street" and enables them to keep using. He condemns the police for trying to "arrest their way out of the heroin epidemic": "There are no actual drug dealers, most of the people are just selling to support a habit that they have. So, and the police know that, they just never try to get no one help."

William is currently in his third year of drug court, an "intense form of proba-tion" that he chose over "going upstate," that is supposed to help him "do some type of work on myself." He elaborates: "Like the first phase, when you're in phase 1 you have to go to get a urine test every week, you do outpatient rehab, you have to go to court every week. I'm in the third phase now. I've been in drug court for over two years now. I'll be done with drug court and probation April next year. And I just go up and take a urine test once a month and go to drug court once a month." He describes the weekly urine tests and meetings with a counselor as "definitely helpful, you need that accountability at first to get clean, you know. Definitely helped." He smokes a pack of cigarettes per day but is not using any other drugs.

His girlfriend, a white longtime resident of the region who is also recovering from heroin addiction, recently gave birth to their daughter. For the first time, he feels optimistic about the future. He wants to get married immediately and assume full responsibility for the household bills. William currently works six nights a week and is hoping to start training on the forklift, which would mean an increase in pay to $18 an hour. But she wants to hold off—"she gets help [med-ical assistance and WIC] now with the baby and stuff, and I could do it, every-thing, like I want to put her on my medical and stuff. But she is like, 'Why? It is extra money.'" He is frustrated by her refusal to get married, especially when the priest at her father's church "found out she was pregnant and that we lived together, he said she couldn't take Communion no more."

Like Jordan in chapter 5, William directs his energy toward managing his own feelings and reactions, telling a story of self-healing and self-change. He says ear-nestly: "I play music, that's one of the biggest things I do. To me keeping healthy means to play music, work, know I'm able to support a family, help around the house as best as I can, and help my girlfriend. I actually worked hard on myself. Like I said before, if nothing changes, nothing changes. So if nothing changed inside of me before I came home, nothing would have changed when I came home." Avoiding "negative" interactions with other people is crucial to his journey of self-management. "Addiction's a powerful thing, you can feed off of someone's negativity," he remarks. "If they're living an unhealthy lifestyle, that can be something I would just feed off of that that would eventually grow into me using." Isolation becomes a strategy for self-protection.

William has "no intention to vote. I don't see no point in voting. I can't, I think it's two years until I'm off probation, but either way I wouldn't vote." He believes unambiguously that "it's rigged or they're going to make whoever they want to be president." He gets all of his information from social media and his girlfriend's father, a vocal Trump supporter. He sighs: "Everything's just all screwed, you know. The government just wants money, so everything comes down to money." Unprompted, he adds: "Cuz all, like all businesses are corrupt in one way or another. They pretty much pay the government to leave them alone. So our country is ran by the government and big business. Which isn't worried about the small guy." William does not believe that either the government or large corporations operate in the interests of the "small guy" and has no faith in the existence of a larger "we" or common good: "like big corporations and big businesses, instead of just having . . . cuz it's cheaper to get something from China than it is to have a factory in the United States. No one's ever worried about America, they just worried about their pocket."

When I ask him if he is proud to be an American, he replies with a lukewarm: "Eh, I guess." He pauses to reconsider. Like Graham, he makes a clear distinction between the government and the people: "But . . . see when I hear we're proud to be an American, like I feel like, you're saying you're proud of our government, which I'm not. So for me to say that, it'd probably be like . . . to be proud of it would be a false sense of pride." If William were forced to choose a candidate—Trump versus Clinton—"It probably would end up being Trump. Cuz he's a businessman." Although it may seem contradictory to denounce politics as being too influenced by big business on the one hand, and then support a famous wealthy businessman on the other, William frames this decision as a vote for the small guy. "Trump's really not like, he didn't grow up in, like all them have a background of being involved in politics, you know? He just wants to take out the bigger people. Which is right, all the big organizations, he wants to split them up. Cuz they take out all the small people."

The promise of an outsider is appealing, yet not appealing enough to pull him toward the polls. For William, change remains an internal battle—"it's all really a perception and about how you adapt." He fundamentally rejects the idea that his larger environment, including who is in political office, exerts any power over his life prospects: "People are like, you got to get out of here, you got to get out. But like why do you have to get out? As long as you take care of what you need to take care of and do what you gotta do, there's nothing really holding you back here. People say this place is a black hole that holds you back, but the only thing that's holding you back is yourself." His skepticism and distrust make withdrawing from the political sphere look like a logical decision, but the necessity of survival—to keep faith in his ability to make the right choices no matter what happens around him—also makes it a powerful moral one.

Literally My Vote Means Nothing

Mo Knight spent several years in a juvenile detention center for assault when he was younger. "There was no justice at all," he states about his trial. He now lives in the coal region with his mother. Mo met his current girlfriend when he was "locked up for stealing from Walmart when we had $25 in food stamps for eight people." They fell in love while passing notes through the prison laundry system. Mo recently quit his job in a warehouse distribution center after his girlfriend had a heroin relapse and left their baby unattended. "She's chasing the high and my daughter's pretty much on the ride with her. That's not going to happen. So my daughter's here with me now," he affirms.

While Mo is not opposed to selling drugs occasionally to support his daughter, he is adamant about not using them: "I don't stay away from them, but I don't do them. If I can make some money, I ain't going to lie I get the money. But no, that's not me. I don't smoke cigarettes, I don't drink coffee, none of that shit." He is frustrated that his plans for improving himself were thwarted by his ex-girlfriend. He says wearily: "I was going to go to [community college] for computer engineering and I had got my FAFSA [federal student aid] approved and I had just got this job, and my girlfriend needed a place to stay so I just said, 'fuck it,' so I had to continue paying for an apartment." Unemployed, unattached, and distrustful, he "stay[s] away from everybody in this community." When I ask him about whether he worries about some of the pressing issues of our time—Black Lives Matter, terrorism, global warming—he articulates his detachment unapologetically: "It's not me getting shot so I don't care."

In response to questions about his sense of allegiance to the United States, he says simply: "I really don't give a fuck. I wouldn't go to another country. But I'm not proud to be an American." Referring to political leaders, he argues: "They're just running this shit into the ground honestly. That's why I don't vote. I don't think anybody has any type of good interest for anything. They're just all about their money." He connects his pervasive distrust to the infiltration of money in politics and his belief in the phoniness of people in power: "Now, you can't just say whatever you want if you're looking for people to hand you money for a campaign. You have to be all what they want you to say. They got an image to maintain, if you have an image to maintain you can't be trusted, period. If you're not you, then I don't like you."

Mo Knight and I meet the day after Donald Trump was elected. Mo did not vote or register to vote. He does not think that his mother has ever voted, either (his father died of cancer two years ago). He muses: "If you look at it, Hillary Clinton won the election, but Trump won the electoral votes that he needed to get. So America voted for Hillary, technically. But Trump is president. So what the fuck does that tell you about me? Literally my vote means nothing."

He trails off: "But yeah, this country is going down. Not saying that it was ever up, since I've been alive it's been going down." Mo is ambivalent about Trump

as his next president. His distrust of people in power leads him to denounce
Trump's comments about a Muslim registry.

> You're talking about name tagging Muslims? Like what are you doing?
> He's just straight discriminating against everything about America.
> America is built on diversity. You can't, how can you be a racist person?
> You can't. But name taggin' the rest of them ain't going to work. We
> don't name tag the Christians, you can't do shit like that. The people
> ain't not the same just because of their religion.

Mo Knight, who believes he was not treated fairly in the past, reflects upon and
questions authority rather than blindly adheres to it. But above all, Mo longs for
authenticity and for a leader who does not care solely about staying in power.
That quality alone is what draws him in and animates his politics. Mo explains:

> When I heard Trump only wanted a dollar, cuz you have to accept the
> salary as the president, he said, "I'll just take a dollar and no vacation."
> I said, "Well then, shit." Say he didn't become president, he don't give
> a fuck. Don't vote for him, whatever. He has money, he doesn't look
> forward to a $400,000 salary. People that run for president, Hillary
> being one of them, she had to raise all the money for her campaign.
> Trump didn't have to, he had all the money for his campaign. That's
> what people hate about Trump too, he don't give a fuck. He's going to
> say whatever the fuck he wants to say. He's not a politician. Politicians
> have images to maintain. He doesn't have one.

"Only wanting a dollar" as a salary becomes the most convincing political slogan
he can imagine. More important than the substance of the politics is the flam-
boyant style of not caring what people think, not being indebted to donors, and
having no image to maintain. "For the country, I don't got too much optimism,"
Mo reflects. "But for myself, yeah. One day I'm going to get a million dollars.
I know I am because I got the motivation to do it." Success is on him, not on anyone else. He does not pay lip service to patriotism or pride, but utterly rejects
anything larger than himself.

The people in this chapter retain a vague sense of connection to the "little
guy" and to "our people," as opposed to the American government, which they
unapologetically dismiss as fraudulent. They firmly believe that their "vote
means nothing" because inauthentic politicians will say or do whatever they
need to in order to attract donors and stay in power. For all of them, "politician"
is such a repellent identity that not being a politician trumps all other characteristics and policy preferences.[19] What they have in common—distrust, a focus

on self-efficacy over collective efficacy, and a dismissal of larger social concerns that do not seem to affect them personally and immediately—prove a shaky foundation for collective action. In the conclusion to this book, we will consider whether affinities built around shared pain might serve as a bridge between working-class people and their broader communities, restoring connection and resilience.

Conclusion

Breathing Life into a Dead Community

The ability to extract coal from the earth and harness its energy fueled the Industrial Revolution.[1] Coal heated homes, won wars, and built fortunes, transforming a predominantly rural nation into the world's greatest power-house. But coal companies also stripped the land, poisoned the sky, and treated workers' bodies as cheap and disposable.[2] The discipline of sociology arose in the nineteenth century, in part, to make sense of the widespread suffering and exploitation that came hand in hand with rapid economic growth and techno-logical progress.[3] Scholars from sociology's founding figures up to the present have struggled to explain the puzzling relationship between social class and political behavior.[4] Many prominent thinkers predicted that if the industrial working class were not tricked by ideology, or subjected to divide-and-conquer strategies by the elites, then they would unite, rise up, and overthrow their oppressors. "Working Men of All Countries, Unite!" the *Communist Manifesto* famously urged. "Workers have nothing to lose but their chains. They have a world to win."[5]

Yet many workers did, in fact, have too much to lose. Inequalities of mate-rial resources during the industrial era were bound up with, and dependent on, inequalities of recognition. Through the meanings we attach to identities, in the constant interplay between history, hierarchy, and self-worth, recognition is something we can give or deny each other. When members of particular groups are denied the ability to participate in social life as equals because of the way our society has assigned moral worth to them, they can feel inferior, excluded, and demonized. Many studies have observed how industrial working-class white men achieved their solidarity as a class by denying recognition to others—whether women, immigrants, racial minorities, or the unemployed. In a society that preaches that one's fate is determined only by one's own efforts, working-class men dealt quietly with what Richard Sennett and Jonathan Cobb called "the hidden injuries of class"—"the feeling of not getting anywhere despite one's efforts, the feeling of vulnerability in contrasting oneself to others at a higher social level, the buried sense of inadequacy that one resents oneself for feeling."[6] As Andrew Cherlin writes, industrial blue-collar workers healed these psychic wounds by redefining alienating, monotonous labor as an expression of masculine superiority. Maintaining control over their families, alongside supporting the household financially, buoyed masculine authority, while differentiating themselves from men of color upheld their sense of self-respect.[7]

Coal companies extracted value from the natural resources until coal was no longer profitable, then deserted mining communities and left behind a reserve army of workers nostalgic for better days.[8] Today, calls for bringing back coal conjure up a spirit of rebellious determination, a refusal to abandon the glory of America's past legacy and the sense of cultural recognition and pride that accompanied it.[9] But the earth's supply of fossil fuel is finite, and the gender and racial hierarchies of recognition that sustained the industrial working class have become sites of violent strife and active contestation. "Class" as a mediating identity between individual troubles and collective action is not working as it once did. It is time to open ourselves up to the challenges of a sharply divided and deeply unequal postindustrial society in which the "working class" is no longer white, no longer male, and sometimes not even working.[10]

This book began as an exploration of the political attitudes and policy preferences of working-class people in the anthracite coal region of Pennsylvania. As I conducted my research, it was difficult to find people who were engaged in and outspoken about politics. Instead, I found individuals who were disconnected from the kinds of institutions that once connected the private self to the political sphere.[11] Moreover, across lines of age, race, and gender, the people I met were deeply mistrustful of the government, of social institutions like education and health care, and of other people to such an extent that participating in conventional politics felt like a joke. As Andres states succinctly in chapter 4, "politicians are selected, not elected." Being openly mocked and laughed at for wearing my "I Voted" sticker on election day—for daring to believe that our democracy would be responsive to my voice—will long linger in my memory.

The men and women in this book suffer from physical pain—muscles torn and backs worn out by heavy lifting and repetitive tasks, and ribs cracked and faces bruised by intimate partner violence. They turn to food and Percocet, heroin and cigarettes, to manage the feelings of anxiety, disappointment, and trauma from their pasts. Sometimes they think about putting a shotgun in their mouth, like Glen in chapter 2, or pray that God will take them out of life, like Lucy in chapter 3. Instead of mobilizing around shared identities, the white residents and the black and Latino newcomers alike harness stories of *individually* managing pain to bridge their personal experiences to the larger social world. They invalidate the pain of others when they fear that their own needs and sacrifices are going unrecognized. The need for self-preservation leaves most of them reluctant to engage in the political sphere. Think back, for instance, to Shelly Moore, the coal miner's granddaughter in chapter 3, who makes her experiences with heroin addiction and violence comprehensible by rejecting social safety nets and framing suffering as a pathway to moral growth. Jordan Madera, in chapter 6, savors online recipes for cooking the perfect chicken and self-help books to endure poverty, infidelity, and isolation. Sometimes their individual approaches to coping with suffering challenge older divisions of class, race, and gender, and sometimes their approaches serve to compound them. None of these changes are going down easy. But in these moments of fracturing, of unanticipated collisions of place and race, in the very fault lines that split open America, new alliances and uncharted possibilities are opening up.

Broken Heroes

Michael Fisher, a muscular, bearded twenty-four-year-old in a T-shirt and baseball cap, slides into the booth of the local pizza parlor, relieved to have a brief respite from the scorching ninety-degree summer day. As we scan our menus and make small talk about the weather, he confides nonchalantly, "You know, this is probably the first time I left the house without carrying anything on me. Usually I carry [a gun]. I usually have a vest on too, so if you try to stab me it won't do anything," he laughs. "But today I'm going to pick up my son after, and it's too hot." Michael already has one assault charge on his record, from when he "got jumped by two guys that were from New York, as [he] was pulling out of the ATM. I automatically got charged. It didn't qualify as self-defense because there was an alley that I could have ran through. But I wasn't going to leave my son laying on the sidewalk, I had to make sure my son was okay. I protect my family." Michael has since put no faith in the police or the criminal justice system, reflecting how, "I was sitting in there waiting and I sat there for about fourteen days afterwards, but they were supposed to have twenty-four hours for me to be released. I sat there for fourteen days, they had no record of me being in that jail. It was ridiculous." He carries his concealed weapon faithfully, convinced that "it's going to be World War III real soon. When all these kids come out of high school they better be prepared because that's where they're going, they're not going into college. They're going to the Marine Corps. This country is going downhill. We'll be in World War III by 2019. I guarantee it."

Michael has been on his own since he was sixteen. From birth, his mother hid him from his biological father. His mother, a Children and Youth Services worker, was murdered when Michael was two years old by a disgruntled parent whose children had been taken away. For a while, his aunt took him in: "They paid her a little bit. But then she had a heart attack, passed away four years after my mom died. It was just too much on her." His grandmother labeled him "the devil's child." Living with her was "the worst period of my life. She hit me with a crow bar. She woke me up with buckets, like cold water. She just drenched me with it one time. Demons coming out of you, went like that." Michael insists on finding a glimmer of positivity in everything from his past: "My grandma was a piece of work. Good cook though. Small Italian lady. She made homemade noodles and everything." After being removed from his grandmother's house, Michael reports living in thirty-seven different foster homes "because they kept quitting. So they had to move me, move me, move me." Finally, another aunt "turned around and said she would take me in, but she couldn't do the adoption process, so they paid her as a foster parent. She did it for the money basically." He says resolutely: "I don't want my kid to grow up with a father and mother like mine."

Three days after he graduated from high school, Michael enlisted in the military with one of his foster brothers, whom he simply calls his brother: "I lived with black foster families, I lived with Puerto Rican foster families, I've lived with white foster families. That don't bother me. My closest brother was African American." As a machine gunner in Iraq, Michael describes the memory that still haunts him when he closes his eyes to sleep at night:

> We have this whole section, it's this big metal disk that's heated and it balances on the floor as you're driving. It's on this big long cable. And the vibration of it hitting the floor and the heat, hits anything within a ten-foot radius of each side, if there's any IEDs [improvised explosive devices] it detonates it. Well, when you go around a turn, that don't help too much. We went around a turn and that's what happened, we got ambushed. I never had my hand shake so much in my life. I think it was twenty-three hundred rounds in the first twenty minutes. It was really intense.

And then, his whole world was shattered: "My brother got killed right in front of me. He did the buddy system with me, and I just shut down. So I got discharged for an anxiety disorder and PTSD." Michael struggles to reconcile how his life has unfolded with visions of who he imagined he would become. He has been "in a lot of pain since coming home," receiving injections in his back and "really struggling" with PTSD. Vicious anxiety and debilitating pain leave him wistful: "If I had finished my four years I probably would, my plan was to retire after the military. Get twenty years in there, retire, would have been like thirty-eight to forty, and still young enough to where I could have put my son in football and still do everything I want to do with my son. That's what I wanted to do. But what you want to do doesn't always happen."

And yet, when he discusses his experiences in the military, he focuses on how there is not *enough* pain—that *not* having to endure basic training like they had in earlier generations has produced an army of weaklings. "I've never seen so many dudes that sounded like little twelve-year-olds in my life," he snickers. "You can go to basic training and get stressed out and they give you a yellow card that you're too stress out. Every time someone gets yelled at they get a little stress card like this. I'm dead serious. You can have your cell phone in basic training in army now. They don't even run, they don't even put shoes on and run on the floors, on the grounds. They are stationary in the barracks. They don't do anything in the rain. What is wrong with you? I'm sorry but I can't trust you." Michael's relationship with himself remains uneasy, as his belief in pain as a virtue doesn't quite square with his PTSD discharge. When I ask him if he is proud that he served his country, he says grimly: "No, because I didn't finish my four years." He believes that he did not rightly earn veterans' benefits such as medical care, disability payments, or college grants, repeating: "I didn't finish."

Michael now works construction, a lucrative but seasonal job that pays $37 an hour plus gas money: "They give you a company gas card, a rental vehicle for as long as I'm down there, they pay for it." He does not have guaranteed hours, and lately "just this rain has been killing me. I can't pour concrete, I can't jack-hammer, I can't do a lot of the stuff." He relies on a second job as a bouncer at a bar in town on the weekends. He is raising his three-year old son with his wife, who does not work. They have been married a year, and he doubts "if it's going much farther," as her credit-card habit of "ordering stuff and only making one payment, not keep the payments going," has sunk his credit score to 540: "I had my credit good enough where I probably coulda got a house." He shrugs: "If I can still get out of bed, I'll work. If I can raise my son, take my son to school, I can work."

Like many of the people in this book, Michael perceives a world of moral unraveling, of unchecked greed and selfishness. "I just don't like it," he sighs. "Like someone will loan me $10, even if I'll be late on rent, I'll make sure she has her $10 before I give that to my rent. I'll take the late fee. You know what I mean? I don't like owing people. I see people all the time in this town I lend money to and I'll turn around and see them buying beer or see 'em sitting in McDonalds or Wendy's buying food for all their friends." He clarifies: "It's not even the principle of getting the money back. If you say you're going to do something, do it. Don't turn around and go, oh I forgot about it. I don't want to hear that. You didn't forget about it. You didn't want to do it." He senses the destruction of the bonds of reciprocity and obligation that once anchored people in relationships of trust. Rather than solely blame people themselves, he points to a corrupt and senseless economic and political system. He expresses support for workers' rights, arguing that the main reason why "our economy is failing" is politicians' refusal to raise the minimum wage: "Everything else keeps going up, you have to raise that too. You keep raising everything else up but keeping that the same you're never going to have money to pay for everything else to keep everything going. So the only option is to raise it. I honestly think $7.25 is ridiculous." He sees poverty as a vicious cycle: "Then you have to use programs they have like food stamps. That stuff should be temporary cause that's what it's made for. Six months, a year at a time. People I know have food stamps for the last five years. That shouldn't be. It's supposed to help you get on your feet, not stay down."

Michael worries about raising his son in a community where "you can't take your kids to the parks because there's heroin needles half the time in the parks." He recently called the owner of a blighted, abandoned building in town to discuss starting an indoor playground that would charge families "$5 a day, which is perfect for this town cuz a lot of people have fixed incomes." He implores: "I've never seen a town where there's ten- and twelve-year-olds in the streets walking around. That's horrible. I don't want my kids outside at twelve years old past ten o'clock at night. There's nothing for kids to do so they get in trouble all the time." So far, his efforts have been unsuccessful—"I tried calling, the guy doesn't call back"—cementing his sense of hopelessness about the town's future.

Michael does not want to talk or think about national politics at all. In July 2016, he refuses to even consider choosing a candidate, even as I gently pressure him to make a choice: "They're both terrible. I heard there's an others box," he says drily. The real problem, as he explains it, is not choosing between one candidate and another, but rather the extreme polarization and lack of transparency that characterizes modern politics: "It's like they just flip everything, everything. Even the most simplest story, they flip it. I hate social media, I hate Facebook completely." He insists, "There's good and bad in everything." As we discuss Syrian refugees, ISIS, Black Lives Matter, and police brutality, he connects these political controversies to a larger conspiracy set up to distract and control the population from above: "It's all a set-up, honestly. Our country could be in martial law soon."

Michael tries to perform the kind of masculinity that industrial blue-collar workers depended on—hard work, integrity, self-sacrifice, and protecting and supporting his wife and son. But the pieces are not coming together for him; by his own logic, he is a failed hero, an undeserving man who let pain get the best of him. His attempts to protect his country, to wield authority within his family, and to earn a steady paycheck, have all failed thus far. Conspiracy theories appeal to his sense of the broken social contract, and withdrawing from all major social institutions seems like the most promising way to survive. But that is not the whole story.

Imperfect Allies

As Michael slowly rebuilds his life, he befriends Derek Grant, twenty-four, who came to the coal region seeking refuge from poverty and violence. Derek grew up with his mother and twelve siblings in North Philly. His family moved all over—from "uptown, Germantown, West Noman, Frankfurt, random areas for a couple years" as "certain things would happen in the neighborhood and you know, one time we moved because you know domestic violence, and we got into a lot of fights. Like we got kicked out of schools, we got sent to another, cuz you always try to avoid like disciplinary schools and all that stuff, until when we got older and it was like, oh well. Now we're not moving no more." He and his twin brother spent three years in juvie for fighting and did not graduate from high school. "Reality didn't really hit nobody until we was like eighteen, nineteen. We was like, oh snap, now what are we gonna do with our lives?"

A gas station and convenience store opened up around the corner from their mother's home, and "hired us on the spot," making $8.50 an hour. Derek worked his way up to maintenance manager and met his girlfriend, who worked next door. They got pregnant with a baby girl soon after, which proved a transformative moment for him: "Like having a kid, like it's not no fun and games no more. Before I wouldn't really like, I was, I would do my, you know, you're nineteen or whatever. We just out and about, just doing whatever you want. You know. You go to work, you come home, you spend your money on whatever you want. You know like, it put a couple years on me." But his girlfriend incessantly worried that he was not committed, and one day, "her crazy ass came to my job thinking I was messing with some chick. Beat up the chick, no my sister beat up the chick. She called my mom before they came down there. Her and my sister came to my job and started causing a scene. I was embarrassed. They came there acting ratchet and I lost my job." He says sadly: "Then after that like, after that I couldn't keep a job. And then once I lost that, I got a couple other jobs. I got a landscaping job, you know, construction job and all that, but I could never keep it."

When Derek's brother Chase was twelve, he and his friends got in a fight with some other kids in the neighborhood. One of the other boys' parents showed up with baseball bats and the violence escalated. Chase was caught in the fray. He has been locked up for two years. A few months later, Derek witnessed his friend getting shot in the head right outside his door—"and it's just like oh man, I gotta get outta here. That and plus all the other stuff that was going on, it was just like, let me just go somewhere. You see someone get shot in the head and it's like man, I don't know if I wanna do this." At just twenty-three, Derek reflects: "I just feel like everything that can go wrong already went wrong so it's nothing but up from now. Nothing but up." When I ask him to clarify, he adds, "Relationships, my goals, everything. I hit rock bottom already. Freakin' depression about my relationship being over, starting over. My brother. You know. No job." At his brother's urging, Derek moved to Coal Brook, even though "at first I was mad. I'm like, I don't wanna be here. I don't know nobody." He stayed when he realized he could "get a house for what, like three hundred dollars a month, like a week worth of pay." He now spends his free time doing "music and stuff," writing songs with his brothers, hoping one day to be "on tour with my music."

Now that everything that could have gone wrong in his life has already happened, as he reports, he "couldn't care less" about politics or anything beyond "putting food on my table and all that. I'm gonna just do what I want to, like do what I do. It ain't got nothing to do with me." But his apathetic stance belies his deep concern for his daughter. He reflects: "The thing I worry about most around here is just the, just the change, if the town is ready for the change that is about to happen. That's one of my biggest worries. One of my biggest. And I'm just, I just want that change to happen. You know my daughter's gonna be in the midst of that change. So I just want everything to be ready for her." For Derek, rural America becomes a refuge from dramatic relationships, violence, and poverty, signaling a chance to rebuild himself and his life.

On his first day in the coal region, he met up with his brother, who informed him, "Oh yeah, this dude just freakin' tried to fight me. He said my kind don't belong here and I'm like oh this is a racist freakin' town. Like in Philly you don't deal with that. In Philly you don't deal with, well you do but you, it's not like it's right there in your face all the time." He tried to go to church one Sunday, but was unsettled by the unwelcoming, blatantly pro-Trump message from the pulpit and did not return. Now, he says, "I just laugh. I'm like, are you serious? They look at me and be like, oh you sell drugs. Like what? Like I'd get in trouble, well I used to get in trouble, in fights. But I didn't, I'm not selling no drugs." When people in town share Facebook posts deriding the newcomers, he responds, "Like all that is for what? All that, like what is that, what is that for? It's unnecessary, like just go live your life. Like what did we, what did we do to you? What did we do to you? We're out here making a living just like you are."

Michael and Derek met at the town's only "black bar," known among many white people as "the ghetto bar," one night when Michael was working as the bouncer. Michael attests firsthand to the virulent racial tensions that the newcomers encounter:

> I come out of the bar sometimes to do my rounds around the building, and if there's anything I have to report it. Just yesterday I was, there was these guys that were about to fight. This white guy said, said oh there was a bunch of monkeys coming to the bar. It was a black guy and four white guys and they turned around and told him right in front of the cop, a good [n-word] is a dead [n-word] and the cop didn't do anything

about it. I've been called a [n-word] lover. It's horrible. Like did the cops say anything, no. I don't even bother calling the cops.

Michael critiques the scapegoating of people of color in town as criminals and addicts, pointing out: "Like I've been looking, like, stuff will pop up on Facebook or on the newspaper, like these meth labs are blowing up. It's like you look at all these people that are selling heroin and all that stuff, they're not even, like there's a couple people that's black that's doing it. But all the people that you catch are like majority of them are white. So how can you say, oh the black people did this?" He becomes especially incensed when discussing the "freakin' Crime Watch walks."

> They say it's a crime watch, but to be honest, that's racist bullshit. They had a group of people that were supposed to be the Crime Watch, walking around town with rifles. Like why are you walking around town with rifles on your back? Yeah. With their guns or with their, like one day we stopped and were like yo, what's this walk for? He's like, oh it's Coal Brook's crime watch, like whatever, man. Cuz they told me they're having a racist meeting to get the black people out this town at that freakin', at that freakin' parking lot. And y'all was gonna have a walk so you can get the black people out, take-our-town-back walk or something like that. He's like, when we confronted him about it, he's like, oh, it's just a crime watch. Yeah, alright.

"So what do me and Michael do?" Derek laughs, recounting the story in a separate conversation. "We walk right with them. They were mad. We were like, we're watching for crime, what are you talking about? We made everything a joke. I was laughing the whole time, I thought it was funny. Real real funny." He shrugs: "But it's like we all just stick together. We all go to the bar, we all pitch in for beer. Like we all just like, it's like a whole, it's like a family basically." Derek has slowly built a circle of new friends, both newcomers and longtime residents, where every morning, "Like people, we check in with everybody and make sure everybody okay." Derek also joined a local football league and his team played to raise money for "Toys for Tots." His coach Glen, the white Trump-supporting PTSD survivor from chapter 2, has become "almost like a father to me."

For Michael Fisher and Derek Grant, turning inward, and focusing only on their own lives, is an appealing strategy to survive contentious relationships, social exclusion, and continual disappointments.[12] But they nonetheless check up on each other every morning, join football leagues, make relationships across lines of race and age, reflect on the kind of world they want their children to grow up in, and march defiantly through town, mocking the armed vigilantes.

Through these everyday moments, they plant the seeds for new forms of social recognition to grow and tentatively reconfigure existing boundaries of inclusion and exclusion. Social change, in this instance, does not spring from informing working-class people about what their best interests are, or from bombarding them with the true facts of politics. Change, infinitesimal and slow, comes in the everyday local challenges to the hostility and isolation that pattern their histories and threaten to occlude their futures. In this continual process of unfolding, in this flux and contingency, hope bubbles up in the shifting alliances, new rituals, and imperfect heroes who imagine new ways of bridging self and community when older models fail them.

Bearing Witness

Some readers might conclude that the injuries of the working-class people in this book—however horrific they may be—are self-inflicted. One prominent iteration of this perspective comes in the form of J. D. Vance's *Hillbilly Elegy*, a memoir of white working-class life, which soared to the top of best-seller lists in summer 2016. The story of a "family and culture in crisis," *Hillbilly Elegy* chronicles the author's childhood of poverty, abuse, and neglect in a declining Appalachian Ohio town. Vance, now a successful Silicon Valley lawyer, points to the "learned helplessness" of his family and friends from his hometown—their willingness to blame the government for their problems, embodied in their "deep skepticism of the very institutions of our society."[13] Drawing explicit connections to pain, Vance suspects that his peers spend their way "into the poor house" to ease their psychic wounds: "We buy giant TVs and iPads. Our children wear nice clothes thanks to high-interest credit cards and payday loans. We purchase homes we don't need, refinance them for more spending money, and declare bankruptcy, often leaving them full of garbage in our wake." Vance muses: "Are we tough enough to look ourselves in the mirror and admit that our conduct harms our children? Public policy can help, but there is no government that can fix these problems for us . . . I don't know what the answer is precisely, but I know it starts when we stop blaming Obama or Bush or faceless companies and ask ourselves what we can do to make things better."

Vance embodies one visible way of managing pain: blaming others for not being strong enough to tough it out on their own, expressing resentment against those who need help to survive, and gaining recognition and a sense of self-worth through cutting oneself off from those who inflicted pain. There are many quotations that echo Vance throughout this book. Denying recognition and dignity to those who cannot fix themselves is a common strategy for glorifying one's own suffering. But the overwhelming majority of the people I met were indeed tough enough to look at themselves in the mirror, account for their failures, and pledge to do better. When Lucy hates herself for needing food stamps, when Ellen declares she will not save her sister from overdose, and when Michael Fisher regrets his inability to triumph over his PTSD, they all reinforce the message that being forced to endure pain produces stronger people. They express disappointment in themselves when they cannot transcend their suffering and grow from it, speedily labeling themselves weak and undeserving.

But when we listen to them reflect carefully on their own lives, most of the men and women in this book are not fully committed to this single, unforgiving approach to pain management. Most are not free-market proponents who believe wholeheartedly that the government's only job is to stay out of people's lives, or that the poor have only themselves to blame for their problems. Rather than carelessly blame Obama, Bush, or faceless companies for their failures, they levy specific and piercing critiques against companies and institutions that have broken the social contract and placed profit over basic fairness and human dignity. Whether pointing to the biased criminal justice system, the dissolution of employer loyalty, the doctors and pharmaceutical companies that profit from addiction, or the for-profit colleges peddling expensive, useless degrees, these working-class observers know that the American Dream has been stolen from the people who once built it. They think it is wrong that the wealthy have politicians "in their pocket." And many of them believe that the pain they feel was not brought on solely by themselves, even as they have only themselves to rely on to escape it.

Even as they are divided by racism, sexism, and xenophobia, the working-class people in this book fundamentally agree that you can't raise a family on nine dollars an hour; that extreme inequality corrupts democracy; and that we have lost essential connections to others. They are frustrated by the impossibility of bipartisanship and public discourse, seeing their current choices, to quote Joshua and his father from chapter 2, as between "shit or a shit sandwich." The sense of meaninglessness and distrust that bridges their different backgrounds and experiences converge in the urgent question of "whom the government is for."[14] Knowing that they are outsiders leads them to embrace conspiracy theories as common sense. Topics such as the World Trade Center attacks on September 11, the Sandy Hook massacre, fluoride in the water, or population control through Ebola and other diseases blur the line between suspicion and paranoia.

But being willing to question some of the central tenets of American patriotism also opens their eyes to the reality that the current system is not working in their favor. Both personal and public causes of pain run through their stories. None of the working-class people in this book fully absolve politicians of serving the needs of their wealthy constituents. And none of them believe wholeheartedly in the innocence of the American dream. In sharing their most intimate pain, they give voice to their awareness of social and economic forces that make their lives unlivable. They bring to light the inequalities and contradictions in which they live. And in understanding the social origins of their suffering, there arises the possibility of pain becoming a vehicle for action—of recognizing, as Pierre Bourdieu writes, that "what the social world has done, it can undo."[15] While many of them are critical of welfare, especially when they believe other groups are benefiting at their own expense, they nonetheless express a great deal of support for policies that expand opportunity in terms of education, health care, fair pay, and good jobs.[16] From their own testimony, it appears possible that a political candidate who puts economic justice for working-class families at the center of their platform, who encourages opportunities for growth for everyday people, and who does not shy away from criticizing the collusion of financial and political elites, could have a shot at gaining their support.[17] Such a candidate would need to carefully balance trust, accountability, an openness to opposing ideas, and a commitment to inclusivity.

Leveraging Pain for Political Mobilization

Dramatic social changes can open up spaces for people to come together and articulate new political identities and concerns for action. But it is tricky to imagine a "we" if one disavows the political sphere all together. This paradox raises the question of whether affinities built around pain could serve as a bridge between individuals and the larger society, perhaps replacing or supplementing older kinds of identity politics like class or race.

As the opioid epidemic ravaged the coal region, a series of open forums was held at high schools and public meeting halls throughout the spring and summer of 2016. During a question and answer session at one such meeting, a local resident angrily recounted how the police used his daughter as a confidential informant, which meant that she was buying and selling heroin, and risking an overdose, for over nine months when she should have been in treatment. Another bemoaned not being able to access painkillers for his debilitating injuries and severe PTSD. An addiction counselor stated frankly that he wished he could solve the addiction epidemic with a machine gun and believes that the "war on drugs" is moving into rural white America because there are "more people with parents who could be robbed." Yet another desperate parent, who had just finished reading Sam Quinone's *Dreamland: The True Tale of America's Opiate Epidemic*, asked earnestly if Trump's wall would keep out black tar heroin from Mexico. Weary but patient, the county officials on the panel—the local judge, coroner, and a state representative—repeatedly

called for a "carrot and stick" approach to addiction: building internal motivation and purpose through education on the one hand, and relying on incarceration for repeat offenders on the other. During the two-and-a-half-hour
meeting, jobs were not mentioned once.

Away from the spotlight, Ellen, the coal miner's granddaughter from
chapter 1, attends a weekly support group for the family and friends of addicts.
This group has no official title or affiliation, and medical experts are noticeably
lacking around the solid oak table. Ellen is there for help coping with her rage
surrounding her sister's heroin addiction. Ellen fumes: "She would rather just lie
on the couch all day and collect food stamps and housing vouchers than work."
As members share their stories of suffering around the circle, Ellen's perspective
shifts. Upon hearing the story of a mother who no longer wants to live with her
heroin-addicted son who steals from her, Ellen offers practical advice on how
to apply for medical insurance and public housing for him. Eva, a Puerto Rican
young woman in recovery whose boyfriend has also been using heroin, powerfully condemns the pharmaceutical companies and doctors who fuel addictions
by creating and prescribing highly addictive opiate painkillers like Oxycontin
and then profit from addiction on the back end through the sale of treatments
like Suboxone. The group criticizes the drugs to prison "pipeline" that traps their
family members and friends. "The system feeds off itself," one man proclaims.
"We have to break the system."

Ellen, who reads self-help literature furiously, brings up the example of a research study that found that rats are less likely to get addicted to heroin water
if they are surrounded by toys and plenty of food. In short, she summarizes, if
they are in "rat heaven," they are less susceptible to dangerous influences. "How
do we make a rat heaven out of the blight of our community?" asks one young
woman. "How do you breathe life into a dead community?" echoes a working-
class white man whose family has lived in Coal Brook for four generations. In
this rare moment, a sense of "we" emerges to confront the desperation facing
working-class families in an unlikely place, in a way that fostered solidarity rather
than undercut it. In place of formal politics and sweeping reforms, camaraderie
was momentarily fused through surprising alliances, skeptical audiences, and
diffuse, local networks coming together to solve problems.

The kinds of stories we tell ourselves can leave us vulnerable to exploitation,
or they can serve as protective shields against self-condemnation and public
scorn.[18] Stories of personal suffering and redemption form the bedrock of the
self for many of the working-class people in this book. Many scholars, myself
included, have worried that narratives of self-healing and self-transformation
privilege the "I" over the "we," trapping sufferers in inward-facing quests that
stymie collective action. As Robin Simon and Kathryn Lively note, "It is ironic
that intense and persistent anger seem to be necessary for the collective redress

of large-scale social inequalities."[19] But perhaps individualistic and communal aspirations do not always have to be at odds with each other. It is possible, as Arlene Stein writes, that "therapeutic politics could encourage individuals, and the groups they are a part of, to display painful feelings in public rather than hold them back, and it could prod them to utilize those feelings as a way of mobilizing politically."[20]

When one reflects on pain, mistreatment, failure, and vulnerability, testifying to a community of witnesses, one is jolted out of the flow of daily life, forced to give an account of why things turned out the way they did.[21] When pain is named, projected outward into the world instead of shrouded in resentment and blame, the possibility of forging social bonds out of what would otherwise be a shameful experience arises.[22] The storyteller can offer his or her story of pain to others, not to speak for them, as J. D. Vance does in *Hillbilly Elegy*, but to speak with them as fellow-sufferers.[23] Building robust public forums that counter self-insulation, and where pain and solutions can be shared openly, could provide a vehicle for collective mobilization among those who are suffering. In her study of marriage education programs, for example, the sociologist Jennifer Randles found that meeting with other couples who shared similarly distressing economic and family circumstances helped low-income parents to validate and support each other, while learning to see poverty, rather than only personal shortcomings, as the cause of their troubles.[24] Similarly, Joan Maya Mazelis documented how poor people in Philadelphia who joined a welfare rights union created lasting ties with each other that allowed them to build networks of mutual reciprocity, share resources, build skills, and mobilize against injustice quickly.[25]

In the coal region, without these kinds of routines and interactions, people are largely on their own to connect their experiences up to politics, which often makes their political worldviews seem fractured, contradictory, or incomplete. Several people in this book complained about the lack of effective civics education in public schools and their frustration at the difficulty of finding valid information. It is possible that a network of trustworthy community organizers, from civic, political, and religious organizations, could help working-class people tie the pain and inequalities that they experience within their own families to the experiences of others, building a compassionate bridge between the individual and the community.[26]

The people I interviewed draw dignity from hard work. They do not like bullies, and they want to be people who can be counted on. They are not ashamed to speak up. In forging a community of sufferers comes the possibility of transformation. To quote Audre Lorde, "I had known the pain, and survived it. It only remained for me to give it voice, to share it for use, that the pain not be wasted."[27] The journey is just beginning.

METHODOLOGICAL APPENDIX

Building comfort and trust with people in the coal region, and convincing them to talk with me, was initially daunting. In small towns where it felt as if everyone knew everything about each other, I immediately stood out as an outsider. I could feel people's eyes on me when I walked into a local bar or restaurant. I worried that I would be seen as a clueless liberal professor, from the wealthier town of Lewisburg, and immediately shunned. This assumption proved to be wrong, as people in the coal region had a favorable opinion of my university and of my town. As a white woman in my early thirties, I likely was not perceived as threatening. While I was asked a few times over the phone or text message if I were a cop, I was generally welcomed into people's homes and allowed to record conversations once we met in person.

My study was approved by Bucknell's institutional review board. I walked participants through a written consent process before I began the interviews, providing the following explanation: "The purpose of my study is to learn about the political beliefs, life experiences, and family histories of residents of central Pennsylvania. I am particularly interested in how you make decisions about who you vote for, what you value, and what kind of country you want America to be." I offered $40 to each interviewee as a token of appreciation for their time. While about half the people made sure that it was "Bucknell's money, not your money," and several older people urged me to "use the money to buy a nice dinner for yourself and your husband," nearly everyone accepted it. I assigned pseudonyms to my respondents to protect their identities. "I have nothing to hide" and "you can use my real name in your book" were common reactions to the consent form; people wanted their stories to be heard and found honor rather than shame in talking about their difficult life experiences. However, my ultimate responsibility lies with protecting them and not creating an additional space where they could be made vulnerable, so I have chosen to de-identify them as much as possible.

One of the first lessons that I learned while collecting the interview material for this book was that it was not prudent to refer to the people I was interviewing as my "informants." In sociology, it is standard practice to refer to the people who share their stories as participants, informants, or respondents. One evening early on in my research in May 2015, I was having nachos at a local diner with Tracy, one of the first coal-region residents who sat down with me to hear about the project. Tracy served as a kind of initial gatekeeper, as she held the potential to introduce me to many families in town who descended from coal miners (sometimes she would text me to say she had heard I had been in a particular area interviewing someone—"not much gets by me!" she would joke). Tracy stopped me cold when I asked about whether I could draw upon her ties to reach more informants: "Are you trying to get me killed? You do not want to use that term!" she exclaimed in horror. "They will think I am a confidential informant for the police!" As I continued to collect data, attending public community events about the opioid crisis, I heard from many parents whose adult children were indeed being used as "confidential informants" by local law enforcement.

Luckily, despite this faux pas, Tracy introduced me to a few people that night at the bar, and the interviews began to take off. I came to be known as "Tracy's friend." I also went off on my own to diversify the networks. I went to volunteer fire stations and bars, police stations, service workplaces like gas stations and convenience stores, local for-profit colleges and community colleges, and temporary employment agencies, asking people if they would participate in a Bucknell study about politics in the area. When Bree Lopez, who opens this book, helped me to cross the racial divide in Coal Brook, I found that the newcomers were shocked when I was not just willing to talk with them but also when I was willing to visit them in their homes.

One of my closest participants, Derek, offered to act as an informal research assistant. He told me he needed something to do, to keep him from "ripping and running" around town. He sometimes accompanied me on interviews and introduced me to friends he had met. He was extremely conscientious, texting me several mornings per week to see if I was going to work that day. I bought him food and toiletries and brought pans of baked ziti and gifts for his daughter. We became friends of a sort, despite our differences in age and background. While I shy away from thinking about my own well-being when conducting research, and usually prioritize gathering rich data over thinking about my own safety, there were certainly times when I would walk up a dimly lit staircase alone and wonder what I would find. Derek's presence added a layer of security and predictability.

I wrote down a long list of interview questions that I memorized, although I would attempt to make the interviews sound more like informal conversations than scripted surveys. I spent two or three hours with each participant, often in their homes with their children running around. I held a lot of babies, helped heat up food, picked up people when they were stranded on the side of the road, donated money to school charities, and handed people tissues when they cried.

Walking through the streets of Coal Brook, I was recognized excitedly as "the person writing the book."

During the interviews, I asked people questions about their childhood background, including their family structure, the jobs their parents held, and their experiences in school, organized religion, and sports. I asked them to self-identify their race and gender identity. I asked them to walk me through their memories of difficult times and happy times. I explored their generational history, including the kinds of memories and stories that had been passed down about their parents and grandparents, especially their involvement in unions, politics, and the military. I asked about their own work history and whether they had considered leaving the area for more opportunity; they walked me through a typical day and gave me an account of their monthly earnings and bills. I asked them about their mental and physical health and whether they had medical care. For example, I asked: "Have you ever received any kind of assistance like WIC or food stamps? How do you feel about it?" Probing more deeply, I questioned how they would compare themselves to their parents and grandparents.

After I established this basic sense of who they were, I asked them to describe the problems in the area, such as drugs, racism, and crime. I also asked about involvement in civic organizations, like volunteer fire companies, ethnic clubs, and youth sports leagues. I explored where they got their news about current events, and how they felt about social movements like Black Lives Matter and Occupy Wall Street. Sometimes we would decide to meet again the following day. Other questions included:

- What do you think the biggest risks to your sense of stability or security are? Walk me through a time when you felt like you just couldn't make it. What happened? Who could you turn to? What did you do?
- Can you remember any times when your race made getting ahead, or achieving a goal, harder for you?
- What types of interactions have you had with the government? Do you feel that leaders and major institutions work in your best interest?
- Are you registered to vote? How have you voted in the past? How do you feel about Democrats/Republicans, liberals/conservatives? Can you walk me through every election you can remember in your life?

I made sure to hit upon social and economic issues including abortion, gay marriage, affirmative action, raising the minimum wage, and Obamacare. I asked them about their heroes, about politicians they admired and disliked, and whether they could name any leaders who cared about "people like you." One question read: Close your eyes and picture the "American Dream." What does the "American Dream" mean to you? Has it changed over time? Are there people who deserve a helping hand?

I recorded all of the interviews (108 total with working-class people, plus 15 additional interviews with community leaders). With my gifted research assistant, Kait Smeraldo, I created a set of initial codes that allowed me to grasp what was happening in the thousands of pages of interview transcripts. We first categorized the participants by age, self-identified race, gender, and sexuality, marital status, place of origin, occupation, education level, whether they had registered to vote, and whom they planned to vote for in 2016. The point was not to reify these categories but to think about how they were historically and socially produced, and how these social locations might link up to different kinds of political interpretations and experiences. Our line-by-line coding led us to document a wide range of details about our sample, including whom they planned to vote for, whether they used government assistance, whether they had health insurance, whether they trusted the government and politicians, and how they remembered their parents' politics. As we dug deeper into the actions and meanings within the interview transcripts, we moved beyond simple categories and into the specific language and topics that interviewees themselves brought up as salient—histories of addiction and sexual abuse, whether they described themselves as suffering from mental illnesses such as anxiety or depression, whether they felt optimistic or gloomy about their futures. We examined how narratives of pain were co-present with narratives of political engagement or withdrawal, and how the ways in which pain and politics connected were both similar and dissimilar by group identity.

I constantly jotted down ideas and wrote ongoing informal memos from before I even started interviewing. It was in that process that I was able to build out, using the interview transcripts as raw material, how people connected their life histories to their politics. Looking back, there were several themes that were familiar to me—racial resentment, fake news, economic anxiety. But the links I uncovered between narratives of suffering and political beliefs did emerge from puzzling over the interview transcripts, reading them line by line. As pain became a sensitizing concept, a central organizing idea that recurred across the transcripts, I began to build a glossary of pain in its many manifestations, tracing how participants' self-described emotional, existential, and physical pain connected to their political stances and analogies. I then divided the sample into groups—white men, white women, black and Latino men, black and Latina women—that corresponded with their histories and experiences. For each group, I read the transcripts and pulled out the following themes:

- identified sources of pain
- responses to pain
- imagined vision of the future
- co-presence of pain and politics in narrative
- forms of civic and political engagement

I also documented what I call "non-pain reasons for voting"—these reasons included loyalty to one's parent's political party, civic duty, or thinking they could not vote because they were on probation or did not know enough about the issues. After this coding, my argument about pain and politics, and how managing suffering coalesces with feelings of distrust and disengagement, took shape. I continued to move back and forth between the data and the themes, crystallizing my findings, writing and rewriting until my analysis did justice to the richness and complexity of the data.

When I present data throughout this book, I have chosen not to use snippets of interview material to support my claims. I intentionally give a great deal of detail in order to allow the reader to follow the narrative connections between identity and life history, and intimate experiences and politics, as produced by the participants themselves. I note that it would be impossible for me, given time and resource limitations, to fact-check all of their stories and memories. However, I am less concerned with what really happened, or whether their beliefs and facts are true, and more concerned with the narrative materials they use to arrive at their positions. That is, I use the interview material to model how working-class people build their own narrative bridges between experience, identity, and politics. I recognize the limits of generalizability in this small study: I do not know if the people I spoke with are representative of working-class populations more broadly. I see my contribution primarily as uncovering mechanisms and processes that help us understand the demographic patterns that we see when relying on quantitative data about political engagement and disengagement. In order to know if people's political ideas shape their behavior, I would have to follow them over time, which is a fruitful area for future research.

When I share this research, I am frequently asked about the toll it has taken on me, physically and emotionally. This question makes me uncomfortable. Although listening to these stories did cause me many sleepless nights, a persistently high level of anxiety, and even physical issues like a recurring sinus infection from breathing in so much smoke, I never wanted this project to be about me or my role. This is a book about the urgency and immediacy of working-class people's suffering; I get to go home at the end of the day.

Nonetheless, there are pieces of me, and where I come from, throughout this story. I come from a family with decidedly working-class roots. My father dropped out of high school at eighteen and joined the military in the early 1970s. He has literally broken his body as a soldier and firefighter for forty years. My mother, who has built a business as a self-trained, high-school-educated landscaper, still works seven days a week, twelve hours a day. From early on, I learned how crucial it was for workers to be paid enough to support themselves, plan for the future, and to give their children a better life. I grew up in a family and community that fiercely believed in patriotism, individual freedom, and sacrificing for their community and country. Many of the people I grew up around have turned to more conservative news outlets over the last decade, as the Democrats are perceived to have turned their back on the very people who built our country and need their support. As I have been upwardly mobile, earning a PhD and working as a professor in elite universities, I do not feel totally at home either in the working-class world I grew up in or the professional academic world I have joined. In the best-selling *Strangers in Their Own Land*, Arlie Hochschild makes a case for working-class conservatives to come over to the liberal side, which she describes as: "people stand around a large public square inside of which are creative science museums for kids, public art and theater programs, libraries, schools—a state of the art infrastructure available to all." But for readers from working-class families like myself, who are the first in our families to attend college, who have felt like unwelcome strangers in liberal-minded elite institutions, and who have been wounded and ashamed by the feeling of being inadequate in museums and schools—this vision does not feel so welcoming.

When I was interviewing for my first job, my father was taking a "sociology of work" class, as one of his major goals in life is to get a four-year degree and he wanted to learn more about what I do. His National Guard unit was deployed for a natural disaster, and he had no choice but to miss an exam. My father wrote several self-prostrating emails, begging to reschedule. The instructor of the course, despite listing social-class inequality as one of his interests, was dismissive and unyielding, insisting that my father would fail the course if he did not show up for the test. Since I could not pick up the phone during my job interview, my dad reached out to one of my close friends, who helped him construct a polished email that persuaded the instructor to allow him to take the exam at a different time. Later, when this sociology instructor learned that my father had a professional sociologist daughter, he was apologetic and bashful. I am sensitive to the hypocrisy of liberal elites who advocate for social justice while remaining blind to the casual cruelty they inflict on the people below them on the class ladder, even as I usually vote with them. And I am uncomfortable around liberal academics who view working-class conservative politics as an obstacle to overcome without trying to understand them. It is from this space of tension and contradiction that I think and write.

In my own family, there are instances of the kinds of pain that runs through this book—addictions and illnesses, poverty and relationship turmoil. Their stories are not mine to tell, but I can empathize deeply with the working-class people of Coal Brook—even when they cut off ties with their own family members or rage against those who seem to refuse to take responsibility for themselves. Yet, at the same time, when I read *Hillbilly Elegy*, a memoir of upward mobility, I felt intense anger and protectiveness toward working-class people. In his book, J. D. Vance escapes the cycle of poverty and hopelessness through the stability of his grandmother, the self-discipline and hard work instilled by the military, and his commitment to realizing his God-given talents. While I might be able to claim that I also worked my way up, *Hillbilly Elegy* smacks of self-righteousness, a harsh unwillingness to acknowledge how economic inequality produces real suffering, or how the barriers to mobility are devastatingly real. It is really hard to leave this community, and the people who trusted me to share their stories. I still feel like I am taking so much more than I could ever give back.

Characteristic of the Sample

	White		Black or Hispanic		Total
	Male	Female	Male	Female	
Registered to vote					
Yes	21	22	15	5	63
No	8	16	11	10	45
Voted for in 2016					
Trump	13	12	1	-	26
Clinton	3	4	3	-	10
Other	1	-	-	-	1
Non-voter	12	22	22	15	71
Education					
Less than HS	-	5	10	6	21
HS or GED	23	21	14	9	66
Certificate	1	5	-	-	6
Some college	1	4	1	-	6
Associate or more	4	3	1	-	8
Relationship status					
Married	11	11	4	1	27
Widowed	1	-	-	-	1
Cohabiting	4	6	7	6	23
Divorced	4	9	1	3	17
Single	9	12	14	5	40
Average age	38	37	29	28	34
Total	29	38	26	15	108

NOTES

Introduction

1. Schlozman, Verba, and Brady (2013).
2. Mayer (2014); Gest (2016); Judis (2016); Lamont (2017).
3. "Coal Brook" is my fictional name for an amalgamation of four small towns in the southern counties of the anthracite coal region. I have changed all names to protect the identities of my respondents. See Methodological Appendix for more detail on the interviewing process and the sample characteristics.
4. Marsh (1987).
5. Frey and Teixeira (2008).
6. A historically Democratic-leaning swing state, Pennsylvania played a deciding role in the victory of Donald Trump in November 2016, with high levels of support streaming from depressed rural areas of the state. National analyses following the 2016 presidential election reveal that nearly one in four of white Democrats with less than a four-year college degree who had voted for Obama in 2012 either supported Trump or voted for a third-party candidate. As researchers Alec Tyson and Shiva Maniam (2016) document, Trump's exit-poll victory margin among whites without a college degree was larger than any candidate's since 1980: two-thirds of noncollege whites voted for Trump, while just 28 percent voted for his opponent, Hillary Clinton. In Schuylkill County, one of the southern counties of the coal region, Trump defeated Clinton 69 percent to 26 percent, a large increase compared to Mitt Romney's 56–42 victory over Obama in 2012. Furthermore, according to an analysis by the *New York Times*, there were 5,995 Schuylkill County registered voters who voted in 2012, remain registered, and did not go to the polls in 2016 (Cohn 2017).
7. Previous research points to the interests of political elites and the barriers to democratic participation that they create as main drivers of inequality in political participation. In their seminal book, *Why Americans Still Don't Vote*, Frances Fox Piven and Richard A. Cloward (2000) describe how the right to vote has been historically contested in the United States and how political elites have been able to build barriers to participation in order to demobilize working-class voters who could use their vote to alter the political direction of the country. For example, the introduction of poll taxes and literacy tests alongside the design of complex voter registration requirements has skewed the electorate toward more privileged voters. My study focuses largely on the ways in which working-class people justify their own disengagement as a choice, as my research was not designed to follow people as they encounter barriers to participation. However, both the external and internal barriers to voting are essential pieces of the puzzle of working-class disengagement.
8. For a discussion about investigating politics in seemingly nonpolitical domains, see Hartmann and Uggen (2015).

9. For rigorous empirical examinations of these trends, see Putnam (2000); Western and Rosenfeld (2011); Rosenfeld (2014); Cherlin (2010); Skocpol and Fiorina (1999).

10. For a compelling case on why policy should focus on investing in workers, whether through vocational training or time off for young parents, rather than on redistribution alone, see Sawhill (2018).

11. For an examination of how children's social security enrollment reduces household poverty, see Duggan and Kearney (2007).

12. See Brooks and Manza (2007).

13. Trump voters were more likely to live in geographically isolated communities like Coal Brook, with few college graduates, high levels of economic insecurity, and low levels of ethnic and cultural diversity. Trump also garnered more voter support than the 2012 Republican presidential candidate Mitt Romney did in small cities and rural areas with the highest drug, alcohol, and suicide mortality rates, hinting at understudied connections among economic decline, emotional despair, and political realignment (Monnat 2016).

14. See Barkun (2006).

15. Haidt (2012).

16. On the connections between narrative, political identity, and suffering, see Gaventa (1980); Alexander (2012).

17. Campbell (2006).

18. Cramer (2016); Polletta (2006).

19. Eliasoph (1998); Bruner (1986).

20. Sherman (2009).

21. Wuthnow (2018).

22. Hochschild (2016).

23. Gest (2016).

24. Achen and Bartels (2016).

25. Weis (2001).

26. Thompson (1966).

27. Keil and Keil (2014:130).

28. Manza and Brooks (1999).

29. Swidler (1986).

30. Furthermore, the concept of "class" stems from a critical tradition that uncovers the relationships of exploitation between social groups, rather than simply explaining advantage in terms of the attributes of individuals climbing and falling, as if on rungs on a ladder. This critical view of inequality runs through the analyses of my interviewees as well as my own (Wright 2008).

31. See Methodological Appendix for the characteristics of the sample. Although I recruited people who had less than a four-year college degree, I allowed for one white respondent who reported she was working on a master's degree from a for-profit online college. As she was working as a home-health aide, married to a day laborer, and raising six children, she was not able to put her degree to use but had acquired significant debt. Another mother in the sample achieved a four-year degree in nutrition after twenty years of taking college classes at different institutions and online but was not using her degree in her service job. None of her children attended a four-year college.

32. Luker (2010:61).

33. Pennsylvania has historically been an overwhelmingly white state, with a minority of African Americans in major cities, but the rural areas are growing more ethnically and racially diverse. In 2000, there were about 157,201 residents, or 5 percent of the total population, who identified as nonwhite and/or Hispanic. In 2015, though, 294,801 rural residents, or 9 percent of the total population, were nonwhite and/or Hispanic. These "newcomers" are generally younger, poorer, less likely to be married, and more likely to be single parents than their rural white counterparts (Center for Rural PA 2015).

34. On racial relations as constantly in flux, produced in micro interactions, see McDermott (2006). My perspective was informed by a critical tradition, which views race as the product of struggles for domination and power, rather than as a fixed biological category (Omi and Winant 1986).

35. On rural transformations, see Marrow (2011).
36. See Lamont, Michele et al. (2016).
37. Lareau and Conley (2008).
38. Lane (1962).
39. Bourdieu (1999).
40. Wailoo (2014); see also Skocpol (1995).
41. Skocpol and Williamson (2016).
42. It is estimated that at least 30,000 men perished while mining anthracite coal, with an additional 50,000 permanently injured and hundreds of thousands dying of black lung later in life. Miners were controlled in every facet of life through dependence on the company store for food and supplies and company homes for shelter, and the threat of starvation, homelessness, and loss of old-age pension kept workers in a state of "industrial feudalism" (Marsh 1987:344).
43. Dublin and Licht (2005:77).
44. Erikson (1978).
45. Hacker (2002, 2008).
46. Reich (2015).
47. Gilens and Page (2014).
48. Bartels (2008).
49. Verba and Nie (1987).
50. Hill et al. (1995).
51. Reich (2015).
52. Schlozman and Brady (2013).

Chapter 1

1. Cherlin et al. (2016).
2. Eatwell and Milgate (2011).
3. Cowie (2016).
4. Taylor-Gooby (2004).
5. Harvey (2005).
6. Western (1997).
7. Edin and Shaefer (2015).
8. Edsall et al. (1992).
9. Morgan and Lee (2017) suggest that circumstances were uncharacteristically propitious for a Republican candidate who could appeal to prospective working-class voters, especially those who had not voted in recent presidential elections but could be mobilized to vote.
10. Unions ignored miner's emphysema, or black lung, a condition caused by inhaling fine coal dust that eventually left hundreds of thousands of miners to die. In1969, the United Mine Workers convinced the US Congress to enact the landmark Federal Coal Mine Health and Safety Act, which provided compensation for miners (and their dependents) disabled by black lung. However, the law was poorly enforced, and mine owners could easily contest the miners' claims (Keil and Keil 2014).
11. Rubin (1976).
12. Komarovsky (1964).
13. Illouz (2007).
14. Lopez (2015).
15. Lakoff (2002).
16. Hochschild (2016).
17. The economist Alan Krueger (2016) posits a relationship between men's employment status and their subjective well-being, finding that prime-age out-of-work men are much more likely to report that their health is "fair" or "poor" than employed men. Three-quarters of prime-age men outside of the labor force do not receive social security disability insurance (SSDI). Furthermore, fully 44 percent of them reported taking pain medication on the previous day.
18. See Mann (1987); Aronowitz (1992).

19. The New Deal and post–World War II era harnessed the support of both African Americans, who were rapidly shifting to the Democratic Party of the New Deal in the 1930s, and white southern segregationists. Southern congressional representatives, for example, insisted that the Social Security Act of 1935 exclude agricultural and domestic workers from coverage—two segments of the American workforce that were overwhelmingly African American in the 1930s (Katznelson 2005).

20. As Edsall and Edsall (1992) explain, taxes "dr[o]ve home the cost to whites of federal programs that redistribute social and economic benefits to blacks and other minorities," mapping onto a whole range of other domestic issues including welfare policy, drug enforcement, housing regulation, and prison construction.

21. McVeigh (2009).

22. Kazin (1998).

23. Alexander (2010).

24. Cherlin (2014).

25. Reich (2014).

26. Cherlin (2014).

27. Sharkey (2015).

28. Wilson (1987).

29. Dunlap et al. (2006).

30. Western (2006).

31. Sharkey (2015).

32. Bentele and O'Brien (2013).

33. In November 2016, both minority and black voter turnout plunged, even in swing states (Frey 2017).

34. Today, as Bennett et al. (2013) argue, more and more Americans are "disavowing" politics—withdrawing from the contentious public sphere and the negative, polluted associations of public political engagement.

35. See Lamont et al. (2013).

36. While several of the young black and Latino men I interviewed believed that they were disenfranchised after being convicted of a felony, voting rights are actually restored in Pennsylvania after a person completes their prison sentence.

37. For an examination of how boys of color are policed in their everyday lives, see Rios (2011).

38. Oliver and Wood (2014).

39. Jolley and Douglas (2014).

Chapter 2

1. In his iconic *America's Working Man*, David Halle (1987:302) discovered that the political culture of the white working class contains seeds of both left-wing progressivism and right-wing populism. On the one hand, he finds, "there is the opportunity for a politics of progress based on the struggle for full democracy, for full employment, for the dignity of the worker, for fair and safe working conditions, for a vigorous trade union movement, for equal treatment of working men and working women and whites and blacks, and for a moderate and balanced foreign policy." On the other hand, "there is also a danger of a domestic policy that draws on hostility toward blacks and Hispanics, women and the poor, and of a foreign policy based on grandiose and reckless images of America's role in the world . . . that could easily destroy the world."

2. Kefalas (2003).

3. It could also be the case that Brian's condemnation of the KKK is a performance of decency for me. Analyses of white separatist publications reveal that white separatist organizations, in their public appeals, often exhibit "a kind of repackaged, relabeled and transformed white supremacy" (Swain 2002:16).

4. On whiteness as an identity in an era of purported color-blindness, see McDermott (2015).

5. Kimmel (2015).

6. Ibid.

7. Hartmann (1981).

8. Willis (1977).
9. See Hochschild (2016:15).
10. As McDermott (2015) demonstrates, this awareness of himself as descending from Irish immigrants leads to a color blindness that denies the existence of racism.
11. MacGaffey (2013).
12. Ibid.
13. Wilcox et al. (2012).
14. Bellah et al. (2017).
15. Cowie (2016).

Chapter 3

1. Putnam (1993).
2. Child sexual abuse occurs across the race and class spectrum, and is less correlated with income than other types of abuse. An estimated 90 percent of offenders are men. Most victims know their offender: about a quarter of them are family members (Douglas and Finkelhor 2005). The lack of resources in rural communities can also make it more difficult for rural victims of sexual abuse and intimate partner violence to get help (McCall-Hosenfeld et al. 2014).
3. According to the National Institute on Drug Abuse, "Synthetic cathinones, more commonly known as 'bath salts,' are synthetic (human-made) drugs chemically related to cathinone, a stimulant found in the khat plant." They are part of a group of "unregulated psychoactive (mind-altering) substances that have become newly available on the market and are intended to copy the effects of illegal drugs." They are seen as a cheaper alternative to methamphetamine and cocaine. They were banned in Pennsylvania in 2011.
4. Women who have experienced or live with intimate partner violence (IPV) are at greater risk of associated depressive symptoms and other mental health problems including posttraumatic stress disorder (PTSD), anxiety, and suicide risk (Bonomi et al. 2006).
5. Uninsured adults are more likely to skip preventative care and screening measures, and are more at risk of being diagnosed with diseases like cancer when they are in later stages, resulting in higher mortality rates. Under the Affordable Care Act, Medicaid coverage was expanded to most adults with incomes at or below 138 percent of the federal poverty line with subsidies available for people with incomes up to 400 percent of the federal poverty line to purchase health insurance through a marketplace. In 2016, the number of nonelderly uninsured people in the US had dropped from 44 million in 2013 to 27 million. However, an access gap and cost poses a major imposition on workers. Workers in small firms like Mary Ann Wilson's find their share of the premium unaffordable. The majority of the remaining uninsured population lives in families with at least one low-income worker. For many uninsured people, "the costs of health insurance and medical care are weighed against equally essential needs, like housing, food, or transportation to work, and many uninsured adults report difficulty paying basic monthly expenses such as rent, food, and utilities" (Garfield et al. 2016).
6. See Carr and Kefalas (2010) on how small towns in rural America "hollow out the middle" by encouraging their best and brightest students to leave their hometowns and build a better life in a new place.
7. Erdmans and Black (2015).
8. In her study of disadvantaged black neighborhoods under heavy police surveillance, Goffman (2014:37) similarly found that "out of frustration and anger at his failures as a father, spouse, brother, or son, his partner or family members may freely call the police on him, taking advantage of his wanted status to get back at him or punish him."
9. The economists Anne Case and Angus Deaton (2017) have drawn attention to a health crisis in rural America, where opioid abuse, cirrhosis of the liver, and suicide are reversing life-expectancy gains among the white working class. They attribute this health crisis to the compounding pain, despair, and social unmooring in the lives of working-class white people that began with the loss of good blue-collar jobs in the 1970s and then got worse during the 2008 financial crisis.

10. Across the United States, nine out of ten rural places experienced increases in diversity between 1990 and 2010, with racial and ethnic minorities moving to whiter areas, and white young adults moving to more diverse urban areas (Barrett and Farrell 2014).

Chapter 4

1. In *Coal Dust on Your Feet: The Rise, Decline, and Restoration of an Anthracite Mining Town*, the anthropologist Janet MacGaffey explains, "a new underclass has emerged in town as a result of demographic change: a new group of migrants, poor and on welfare, have [replaced] some of the population loss" that resulted from the closing of the mines. Labeling these newcomers "welfare migrants" and "poor inner city residents," she claims that these "new arrivals are not integrating into the town community because they are constantly on the move in search of other welfare possibilities." Furthermore, she writes, these new migrants "bring the ways of the inner city into town"—drugs, violence, and a "more confrontational culture and a lifestyle based on overcrowded apartments" (287).
2. King (2001).
3. The years since 2000 have seen the largest wave of migration from Puerto Rico to the US since the Great Migration in the 1950s and 1960s because of economic crisis, low job prospects, and heavy dependence on social assistance on the island. The stateside Puerto Rican origin population once was highly concentrated in the Northeast, especially New York, but is now more widely dispersed (Jensen 2006; Lichter and Johnson 2006).
4. Anderson (2008).
5. From my own investigation into housing in Coal Brook, I learned that there are more than three hundred families, the majority of whom are white, on the waiting list for subsidized housing. The housing authority manages about thirty units through the Section 8 housing choice voucher program. As the poverty scholars Stefanie DeLuca and colleagues (2013) explain, "because housing assistance is not an entitlement, less than a third of eligible households receive any form of subsidy."
6. On racial discrimination in hiring, see Pager et al. (2009).
7. Lamont et al. (2013).
8. Bell (2017).
9. Lamont (2000).
10. Lamont et al. (2013).
11. Fields (2016).
12. On the experience of leaving prison and attempting to integrate back into society, see Western (2018).

Chapter 5

1. Hays (2004).
2. Hill (2005).
3. Collins (2000).
4. See Cottom (2016).
5. As Shirley Hill explains, people of color in the United States have long been at odds with dominant societal ideals about the proper roles of men and women. Indeed, black men have been seen as particularly "emasculated" by racism because it robbed them of authority over their wives and children, which is granted to white men as primary breadwinners.
6. Wilson (1987); Edin and Kefalas (2005).
7. The incarceration of a parent has been linked with worsening behavioral and mental health outcomes among children, including increased aggression and delinquency, decreased educational attainment, and exposure to social stigma, in addition to loss of an involved parent (Wildeman 2009; Haskins 2016; Turney and Haskins 2014).

Chapter 6

1. Hacker and Pierson (2010) argue that both Democrats and Republicans have worked against the economic interests of the American people by allowing the top 1 percent to accumulate enormous wealth gains while income growth has remained flat among the middle class and poor since the 1970s. This soaring inequality is problematic because political parties have adjusted their platforms to respond to the policy concerns of the wealthy elite rather than the average voter—whether by cutting capital gains taxes or failing to penalize corporations for wrongdoing, such as during the 2008 financial crisis. Importantly, Hacker and Pierson push back against the idea that inequality is the inevitable result of globalization and technological change, focusing on how corporate and financial actors have lobbied for government policies in their favor.
2. Lane (1962: 164–176).
3. Lane (1962).
4. Kenworthy and Owens (2012).
5. Tocqueville (2003); Arendt (1951); Putnam (1993); Warren (2001).
6. Pilkington and Polluck (2015) have found that European young adults are "fed up" with the politics of their parents' generation and are searching for new forms of civic engagement that happen outside of traditional arenas.
7. The transmission of party identification from parent to child is a key element of political social-ization in the US, but children do not automatically take on their parents' views. Intriguingly, social support, shared activities, and feelings of belonging within the family does not affect whether children know their parents' political views, but this makes it more likely that children will adopt their parents' perceived political affiliations and identities (Ojeda and Hatemi 2015).
8. Horkheimer and Adorno (1972).
9. Walker (2013).
10. Hofstadter (1964).
11. Barkun (2006).
12. Bader and Gordon (2017).
13. DiGrazia (2017).
14. Barkun (2006).
15. Sunstein (2017).
16. The legal scholar Michelle Alexander (2010) writes extensively about the penalties that are applied to people who have been convicted of crimes after they serve their time and are released back into society.
17. LeBlanc (2003).
18. See, for example, Illouz (2007); Silva (2013); hooks (1989).
19. Bennett et al. (2013).

Conclusion

1. McKerns (2007).
2. Klein (2015).
3. Giddens (1984).
4. See, for example, Marx and Engels (1848); Gramsci (1985); Adorno et al. (1950); Mann (1986); Aronowitz (1992).
5. https://www.marxists.org/archive/marx/works/1848/communist-manifesto/.
6. Sennett and Cobb (1973).
7. Cherlin (2014).
8. Lyson and Falk (1993).
9. Goodell (2007).
10. See Milkman (1997); Bettie (2003).

11. See Berezin (1997).
12. Hall and Lamont (2013).
13. Vance (2016).
14. Reich (2015).
15. Bourdieu (2000:629).
16. McCall (2013).
17. For a discussion of the potential for multiracial coalitions among Democratic voters, see Bobo (2017); on the appeal of Trump to white working-class men in search of recognition, see Lamont (2017).
18. Ewick and Silbey (2003).
19. Simon and Lively (2010).
20. Stein (2011).
21. Kleinman (1997).
22. Scheff (2000).
23. Frank (1995).
24. Randles (2017).
25. Mazelis (2017).
26. Nussbaum (1996).
27. Lorde (1992).

REFERENCES

Achen, Christopher H., and Larry M. Bartels. 2016. *Democracy for Realists: Why Elections Do Not Produce Responsive Government.* Princeton, NJ: Princeton University Press.

Adorno, Theodor W., Elise Frenkel-Brunswik, Daniel Levinson, and Nevitt Sanford. 1950. *The Authoritarian Personality.* New York: Harper & Brothers.

Alexander, Jeffrey C. 2012. *Trauma: A Social Theory.* Cambridge, UK: Polity.

Alexander, Michelle. 2010. *The New Jim Crow: Mass Incarceration in the Age of Colorblindness.* New York: Free Press.

Anderson, Elijah. 2008. *Against the Wall: Poor, Young, Black, and Male.* Philadelphia: University of Pennsylvania Press.

Arendt, Hannah. 1951. *The Origins of Totalitarianism.* 1st ed. New York: Harcourt, Brace.

Aronowitz, Stanley. 1992. *False Promises: The Shaping of American Working Class Consciousness.* Durham, NC: Duke University Press.

Aughtmon, Susanna Foth. 2009. *All I Need Is Jesus and a Good Pair of Jeans: The Tired Supergirl's Search for Grace.* Grand Rapids: Revel, a division of Baker Publishing House.

Bader, Christopher, Edward Day, and Ann Gordon. 2017. "What Aren't They Telling Us?—Chapman University Survey of American Fears." Wilkinson College of Arts, Humanities, and Social Sciences. Retrieved July 17, 2017 (https://blogs.chapman.edu/wilkinson/2016/10/11/what-arent-they-telling-us/).

Barkun, Michael. 2006. *A Culture of Conspiracy: Apocalyptic Visions in Contemporary America.* Berkeley: University of California Press.

Barrett, John Iceland, and Chad Farrell. 2014. "Is Ethnoracial Residential Integration on the Rise? Evidence from Metropolitan and Micropolitan Since 1980." In *Diversity and Disparities: America Enters a New Century,* 415–56. New York: Russell Sage Foundation.

Bartels, Larry. 2008. *Unequal Democracy: The Political Economy of the New Gilded Age.* New York: Russell Sage Foundation.

Beattie, Melody. 1986. *Codependent No More: How to Stop Controlling Others and Start Caring for Yourself.* Center City: Hazelden.

Bell, Monica. 2017. "Police Reform and the Dismantling of Legal Estrangement." *Yale Law Journal* 126(7):2054.

Bellah, Robert, Richard Madsen, William Sullivan, Ann Swidler, and Steven Tipton. 2017. *Habits of the Heart: Individualism and Commitment in American Life.* Berkeley: University of California Press.

Bennett, Elizabeth A., Alissa Cordner, Peter Taylor Klein, Stephanie Savell, and Gianpaolo Baiocchi. 2013. "Disavowing Politics: Civic Engagement in an Era of Political Skepticism." *American Journal of Sociology* 119(2):518–48.

Bentele, Keith Gunnar, and O'Brien, Erin E. 2013. "Jim Crow 2.0?: Why States Consider and Adopt Restrictive Voter Access Policies." *Sociology Faculty Publication Series*. 11(4):1088–116.

Berezin, Mabel. 1997. *Making the Fascist Self: The Political Culture of Interwar Italy*. Ithaca, NY: Cornell University Press.

Bettie, Julie, 2003. *Women without Class: Girls, Race, and Identity*. Berkeley: University of California Press.

Bobo, Lawrence. 2017. "Racism in Trump's America: reflections on culture, sociology, and the 2016 US presidential election." *British Journal of Sociology* 68(1): S85–S104.

Bonomi, Amy E. et al. 2006. "Intimate Partner Violence and Women's Physical, Mental, and Social Functioning." *American Journal of Preventive Medicine* 30(6):458–66.

Bourdieu, Pierre. 1999. *The Weight of the World: Social Suffering in Contemporary Society*. Redwood City, CA: Stanford University Press.

Brooks, Clem, and Jeff Manza. 2007. *Why Welfare States Persist: The Importance of Public Opinion in Democracies*. Chicago: University of Chicago Press.

Bruner, Jerome Seymour. 1986. *Actual Minds, Possible Worlds*. Cambridge, MA: Harvard University Press.

Campbell, David E. 2006. *Why We Vote: How Schools and Communities Shape Our Civic Life*. Princeton, NJ: Princeton University Press.

Carr, Patrick J., and Maria J. Kefalas. 2010. *Hollowing Out the Middle: The Rural Brain Drain and What It Means for America*. Boston: Beacon Press.

Case, Anne, and Angus Deaton. 2017. "Mortality and Morbidity in the 21st Century | Brookings Institution." Brookings. Retrieved March 29, 2017 (https://www.brookings.edu/bpea-articles/mortality-and-morbidity-in-the-21st-century/).

Center for Rural PA. 2015. "Fact Sheet: Rural Pennsylvania Minority Population." The Center for Rural Pa. Retrieved June 8, 2017 (http://www.rural.palegislature.us/documents/factsheets/Minorities2012.pdf).

Cherlin, Andrew J. 2014. *Labor's Love Lost: The Rise and Fall of the Working-Class Family in America*. New York: Russell Sage Foundation.

Cherlin, Andrew. 2010. *The Marriage-Go-Round: The State of Marriage and the Family in America Today*. New York: Vintage.

Cherlin, Andrew J., David C. Ribar, and Suzumi Yasutake. 2016. "Nonmarital First Births, Marriage, and Income Inequality." *American Sociological Review* 81(4):749–70.

Chetty, Raj et al. 2016. "The Fading American Dream: Trends in Absolute Income Mobility Since 1940." National Bureau of Economic Research. Available online: http://www.nber.org/papers/w22910.

Cohn, Nate. 2017. "A 2016 Review: Turnout Wasn't the Driver of Clinton's Defeat." *New York Times*. Available online: https://www.nytimes.com/2017/03/28/upshot/a-2016-review-turnout-wasnt-the-driver-of-clintons-defeat.html.

Collins, Patricia Hill. 2000. *Black Feminist Thought: Knowledge, Consciousness, and the Politics of Empowerment*. New York: Routledge.

Cottom, Tressie McMillan. 2016. *Lower Ed: The Troubling Rise of For-Profit Colleges in the New Economy*. New York: New Press.

Cowie, Jefferson. 2016. *The Great Exception*. Princeton, NJ: Princeton University Press.

Cramer, Katherine. 2016. *The Politics of Resentment*. Chicago: University of Chicago Press.

DeLuca, Stefanie, Philip M. E. Garboden, and Peter Rosenblatt. 2013. "Segregating Shelter: How Housing Policies Shape the Residential Locations of Low-Income Minority Families." *Annals of the American Academy of Political and Social Science* 647:268–99.

DiGrazia, Joseph. 2017. "The Social Determinants of Conspiratorial Ideation." *Socius*. Available online: https://doi.org/10.1177/2378023116689791.

Douglas, Emily M., and David Finkelhor. 2005. *Childhood Sexual Abuse Fact Sheet*. Crimes Against Children Center. Durham: University of New Hampshire. Retrieved July 9, 2017 (http://www.unh.edu/ccrc/factsheet/pdf/CSA-FS20.pdf).

Dublin, Thomas, and Walter Licht. 2005. *The Face of Decline: The Pennsylvania Anthracite Region in the Twentieth Century.* Ithaca, NY: Cornell University Press.

Duggan, Mark G., and Melissa Kearney. 2007. "The Impact of Child SSI Enrollment on Household Outcomes." *Journal of Policy Analysis and Management* 26(4):861–85.

Dunlap, Eloise, Andrew Golub, and Bruce D. Johnson. 2006. "The Severely-Distressed African American Family in the Crack Era: Empowerment Is Not Enough." *Journal of Sociology and Social Welfare* 33(1):115–39.

Eatwell, John, and Murray Milgate. 2011. *The Fall and Rise of Keynesian Economics.* Oxford: Oxford University Press.

Edin, Kathryn, and Maria Kefalas. 2005. *Promises I Can Keep: Why Poor Women Put Motherhood before Marriage.* Berkeley: University of California Press.

Edin, Kathryn, and Luke Shaefer. 2015. *$2.00 a Day: Living on Almost Nothing in America.* Boston: Houghton Mifflin Harcourt.

Edsall, Thomas B., and Mary D. Edsall. 1992. *Chain Reaction: The Impact of Race, Rights, and Taxes on American Politics.* New York: W. W. Norton.

Eliasoph, Nina. 1998. *Avoiding Politics: How Americans Produce Apathy in Everyday Life.* New York: Cambridge University Press.

Eliasoph, Nina, and Paul Lichterman. 2003. "Culture in Interaction." *American Journal of Sociology* 108(4):735–94.

Erdmans, Mary Patrice, and Timothy Black. 2015. *On Becoming a Teen Mom: Life before Pregnancy.* Berkeley: University of California Press.

Erikson, Kai T. 1978. *Everything in Its Path: Destruction of Community in the Buffalo Creek Flood.* New York: Simon & Schuster.

Ewick, Patricia, and Susan S. Silbey. 2003. "Narrating Social Structure: Stories of Resistance to Legal Authority." *American Journal of Sociology* 108(6):1328–72.

Fields, Corey. 2016. *Black Elephants in the Room: The Unexpected Politics of African American Republicans.* Berkeley: University of California Press.

Frank, Arthur. 1995. *The Wounded Storyteller: Body, Illness, and Ethics.* Chicago: University of Chicago Press.

Frey, William. 2017. "Census shows pervasive decline in 2016 minority voter turnout." Available at: https://www.brookings.edu/blog/the-avenue/2017/05/18/census-shows-pervasive-decline-in-2016-minority-voter-turnout/.

Frey, William H., and Ruy Teixeira. 2008. *The Political Geography of Pennsylvania: Not Another Rust Belt State.* Washington, DC: Brookings. Retrieved June 7, 2017 (https://www.brookings.edu/wp-content/uploads/2016/06/04_political_demographics_frey_teixeira.pdf).

Garfield, Rachel, Melissa Majerol, Anthony Damico, and Julia Foutz. 2016. "The Uninsured: A Primer—Key Facts about Health Insurance and the Uninsured in the Wake of National Health Reform." Henry J. Kaiser Family Foundation. Retrieved July 19, 2017 (https://www.kff.org/uninsured/report/the-uninsured-a-primer-key-facts-about-health-insurance-and-the-uninsured-under-the-affordable-care-act/).

Gaventa, John. 1980. *Power and Powerlessness. Quiescence and Rebellion in an Appalachian Valley.* Urbana: University of Illinois Press

Gest, Justin. 2016. *The New Minority: White Working Class Politics in an Age of Immigration and Inequality.* Oxford: Oxford University Press.

Giddens, Anthony. 1984. *The Constitution of Society: Outline of the Theory of Structuration.* Berkeley: University of California Press.

Gilens, Martin, and Benjamin I. Page. 2014. "Testing Theories of American Politics: Elites, Interest Groups, and Average Citizens." *Perspectives on Politics* 12(3):564–81.

Goffman, Alice. 2014. *On the Run: Fugitive Life in an American City.* Chicago: University of Chicago Press.

Goodell, Jeff. 2007. *Big Coal: The Dirty Secret Behind America's Energy Future.* Boston: Houghton Mifflin.

Gramsci, Antonio. 1985. "The Intellectuals." In *Selections from the Prison Notebooks*, 5–14. New York: International Publishers.

Hacker, Jacob S. 2008. *The Great Risk Shift: The New Economic Insecurity and the Decline of the American Dream*. New York: Oxford.

—–. 2002. *The Divided Welfare State: The Battle over Public and Private Social Benefits in the United States*. New York: Cambridge University Press.

Hacker, Jacob S., and Paul Pierson. 2010. *Winner-Take-All Politics: How Washington Made the Rich Richer-and Turned Its Back on the Middle Class*. New York: Simon & Schuster.

Haidt, Jonathan. *The Righteous Mind: Why Good People are Divided by Politics and Religion*. 2012. New York: Vintage.

Hall, Peter A., and Michèle Lamont, eds. 2013. *Social Resilience in the Neo-Liberal Era*. Cambridge: Cambridge University Press.

Halle, David. 1987. *America's Working Man: Work, Home, and Politics among Blue-Collar Property Owners*. Chicago: University of Chicago Press

Hartmann, Douglas, and Christopher Uggen. 2015. *The Social Side of Politics*. New York: W. W. Norton.

Hartmann, Heidi. 1981. "The Unhappy Marriage of Marxism and Feminism." In *Women and Revolution: A Discussion of the Unhappy Marriage of Marxism and Feminism*. South End Press Political Controversies, edited by L. Sargent. Boston: South End Press.

Harvey, David. 2005. *A Brief History of Neoliberalism*. Oxford: Oxford University Press.

Haskins, Anna. 2016. "How Does Parental Incarceration Affect Children's Cognitive and Noncognitive Development?" *Focus* 23:18–22.

Hay, Louise and David Kessler. 2014. *You Can Heal Your Heart: Finding Peace After a Breakup, Divorce, or Death*. Carslbad: Hay House Inc.

Hays, Sharon. 2004. *Flat Broke with Children: Women in the Age of Welfare Reform*. New York: Oxford University Press.

Hill, Kim Quaile, Jan E. Leighley, and Angela Hinton-Andersson. 1995. "Lower-Class Mobilization and Policy Linkage in the US States." *American Journal of Political Science* 39:75–86.

Hill, Shirley. 2005. *Black Intimacies: A Gender Perspective on Families and Relationships*. Lanham, MD: AltaMira.

Hochschild, Arlie Russell. 2016. *Strangers in Their Own Land: Anger and Mourning on the American Right*. New York: New Press.

Hofstadter, Richard. 1964. "The Paranoid Style in American Politics." *Harper's Magazine*, November. Available at: https://harpers.org/archive/1964/11/the-paranoid-style-in-american-politics/.

hooks, bell. 1989. *Talking Back: Thinking Feminist, Thinking Black*. 1st ed. Toronto: Between the Lines.

Horkheimer, Max, and Theodor W. Adorno. 1972. *Dialectic of Enlightenment*. New York: Crossroad Publishing Company.

Illouz, Eva. 2007. *Cold Intimacies: The Making of Emotional Capitalism*. Cambridge: Polity.

Jensen, Leif. 2006. *New Immigrant Settlements in Rural America: Problems, Prospects, and Policies*. Durham, NH: Carsey Institute.

Jolley, Daniel, and Karen M. Douglas. 2014. "The Social Consequences of Conspiracism: Exposure to Conspiracy Theories Decreases Intentions to Engage in Politics and to Reduce One's Carbon Footprint." *British Journal of Psychology* 105(1):35–56.

Kalleberg, Arne L. 2009. "Precarious Work, Insecure Workers: Employment Relations in Transition." *American Sociological Review* 74(1):1–22.

Katznelson, Ira. 2005. *When Affirmative Action Was White: An Untold History of Racial Inequality in Twentieth-Century America*. New York: W. W. Norton.

Kazin, Michael. 1998. *The Populist Persuasion: An American History*. Rev. ed. Ithaca, NY: Cornell University Press.

Kefalas, Maria. 2003. *Working-Class Heroes: Protecting Home, Community, and Nation in a Chicago Neighborhood*. Chicago: University of Chicago Press.

Keil, Thomas J., and Jacqueline M. Keil. 2014. *Anthracite's Demise and the Post-Coal Economy of Northeastern Pennsylvania*. Lanham, MD: Rowman & Littlefield.

Kenworthy, Lane, and Lindsay Owens. 2012. *Political Attitudes, Public Opinion, and the Great Recession*. Stanford, CA: Russell Sage Foundation and the Stanford Center on Poverty and Inequality.

Kimmel, Michael. 2015. *Angry White Men: American Masculinity at the End of an Era*. New York: Nation Books.

King, Laura. 2001. "The Hard Road to the Good Life: The Happy, Mature Person." *Journal of Humanistic Psychology* 41(1):51–72.

Klein, Naomi. 2015. *This Changes Everything: Capitalism vs. the Climate*. New York: Simon & Schuster.

Kleinman, Arthur. 1997. *Writing at the Margin: Discourse Between Anthropology and Medicine*. Berkeley: University of California Press.

Komarovsky, Mirra. 1964. *Blue-Collar Marriage*. With the collaboration of Jane H. Phillips. New York: Random House.

Krueger, Alan B. 2016. "Where Have All the Workers Gone?" Paper presented at the Federal Reserve Bank of Boston 60th Economic Conference.

Lakoff, George. 2002. *Moral Politics: How Liberals and Conservatives Think*. 2nd ed. Chicago: University of Chicago Press.

Lamont, Michele. 2000. *The Dignity of Working Men*. Chicago: University of Chicago Press.

Lamont, Michele. 2017. "Addressing the Recognition Gap: Destigmatization and the Reduction of Inequality." Presidential Address at the 112th Annual Meeting of the American Sociological Association in Toronto, ON, Canada, August 13, 2017.

Lamont, Michele, Graziella Morales Silva, Jessica S. Welburn, Joshua Guetzkow, Nissim Mizrachi, Hanna Herzog, and Elisa Reis. 2016. *Getting Respect: Responding to Stigma and Discrimination in the United States, Brazil, and Israel*. Princeton, NJ: Princeton University Press.

Lamont, Michèle, Jessica S. Welburn, and Crystal M. Fleming. 2013. "Responses to Discrimination and Social Resilience Under Neoliberalism: The United States Compared." In *Social Resilience in the Neoliberal Age*, edited by P. Hall and M. Lamont, 129–57. Cambridge: Cambridge University Press.

Lane, Robert. 1962. *Political Ideology: Why the American Common Man Believes What He Does*. New York: Free Press.

Lareau, Annette, and Dalton Conley. 2008. *Social Class: How Does It Work?* New York: Russell Sage Foundation.

LeBlanc, Adrian Nicole. 2003. *Random Family: Love, Drugs, Trouble, and Coming of Age in the Bronx*. New York: Simon & Schuster.

Lichter, Daniel, and Kenneth Johnson. 2006. "Emerging Rural Settlement Patterns and the Geographic Redistribution of America's New Immigrants." *Rural Sociology* 71(1):109–31.

Lopez, Ian Haney. 2015. *Dog Whistle Politics: How Coded Racial Appeals Have Reinvented Racism and Wrecked the Middle Class*. Reprint. Oxford: Oxford University Press.

Lorde, Audre. 1992. *The Cancer Journals: Special Edition*. San Francisco: Aunt Lute Books.

Luker, Kristin. 2010. *Salsa Dancing into the Social Sciences*. Cambridge, MA: Harvard University Press.

Lyson, Thomas A., and William W. Falk. 1993. *Forgotten Places: Uneven Development in Rural America*. Lawrence: University Press of Kansas.

MacGaffey, Janet. 2013. *Coal Dust on Your Feet: The Rise, Decline, and Restoration of an Anthracite Mining Town*. Lewisburg, PA: Bucknell University Press.

Mann, Michael. 1986. *The Sources of Social Power*. Cambridge: Cambridge University Press.

Mann, Michael. 1987. "Ruling Class Strategies and Citizenship." *Sociology* 21(3):339–54.

Manza, Jeff, and Clem Brooks. 1999. *Social Cleavages and Political Change: Voter Alignments and U.S. Party Coalitions*. New York: Oxford University Press.

Marrow, Helen B. 2011. *New Destination Dreaming: Immigration, Race, and Legal Status in the Rural American South*. Stanford, CA: Stanford University Press.

Marsh, Ben. 1987. "Continuity and Decline in the Anthracite Towns of Pennsylvania." *Annals of the Association of American Geographers* 7(3):337–52.

Marx, Karl, and Friedrich Engels. 1848. *The Communist Manifesto.* Available at: https://www.marxists.org/archive/marx/works/1848/communist-manifesto/.

Mazelis, Joan Maya. 2017. Surviving Poverty: Creating Sustainable Ties Among the Poor. New York: NYU Press.

Mayer, Nonna. 2014. "Bring the Poor Back In! Inequalities, Welfare and Politics." *European Political Science* 13(2):187–200.

McCall, Leslie. 2013. *The Undeserving Rich: American Beliefs about Inequality, Opportunity, and Redistribution.* New York: Cambridge University Press.

McCall-Hosenfeld, Jennifer S., Carol S. Weisman, Amanda N. Perry, Marianne M. Hillemeier, and Cynthia H. Chuang. 2014. "'I Just Keep My Antennae out'—How Rural Primary Care Physicians Respond to Intimate Partner Violence (IPV)." *Journal of Interpersonal Violence* 29(14):2670–94.

McDermott, Monica. 2006. *Working-Class White: The Making and Unmaking of Race Relations.* Berkeley: University of California Press.

McDermott, Monica. 2015. "Color-Blind and Color-Visible Identity Among American Whites." *American Behavioral Scientist* 59(11):1452–73.

McKerns, Gerald. 2007. *The Black Rock that Built America: A Tribute to the Anthracite Coal Miners.* New York: Xlibris.

McVeigh, Rory. 2009. *The Rise of the Ku Klux Klan: Right-Wing Movements and National Politics.* Minneapolis: University of Minnesota Press

Milkman, Ruth. 1997. *Farewell to the Factory: Auto Workers in the Late Twentieth Century.* Berkeley: University of California Press

Monnat, Shannon M. 2016. "Deaths of Despair and Support for Trump in the 2016 Presidential Election." Department of Agricultural Economics, Sociology, and Education: University Park, PA: Pennsylvania State University.

Morgan, Stephen L., and Jiwon Lee. 2017. "Social Class and Party Identification During the Clinton, Bush, and Obama Presidencies." *Sociological Science* 4:394–423.

Nakano Glenn, Evelyn, Grace Chang, and Linda Rennie Forcey, eds. 1994. *Mothering: Ideology, Experience, and Agency.* New York: Routledge.

Nussbaum, Martha. 1996. "Compassion: The Basic Social Emotion." *Social Philosophy and Policy* 13(1):27–58.

Ojeda, Christopher, and Peter K. Hatemi. 2015. "Accounting for the Child in the Transmission of Party Identification." *American Sociological Association* 80(6):1150–74.

Oliver, J. Eric, and Thomas J. Wood. 2014. "Conspiracy Theories and the Paranoid Style(s) of Mass Opinion." *American Journal of Political Science* 58(4):952–66.

Omi, Michael, and Howard Winant. 1986. *Racial Formation in the United States.* 1st ed. New York: Routledge.

Pager, Devah, Bruce Western, and Bart Bonikoswki. 2009. "Discrimination in a Low Wage Labor Market: A Field Experiment." *American Sociological Review* 74:777–99.

Pilkington, H. and Pollock, G., eds. 2015. *Radical Futures? Youth, Politics and Activism in Contemporary Europe.* Oxford: Wiley-Blackwell.

Piven, Frances Fox, and Richard A. Cloward. 2000. *Why Americans Still Don't Vote.* New Democracy Forum Series. Boston: Beacon Press.

Polletta, Francesca. 2006. *It Was Like a Fever: Storytelling in Protests and Politics.* Chicago: University of Chicago Press.

Putnam, Robert. 1993. *Making Democracy Work: Civic Traditions in Modern Italy.* Princeton, NJ: Princeton University Press.

Putnam, Robert D. 2000. *Bowling Alone: The Collapse and Revival of American Community.* New York: Simon & Schuster.

———. 2015. *Our Kids: The American Dream in Crisis.* New York: Simon and Schuster

Randles, Jennifer. 2017. *Proposing Prosperity? Marriage Education Policy and Inequality in America.* New York: Columbia University Press.

Reeves, Richard V. 2017. *Dream Hoarders: How the American Upper Middle Class Is Leaving Everyone Else in the Dust, Why That Is a Problem, and What to Do about It.* Washington. DC: Brookings Institute.

Reich, Robert. 2015. *Saving Capitalism: For the Many, Not the Few.* New York: Vintage Books.

Reich, Steven Andrew. 2014. *The Great Black Migration: A Historical Encyclopedia of the American Mosaic.* Santa Barbara, CA: Greenwood Press.

Rios, Victor M. 2011. *Punished: Policing the Lives of Black and Latino Boys.* New York: NYU Press.

Rosenfeld, Jake. 2014. *What Unions No Longer Do.* Cambridge, MA: Harvard University Press

Rubin, Lillian. 1976. *Worlds of Pain: Life in the Working-Class Family.* New York: Basic Books.

Sawhill, Isabel. 2018. *The Forgotten Americans: An Economic Agenda for a Divided Nation.* New Haven, CT: Yale University Press.

Scheff, Thomas. 2000. "Shame and the Social Bond: A Sociological Theory." *Sociological Theory* 18(1):84–99.

Schlozman Verba, and Henry Brady 2013. *The Unheavenly Chorus: Unequal Political Voice and the Broken Promise of American Democracy.* Princeton, NJ: Princeton University Press.

Sharkey, Patrick. 2015. "Geographic Migration of Black and White Families over Four Generations." *Demography* 52(1):209–31.

Sherman, Jennifer. 2009. *Those Who Work, Those Who Don't: Poverty, Morality, and Family in Rural America.* Minneapolis: University of Minnesota Press.

Sennett, Richard, and Jonathan Cobb. 1973. *The Hidden Injuries of Class.* New York: Vintage.

Silva, Jennifer M. 2013. *Coming Up Short: Working-Class Adulthood in an Age of Uncertainty.* New York: Oxford University Press.

Simon, Robin W., and Kathryn Lively. 2010. "Sex, Anger and Depression." *Social Forces* 88(4):1543–68.

Skocpol, Theda. 1995. *Protecting Soldiers and Mothers: The Political Origins of Social Policy in the United States.* Cambridge, MA: Harvard University Press.

Skocpol, Theda, and Morris Fiorina. 1999. "Advocates without Members: The Recent Transformation of American Civic Life". In *Civic Engagement in American Democracy,* 461–509. Washington, DC: Brookings Institution.

Skocpol, Theda, and Vanessa Williamson. 2016. *The Tea Party and the Remaking of Republican Conservatism.* New York: Oxford University Press.

Stein, Arlene. 2011. "Therapeutic Politics: An Oxymoron?" *Sociological Forum* 26(1):187–93.

Sunstein, Cass. 2017. *#Republic: Divided Democracy in the Age of Social Media.* Princeton, NJ: Princeton University Press.

Swain, Carol M. 2002. *The New White Nationalism in America: Its Challenge to Integration.* New York: Cambridge University Press.

Swidler, Ann. 1986. "Culture in Action." *American Sociological Review* 51:273–86.

Taylor-Gooby, Peter. 2004. *New Risks, New Welfare.* Oxford: Oxford University Press.

Thompson, E. P. 1966. *The Making of the English Working Class.* New York: Vintage.

Tocqueville, Alexis de. 2003. *Democracy in America and Two Essays on America.* Edited by I. Kramnick. London: Penguin Classics.

Tolle, Eckhart. 1999. *The Power of Now: A Guide to Spiritual Enlightenment.* Novato: New World Library.

Turney, Kristin, and Anna R. Haskins. 2014. "Falling Behind? Children's Early Grade Retention after Paternal Incarceration." *Sociology of Education* 87(4):241–58.

Tyson, Alec, and Tyson Maniam. 2016. "Behind Trump's Victory: Divisions by Race, Gender, Education." Pew Research Center. Retrieved July 18, 2017 (http://www.pewresearch.org/fact-tank/2016/11/09/behind-trumps-victory-divisions-by-race-gender-education/).

Vance, J. D. 2016. *Hillbilly Elegy: A Memoir of a Family and Culture in Crisis.* New York: HarperCollins.

Verba, Sidney, and Norman H. Nie. 1987. *Participation in America: Political Democracy and Social Equality.* Chicago: University of Chicago Press.

Wailoo, Keith. 2014. *Pain: A Political History.* Baltimore, MD: Johns Hopkins University Press.

Walker, Jesse. 2013. *The United States of Paranoia: A Conspiracy Theory.* New York: Harper.

Warren, Mark. 2001. *Democracy and Association.* Princeton, NJ: Princeton University Press.

Weis, Lois. 2001. *Class Reunion: The Remaking of the American White Working Class.* New York: Routledge.

Western, Bruce. 1997. *Between Class and Market: Postwar Unionization in the Capitalist Democracies.* Princeton, NJ: Princeton University Press.

———. 2006. *Punishment and Inequality in America.* New York: Russell Sage Foundation.

——— 2018. *Homeward: Life in the Year After Prison.* New York: Russell Sage.

Western, Bruce, and Jake Rosenfeld. 2011. "Unions, Norms, and the Rise in U.S. Wage Inequality." *American Sociological Review* 76(4) 513–37.

Wilcox, W. Bradford, Andrew J. Cherlin, Jeremy E. Uecker, and Matthew Messel. 2012. "No Money, No Honey, No Church." *Research in the Sociology of Work* 23:227–50.

Wildeman, Christopher. 2009. "Parental Imprisonment, the Prison Boom, and the Concentration of Childhood Disadvantage." *Demography* 46(2):265–80.

Willis, Paul E. 1977. *Learning to Labor: How Working Class Kids Get Working Class Jobs.* Morningside ed. New York: Columbia University Press.

Wilson, William Julius. 1987. *The Truly Disadvantaged: The Inner City, the Underclass, and Public Policy.* Chicago: University of Chicago Press.

Wright, Erik Olin. 2008. "Logics of Class Analysis." In *Social Class: How Does It Work?* Edited by Annette Lareau and Dalton Conley. New York: Russell Sage Foundation.

Wuthnow, Robert. 2018. *The Left Behind: Decline and Rage in Rural America.* Princeton, NJ: Princeton University Press.

INDEX